T0163566

THE DIARY OF ALMON HARRIS THOMPSON

THE DIARY OF
ALMON HARRIS THOMPSON

Explorations of the Colorado River of the West
and Its Tributaries, 1871–1875

Edited by Herbert E. Gregory

The University of Utah Press

Utah State Historical Society

Salt Lake City

Copyright © 1939 by the Utah State Historical Society. All rights reserved.
First published in the *Utah Historical Quarterly*, volume 7, numbers 1, 2, and 3
Reprint edition 2009

 The Defiance House Man colophon is a registered trademark of the University of Utah Press.
It is based upon a four-foot-tall, Ancient Puebloan pictograph (late PIII) near Glen Canyon,
Utah.

13 12 11 10 09   1 2 3 4 5

LIBRARY OF CONGRESS CATALOGING-IN-PUBLICATION DATA

Thompson, A. H. (Almon Harris), 1839-1906.
  The diary of Almon Harris Thompson : geographer, explorations of the Colorado River of the West
and its tributaries, 1871-1875 / edited by Herbert E. Gregory ; preface by J. Cecil Alter. -- Reprint ed.
2009.
    p. cm.
  First published in the Utah Historical Quarterly, v. 7, nos. 1, 2, and 3, 1939.
  Includes bibliographical references and index.
  ISBN 978-0-87480-962-6 (pbk. : alk. paper) 1. Colorado River (Colo.-Mexico)--Description and
travel. 2. Colorado River (Colo.-Mexico)--Discovery and exploration. 3. Thompson, A. H. (Almon
Harris), 1839-1906--Diaries. 4. Thompson, A. H. (Almon Harris), 1839-1906--Travels--Colorado
River (Colo.-Mexico) 5. Powell, John Wesley, 1834-1902--Travel--Colorado River (Colo.-Mexico) 6.
Canyons--Colorado River (Colo.-Mexico)--History--19th century. 7. Southwest, New--Description and
travel. 8. Southwest, New--Discovery and exploration. I. Gregory, Herbert E. (Herbert Ernest), 1869-
1952. II. Title.
  F788.T49 2009
  917.91'3044--dc22

                                                                    2009030511

Printed and bound by Sheridan Books, Inc., Ann Arbor, Michigan.

CONTENTS

ILLUSTRATIONS

Utah State Historical Society

State Capitol—Salt Lake City, Utah

| Volume VII | January, April and July, 1939 | Nos. 1, 2 & 3 |

DIARY OF ALMON HARRIS THOMPSON

GEOGRAPHER, EXPLORATIONS OF THE COLORADO RIVER OF THE
WEST AND ITS TRIBUTARIES. 1871-1875

PREFACE

As documentary evidence relating to the navigability of the
Colorado River, the diaries of Almon Harris Thompson were in-
troduced by the United States Geological Survey as part of the
Government exhibit in the case of United States vs. Utah, 1930.
In 1932 the Diary was transmitted by the Survey to Prof. Herbert
E. Gregory for study, with permission to publish such parts as he
deemed of sufficient interest to historians and geographers. View-
ing the diary as a document of importance in the history of Utah,
Professor Gregory kindly offered it to the Utah State Historical
Society for publication.

The manuscript as received bears the following notation:
"Diaries of Almon Harris Thompson (1839-1906). Astronomer
and topographer, second Powell expedition and Rocky Mountain
exploration expedition.

"May, 1871 to November 28, 1871. Down the Green and
Colorado Rivers. November 29, 1871 to August 13, 1872; Field-
work. Kanab to mouth of Dirty Devil, overland. August 13, to
September 1871. Through the Grand Canyon.

"September 1, 1872 to June 4, 1873. Topographic work,
Kanab, St. George, Pipe Springs, Paria, etc. September 8th to
December 24, 1873, ditto. 1875. Topographic work. Gunnison,
Castle Valley, Kaiparowitz Plateau, Warm Creek, Paria."

The manuscript was typewritten in Salt Lake City, from
photostat copies of the original in the New York City Library,
and introduced as part of Government Exhibit 627 in the case of
U. S. versus Utah, No. 15, original U. S. Supreme Court. 590
(270). G. T. 37—Library reference number U. S. Geological Survey, Washington, D. C.

Original clippings from photostats, pasted in here and there,
such as diagrams and drawings, also a few undecipherable notes,
have not been reproduced.

In most respects however, the Diary as here published faithfully reproduces the arrangement and wording of the author. The liberty has been taken to correct obvious errors in capitalization, spelling and grammar incident to note-writing in the field, and to omit certain phrases that could not be deciphered with assurance. Also omitted are certain mathematical notes, compass bearings and figures relating to heights and distances that appear in final form on the published maps. It is hoped that these alterations and omissions have made the Diary more easily read without losing any of its value as a story of exploration.

The Diary as here printed is supplemented by Dellenbaugh[1] who served as assistant to Thompson during the trip from Green River to the mouth of Kanab Creek and in the survey of the region between Mount Trumbull and Henry Mountains. Dellenbaugh acknowledges his indebtedness for the use of the Thompson Diary "as a check on my own", and also "for many photographs now difficult to obtain". However, the Thompson Diaries herewith are the originals, and form the authentic primary record of one of the most important exploration surveys of the West.

Part of the Diary describing the route overland (1872) from Kanab to the mouth of the "Dirty Devil" [Fremont] was published in somewhat expanded form by Powell.[2] Nevertheless many of the more intimate interesting details there omitted are here reproduced as originally written.

The following "Introduction" to the Thompson Diary, and the footnotes throughout the text, were prepared at my suggestion by Dr. Herbert E. Gregory, whose work with the United States Geological Survey for many years has made him familiar with the plateau country of Utah and Arizona. Dr. Gregory's work on the Diaries was completed some years ago, but publication has been deferred until now for want of funds.

The Utah State Historical Society and the general public are much indebted to Dr. Gregory for his courtesy and generous cooperation in thus reproducing herewith the most important, at least in some respects, of the early Colorado River exploration journals, together with interesting elucidating annotations, which no living person other than Dr. Gregory could present; for the region covered by the Thompson Diary is about as much an uninhabited wilderness today as it was when Professor Thompson saw it.

J. Cecil Alter.

[1]Dellenbaugh, F. S., A Canyon Voyage, New York, 1908.
[2]Powell, J. W., Exploration of the Colorado River of the West and its tributaries, Washington, 1875.

THE COLORADO RIVER EXPLORING PARTY, 1871—THE START AT GREEN RIVER, WYOMING
Boats and Occupants left to right:

First boat (Canonita)   Second boat (Emma Dean)   Third boat (Nellie Powell)
Beaman, Hatten, C. Powell   Jones, Hillers, Maj. Powell, Dellenbaugh   Thompson, Steward, Bishop, Richardson

INTRODUCTION

Almon Harris Thompson was born at Stoddard, New Hampshire, September 24, 1839. Elementary instruction at home was followed by training in the schools of Southboro, Massachusetts (1848-1856) and at Wheaton College, Illinois (1857-1861). Soon after graduation, he married Ellen L. Powell, sister of his life-long friend, Major J. W. Powell. During the Civil War he served as First Lieutenant. 139th Illinois Volunteer Infantry. After the war, he returned to Illinois where he served as Superintendent of Schools at Lacon (1865-1867) and Bloomington (1867-1868) and as Acting Curator of the Illinois Natural History Society (1869). These experiences as student, soldier, teacher, and curator seem to have been natural steps in a life work which called for a knowledge of mathematics and science, an enthusiasm for collecting and recording field data, and reliability in "team work." His career as professional geographer began at the age of 31 when Powell selected him as scientific associate on a reconnaissance traverse from Salt Lake through southern Utah, across the Colorado and through the Navajo country which ended at Fort Defiance, December 5, 1870. The purpose of this traverse was to make preparations for the systematic exploration and mapping of the Colorado River and its adjoining lands—the task assumed by Thompson for the period 1871-1878, part of which (1871-1875) is covered by the Diary. In 1879 when the United States Geographical and Geological Survey of the Rocky Mountain Region (the "Powell Survey") was enlarged and redefined as the United States Geological Survey, Thompson became Chief Geographer of the new organization, and continued in that service until his death, July 31, 1906.

In Washington, Thompson took a leading part in the organization of the National Geographic Society (1889), and was active in many other scientific societies. His surviving associates in the Geological Survey speak of him with affection and recall many acts of kindness and generosity. Among his scientific colleagues, his assistants, and the men in Utah with whom he came in touch, Thompson was known as "Prof." Originally applied perhaps because of his service as a school teacher, his readiness to train young men and his obvious scholarship made the term appropriate.

Thompson possessed that rare combination of qualities that brings success to the explorer: a rigid insistence on discipline and order of procedure, kindness toward his subordinates, and sympathetic interest in the native people with whom he came in contact. Though in no sense egotistical, he had the confidence that views difficulties merely as routine problems capable of solution. His peace of mind seems to have been little disturbed by the dangers and hardships of field work, and though his appreciation of the beauty of the canyons is evident he gave little thought to flowery writing. Of himself he wrote, "I cannot gush. I leave this writing to read Miles Standish."

The few men familiar with the canyons of Green River, with Cataract Canyon, Glen Canyon, and with the tangle of cliffs and gorges in the region east of the Paria and Aquarius Plateaus will see events of dramatic meaning in such cryptic phases as "distribute food to the Indians." "Got up, ran rapids, went to bed," "Cached the Canonita this morning," "Sick ones getting better," "Took hammer and chisel and cut 'holds' in the sandstone." "Climbed 850 feet. Got bearings," "Ran as close to the rocks as we dared, then pulled. Made it all right," "Worked in camp mending shoes, etc,," "Cold as thunder!" "Steward was taken down three times but managed to come to the surface," "Laughed and talked over the adventures of the day."

Thompson's lack of "gush" and of interest in self-advertising is vividly shown in the Diary entry for February 17, 1873: "Got map finished. Fred and Jack started for Panguitch or farther." In these few words are recorded the completion and dispatch to Washington of the first map ever made of southern Utah and of the canyon of the Green and the Colorado—a map resulting from nearly two years of arduous and skillful work in a region largely uninhabited.

Dellenbaugh, who served as Thompson's assistant for two years, records interesting incidents of field work: "Heavy sand blew all over us." To permit Beaman to get a good photograph, "Thompson waited three days." After a day of particular hardship and danger, "Prof read aloud to us, and we went to sleep satisfied." "The boat rolled over, Fred slid under. Prof pulled him back while the men all sprang to the rocks and were saved." At the Crossing of the Fathers, though eager to proceed, "Prof persuaded Powell to wait a day for none of us had a chance to write a line" since leaving Uinta. "Prof decided to go across the Kiabab to Kanab with the two very sick men." "Prof climbed the heights for topographical purposes, reaching an altitude of 4,000 feet above the river." "His foresight and resourcefulness were phenomenal, and no threatening situation found him without some good remedy." Thompson was "always level headed and never went off on a tangent doing wild and unwarranted things."

The work of Thompson as recorded in the Diary falls naturally into three sections: navigation of the Green-Colorado; exploratory traverse from Kanab to the mouth of Fremont River; and the systematic mapping of central, eastern and southern Utah, and of Arizona north of the Grand Canyon.

The river trip was made in two stages—Green River, Wyoming, to Lees Ferry (May 22 to Oct. 26, 1871) and Lees Ferry to the mouth of Kanab Creek (August 1 to September 7, 1872)—and leisurely enough to permit mapping, the collection of specimens, and detailed observations on geology, archaeology, and botany. Compass direction and estimates of distance were made continuously and checked at frequent intervals by astronomical observations for latitude and longitude. Arrangements for bringing provisions by pack train to the mouth of the Duchesne River, the mouth of the Fremont to Ute Ford (Crossing of the Fathers) and to the mouth of the Paria (Lees Ferry) made it seem unnecessary to carry large stocks of food or to hasten the journey to avoid starvation. Though the pack trains could not reach the mouth of the Fremont and the land supporting parties were delayed in reaching Ute Ford and Lees Ferry, the river party completed their traverse before their meager supplies were exhausted.

Green River, referred to in some early accounts as Rio Verde River and Spanish River, [but usually as Seedskeedee (Prairie Hen), or San Buenaventura] was fairly well known before the Powell-Thompson traverse. It had long been a favorite hunting ground for Indians and was the seat of a successful trapping industry, particularly during the period 1825-1850. The camp sites, ruined stockades and cabins, broken boats, skeletons, and unmarked graves mentioned by Thompson are records of a past age. The few stockmen and farmers whom he met with were the vanguard of the present settlements of Uinta County. Below the mouth of the Uinta no one lived along the Green or the Colorado in Utah and few Indians or white men had ventured into the desert lands that border the streams. In their course through Labyrinth Canyon, Cataract Canyon, and Glen Canyon the boat party was peculiarly isolated, far beyond the reach of help if needed. Realizing this situation, few risks were taken. At the rapids, where at low water the danger is chiefly protruding rocks, the boats were let down by lines held in the hand or attached to snubbing posts.

After four and a half months on the river, Thompson's party lacking one boat met white men at the Crossing of the Fathers (October 6) and twenty days later reached the mouth of the Paria, the end of the river traverse planned for 1871. The continuation of the trip to the mouth of Kanab Canyon (August 17-September 7, 1872) duplicated the hazardous journey of 1869 so vividly described by Powell (Exploration, pp. 73-90). The decision to forego the traverse of the Colorado below Kanab Creek was a triumph of practical sense over the love of adventure. No scientific purpose would have been served by continuing a route previously explored. The south side of the river had been mapped by Ives in 1861; the north side and the canyon itself could be mapped most advantageously by land parties.

The contribution to knowledge made by the 1871-1872 traverse of the Green-Colorado canyons seems not to have been fully recognized. Strangely enough, Powell's story of the "Explorations of the Colorado of the West and its tributaries," published in 1875, though embodying the results of work done in 1871, 1872, and 1873, is written as the account of a traverse made in 1869. For reasons never explained, the maps, field notes, and collections made by Thompson and his other colleagues were used without referring to their source. As a matter of fact, the first boat trip through the Green and Colorado canyons, conducted by Powell in 1869, was primarily a daring adventure conceived and carried to success by a resolute, resourceful mind. It ranks among the most distinguished feats in the history of exploration. The scientific results were, however, meager. Guiding boats along an unknown stream at the rate of 23 miles a day left scant time for measurements and writing of notes. The chief reason for the second traverse of the river, described in the Diary, herewith, was to prepare a topographic map, and record geographic and geologic features with detail sufficient to permit the publication of reports descriptive of a heretofore unknown region.

To make the second expedition a record of scientific achievement, Powell states he put the "entire charge of the geographic work" in the hands of Thompson, "my companion and collaborator." In the absence of Powell, Thompson assumed command of the boat party between Ouray and Gunnison Crossing (now Green River, Utah) and from the Crossing of the Fathers to Paria.

Thompson's exploratory traverse of the region between the Colorado and the High Plateaus (May 29-July 7, 1872) seems to have had a two-fold purpose—the recovery of the boat (Canonita) abandoned the previous year at the mouth of the Fremont and to learn something of a region that had proved inaccessible to scouting parties. In 1870 this region of some 10,000 square miles embracing the eastern parts of the present Kane, Garfield, Emery, and Wayne Counties was unknown. In 1871 attempts to bring supplies to the mouth of the Fremont for use of the boat party resulted in complete failure. The party from Glencove (now Glenwood) in Sevier Valley turned back after going but fifty miles, and a party from Kanab in charge of the veteran scout, Jacob Hamblin, became lost in the region north of Kaiparowits Plateau and followed an unknown river (Escalante) thinking it the Fremont fifty miles farther north. Even the trail to the mouth of the Paria followed by Powell, Thompson, and Hamblin in 1870 was so little known that the packers sent with supplies for the river party of 1871 wandered so long among the cliffs and canyons that eleven days were needed to make the usual four-day trip from Kanab.

This traverse of Thompson made known the agricultural possibilities of the region at the head of the Paria and the Escalante, the remarkable Aquarius and Kaiparowits Plateaus, Water Pocket

Fold, and Henry Mountains that formed the basis of the classic works of Dutton and of Gilbert (1875).

Systematic mapping by Thompson began in northern Coconino County, Arizona, and central Kane County, Utah (1871), and without interruption was extended into the region now organized as Washington and Iron counties, Utah, and Mohave County, Arizona (1872-1873). It was carried northward into the present Wayne, Piute, Sevier, and Emery Counties (1874-1875). Not recorded in the diary is the continuation of this work into the Wasatch Plateaus (1875) and northeastward to the Wyoming and Colorado lines (1877, 1878).

As no geographic study of the region north of the Colorado canyons had previously been made, Thompson necessarily began his field work by astronomical and time observations sufficient to establish a base line accurately located in latitude and longitude. A line 9 miles in length was measured on flat land (Nine-mile valley) southeast of Kanab (1871). From this reference base, the position of prominent topographic features was established by triangulation, and with these in turn as guides the topography of south-central Utah was mapped in detail by plane table. A second base line measured at Gunnison and a second set of triangulation control points served for east-central Utah. The maps thus made are still in use and for parts of Utah and Arizona are the only ones available. On them are recorded the geological observations of Thompson's contemporaries—Powell, Dutton, and Gilbert, of later geologists and students of natural history.

Most of the names of geographic features mentioned in the Diary, both those in use previous to 1871 and those given by Thompson, have become part of the accepted terminology and appear on maps issued by Government bureaus. Some of those not mapped and some now known by other names may be located with reference to nearby features that are known. A few cliffs, ridges, and stretches of river, however, seem to have only "note book" names and are not identifiable. In selecting geographic names and in adopting those proposed by Powell and his other associates, Thompson showed a feeling for appropriate nomenclature. He uses such discriminating Piute terms as Kaibab (mountain lying down*), Uinkaret (home of the pines), Toroweap (gulley or dry wash), Paunsaungunt (Paunsagunt) (home of the beaver), Shinumo (old people; cliff dwellers), Markagunt (highland of trees), Parunuweap (water that roars), Paria (pah rea: elk river), Wonsits (antelope plain).

_____

*Kai-bab is the generally accepted pronunciation lately, but the sometimes-difficult Indian articulation was first given by Major Powell (Progress Report, April 30, 1874) as follows: "With a certain tribe in Northern Arizona, kaivw is the word signifying mountain; a-vwi means reclining or lying down; Kai-vav-wi, a mountain lying down, is the name for a plateau. A great plateau north of the Grand Canyon of the Colorado is called by them Kai-vav-wi, and the small tribe of Indians inhabiting it are Kai-vav-wits." — (J. C. A.)

He records the usage of the Mormon pioneers in such names as Berry Spring, Potato valley, Pipe Spring, Wild Band Pockets, Kolob, Eight-Mile Spring, Long Valley, Hidden Spring, and the history of exploration in Escalante River, Fremont River, Dellenbaugh Butte, Mount Hilgard, Mount Marvine, and other features. As descriptive terms, Thousand Lake Mountain, Table Cliffs, Hurricane Cliffs, Aquarius Plateau, Tantalus Creek, Waterpocket Fold, Crescent Wash, Warm Creek, Sentinel Rock Creek, Echo Cliffs, and Boulder Creek are peculiarly fitting.

The maps of the Colorado drainage basin place Thompson in the front rank of geographic explorers. Entries in the Diary and his paper on "The Irrigable Lands of Utah" that reveal keen insight into utilization of natural resources add to his reputation.

As an historical document the Diary has high value. It is a story of colonization in southern Utah, an impartial first hand account of the purpose and methods of the Mormon Church in extending its settlements in Virgin and Sevier Valleys eastward across the High Plateaus to and beyond the Colorado River. During the year that Thompson began his systematic study of Utah geography (1871-1872), Paria was settled, the rock fort at Pipe Spring built, Lees Ferry established as a ranch, and the scattered farms in Long Valley, Johnson Valley, Upper Kanab Valley, at Moccasin Springs and Panguitch, abandoned during "Indian disturbances," were reoccupied. While his work was in progress, Thompson witnessed the settlement of Orderville, the expansion of Paria into a precinct, the establishment of Cannonville, Henrieville, and Escalante, and the selection of ranch sites about Kaibab Plateau and along streams tributary to the Paria, the Escalante, the upper Sevier, and the east fork of Virgin River. In 1872 Kanab was "a stockaded square of log houses with some few neat adobe houses outside." By 1878 it had become a prosperous village of some 400 farmers and stockmen. Adjoining it, 1100 acres of grain fields and orchards were watered by four miles of irrigation ditches.

—*Herbert E. Gregory.**

*GREGORY, HERBERT ERNEST—Geologist, b. Middleville, Michigan, Oct. 15, 1869, s. George and Jane (Bross) G. A. B. Yale 1896, Ph. D. 1899, m. Edna Earle Hope of Charleston, S. C. June 30, 1908. Asst. in biology 1896-98—instr. physical geography 1898-1901, asst. prof. physiography 1901-04, Silliman prof. geology 1904-36; prof. emeritus since 1936, Yale; also Director Bernice P. Bishop Museum 1919-36. Geologist U. S. Geological Survey, Regent U. of Hawaii, Chmn. Com. on Pacific Investigations of Nat. Research Council and Fellow Geological Society America, Assn. Am. Geographers, Am. Academy Arts & Sciences, American Philos. Society, and author of various papers on geology in Government and scientific publications. Address: Bishop Museum, Honolulu, T. H.—From—WHO'S WHO IN AMERICA—1938-39.

ALMON HARRIS THOMPSON
September 24, 1839—July 31, 1906.

DIARY OF ALMON HARRIS THOMPSON

(Green River, Wyoming.) May 22d, 1871. Turned out early, carried rest of things to boats; breakfast at Mr. Fields at 7:00; got started at 10:00; made 2¾ miles to dinner camp on island. Broke steering oar of Emma Dean; Richardson and Clement went back to town for another oar. After dinner the "Emma Dean" and "Nellie Powell" pulled out leaving the C. [Canonita]† to take Clement and Richardson.[1] * Run about 1¾ miles to camp; came near running against a cliff; went back to foot of dinner island to warn the Canonita. Got in with Beaman and managed to get his boat in the same place with mine. Ran down ½ mile when we came to a small rapid; ran it easily; bluffs on left bank often 200 feet high—in one place colored with iron; ran down about eight miles from Green River to a place where Tertiary coal is found. Camped on right bank.

May 23d. Sent out box of fossils by some men to Green River. Last night was half sick. In middle of night was waked by Ford's crying out. He was choking Jones in his sleep. It startled me a

---

†Bracketed entries throughout the text are by Dr. Gregory.—J.C.A.

[1]As recorded in an unpublished report to the Smithsonian Institution, also by Dellenbaugh, the "River Party" of 1871 comprised J. W. Powell, A. H. Thompson, J. K. Hillers, F. S. Dellenbaugh, E. O. Beaman, S. V. Jones, J. F. Steward, F. M. Bishop, F. A. Richardson, W. C. Powell, and A. J. Hatten.

In selecting this personnel, J. W. Powell (Major), organizer and leader of the expedition, filled the key positions with men of special training and experience. Thompson (Prof) had demonstrated his ability as a geographer. Jones, assigned as topographer, was a student of mathematics and surveying. Beaman was professional photographer, and Dellenbaugh (Fred) a young artist of promise. Powell himself served as geologist. The other members of the party had no demonstrated fitness for the work in hand. They seem to have been chosen from among the friends and war-time associates of Powell and Thompson. W. C. Powell (Clem), assigned as assistant photographer, was Powell's nephew. Hillers (Jack), general assistant, Bishop (Cap), assistant topographer, Steward (Ford, Sergeant), assistant geologist, and Hatten (Andy) cook, were veterans of the Civil War. Richardson (Frank) was a family friend. Nine of the 11 members of the party were from Illinois.

The crews of each of the three boats used by the expedition were so selected as to provide a helmsman and two oarsmen. As his companions on the Emma Dean (named for Mrs. Powell), Powell chose Jones, Hillers, and Dellenbaugh. To the Nellie Powell (named for Mrs. Thompson) he assigned Thompson, Steward, Bishop, and Richardson, and to the Canonita, Beaman, W. C. Powell, and Hatten.

Dellenbaugh reports: Every morning the cabins of the boats were packed like so many trunks. The blankets were rolled up and put in their rubber cases, all bags of supplies were secure-ly tied and stowed away; in short, every article was placed in the cabins and the hatches firmly buttoned in place, with the canvas cover drawn snugly over the deck. Only a grand smash-up could injure these things. Nothing was left out but such instruments as were hourly needed, the guns, life preservers, and a camp kettle in each boat for bailing purposes. On each of two boats there was a topographer, whose duty was to sight the direction of every bend of the river and estimate the length of the stretch. Thompson on his boat also kept a similar record. The sighting was done with a prismatic compass.

*In the notes, references to Dellenbaugh are from A Canyon Voyage: Yale Press, 1908. Material has been taken also from the following publications of the U. S. Geological Survey: Water Power and Flood Control of Colorado River below Green River, by E. C. LaRue: Water-Supply Paper 556, 1925; The Green River and its Utilization, by Ralf R. Woolley: Water-Supply Paper 618, 1930; Geology of the Navajo Country, by Herbert E. Gregory: Prof. Paper 93, 1917; The Kaiparowits Region, by Herbert E. Gregory: Prof. Paper 164, 1931.

good deal. Commenced raining and snowing about daylight; we stayed in camp until about 1:00 o'clock p. m. Pulled out and ran about six miles; camped in a grove of cottonwoods. Boys caught a mess of fish. Ran one small rapid. Cold as thunder.

May 24th. Dinner at Station 12. Where cliff breaks down a creek supposed to be Sage comes in; valley covered with grease-wood, currant, and sage. Landed to hike the valley. Valley wider; saw three deer at Station 18. Took two pictures. Measured height of Needle and Boston Loaf Buttes. Saw a good many ducks and geese. Took observation for latitude and time.

Thursday, May 25th. Islands in stream all along. Valley on both sides. River 250 feet. Current 1½. When this station was about half run the crew of the Emma Dean saw a deer on the bank of a low willow covered island. The Major shot at but missed it. All the boats landed and we had a good hunt. Got three—two bucks and one doe. Camped, skinned our game and feasted on venison.

Friday, May 26th. [Records current, width of river, and height of walls at 13 stations.] Saturday, May 27th. Left camp at 7:05. Left Steward behind and took Hillers. Dinner camp at Station 11½. Observation Butte on right 275 feet high. River 75 yards; current 2 miles. Valleys on left. Climbed Observation Butte; from top towards north the whole country is low rolling tableland into which the river has cut its valley; towards south the same until the foothills of Uinta Range are reached. Needle Buttes bear N. 12 E. Our general course since moving has been S. 12 W. The Uinta Range bears west and S.W.; are a low range of hills with considerable timber; N. E. are the Quin Horne mountains with bearing timber from the N.E. to the N.W., the country seems about the same level and covered only with sage, etc. After leaving camp we passed through low rolling hills. The river sweeps from right to left through a system of continuous curves that remind one of figure 8. The wind blew with great violence from the west, often lifting the crest of a wave over the side of the boat. We pulled steadily on for four miles, nearing the ridges when suddenly a sharp turn to left, a wheel back to right, and the river dashed itself against a ridge which receiving the shock, throws the waters to left and maddened waters rush down toward the west, and the south. Flaming Gorge hard into view, the right side a dark red flame below in the morning sun with a grey cap of sandstone overtopped with brown, the whole cliff rising to 1000 feet. While on the left the quiet green of a lovely grove of cottonwoods heightened by its contrast the beauty and grandeur of the scene. Not long can we admire for our camp lay in those trees so bending with a will to the oars we soon beached the boat on a sandy beach; and set about making ourselves comfortable. Seeing fresh track of deer and sheep I took my rifle and set off to examine the willow thickets.

May 29th. Camp No. 9. Left camp at 8:00. High wind— Flaming Gorge River 300, current $3\frac{1}{2}$, 900 feet high on right. Station 4. Commencement of Horse Shoe Canon. In camp when Station 13 half run; lower end of station, commencement of Kingfishers Canon. When we left Camp No. 7 the wind was blowing a perfect gale. Before we could get around we shipped a lot of water. A few minutes of sharp pulling and we were all right. Nothing occurred until Station 4, when we reached the commencement of Horse Shoe Canon. The Canon at commencement runs south of east, then east, then south, then west and north west; water still and quiet, until you turn from south to west—then as you round the point the river narrows to——in width, makes a smooth rapid of perhaps three rods, then waves. It was our first real rapid and was exciting. I was a little anxious as to how the boat rides, but she rode the waves nicely. We ran down perhaps $\frac{1}{2}$ mile to dinner camp. The Major and myself went over the hills to view. After dinner the Captain and myself went to the top of Horse Shoe bend for bearings. At 5:00 we pulled out; run 1 mile to camp; Major and myself took a long walk over the hills to K. C. J. [Kingfisher Canyon Junction.]

Tuesday, May 30th. In camp all day. Rainy. In morning went hunting. Forded creek. Kingfisher [Sheep Creek?] is a beautiful clear stream that ought to contain trout. When we came to the cliff and looked down on its valley I thought it as lovely as we ever saw. The stream has cut a canon at level 500 feet deep through Carboniferous rocks and carried out a valley $\frac{1}{8}$ mile wide. The valley is thick with cottonwoods, willows, alders, and box elders. The water is clear of a slight reddish tinge, cold, and where it empties into the Green the color of the two streams is brought into vivid contrast. The clay colored Green soon absorbs the blue Kingfisher.

Wednesday, May 31st. Stopped to take pictures—Kingfisher creek. Stopped on an eddy to take on Bishop; Beehive rapids just as you turn the point. [Beehive Point.] Rapids $\frac{1}{8}$ mile long; current $5\frac{1}{2}$ miles. An exciting ride. We shipped a little water in the bow. Caused by rowing too fast. Camped for dinner. Station 6. Mouth [upper end] of Red Canon. Rapids below; go into a nice camp.

Thursday, June 1, 1871. In camp No. 9 all day. After breakfast Bishop went over the river for topography; Steward and Richardson for geology; Beaman for pictures, while Jones and myself climbed the mountains back, south of camp. After a climb of an hour and a half we reached the top some 1800 feet above the river. We then went along the ridge three miles to a still higher point; from there we took the topography of the country, then back to

camp. After a long walk we reached camp at 2:00 P. M. Stayed
in camp with the exception of a short walk to run the rapids the
rest of the day.

Friday, June 2d. Camp 10. River narrows suddenly then
plunges off into rapid after rapid. They are not very bad I think,
but we shall ship some water. Well, we went into the rapids; ran
three, when we came to a short turn in the river to right, then im-
mediately to left with rocks in both bends. We were steering all
right to take advantage of the current when the Major motioned
us in farther to the right. He made motions so energetically that we
thought we must come in, so putting forth all our strength I threw
her bow up stream and made for the bank. I soon found that we
were too far in, so tried all we could to bring her round. It was
too late, we could not come in and drifted on the rocks in an awful
current, struck just aft the main hatch on left side broke the upper
planks, sprung the ribs, careened her so she filled and rolled over.
We sprang upon the rocks just as she filled, caught the rope and
held her. In about a minute we got the rope up stream, pulled the
boat out from the bank when she righted and we pulled her up on the
beach. Partially unloaded, repaired the broken side, towed up to
a good point for a start, took the very same course as we were taking at first, ran the rapid without shipping a drop. Found the other
boats about an eighth below, waiting for us. We ran in, shipping
a little water. Found that the Emma Dean had struck the rocks
and torn off a row lock. We lost in the affair a sponge, camp kettle,
and compass. We also lost two oars but picked them up below.
We ran a rapid or two, then went into camp for dinner. Took
two pictures—ran a mile and a half when we came to a long rapid;
landed on the left bank and the Major and myself went down to
reconnoiter. Found it too hard to run. Went back and decided
to cross the river and let down on the other bank. Had a hard pull.
The Emma Dean went over first. We followed and landed in the
same place. The crew of the Dean caught our boat before we
struck. The Canonita followed but landed below, was caught by
the other crews. Then we took the load out of the E. D. and let
her over the worst. Loaded her up and let her down to a bad
place and decided to camp. Took part of the load out of the N. P.
and C., let them down to camp. Got in before dark and found that
we were camped on the very same ground that the Major camped
on two years ago the same night. Laughed and talked over our
adventures of the day. The river is not over 250 feet wide, current
at least 6 miles per hour. Tumbles over rocks, waves at least 5 feet
high. Our boats ride the waves nicely. The Nellie Powell carries
the heaviest load, ships the most water of course, but I think that
we manage first rate. I think we get along fully as well as I expected, and the rapids are no worse. We shall go through.

Saturday, June 3rd. Camp No. 11. We decided not to move

out today. Sent Jones and Bishop to the top of the cliff to get the topography. I stayed in camp. Beaman took pictures. We shall take the river again tomorrow.

Sunday, June 4th. Camp No. 11. Left camp at 7:30 o'clock. Ran the lower part of the rapid. It was rather bad, but we got through without shipping much water. We soon ran another rapid and then came to a bad one; we looked it over and concluded to cross over and let down with ropes. The E. D. ran over first, but got aground just above our point of landing. We followed and landed just where we wished, but had hard pulling. The C. followed but hardly made it. Bishop caught her and prevented her from striking hard. We let down past the rocks, then in the boats, ran another rapid when we came to a place where the river suddenly narrowed and caused high waves; reconnoitered and decided to run it. Got through nicely; then ran some rapid places until we came to a nice place to camp. Decided to sleep the rest of the day. Made 3½ miles; ran four rapids and let down past one. In the afternoon the Major and myself climbed a hill 1200 feet high west of camp. Had a magnificent view. To the south the Uintah mountains appeared broken down to low hills forest crowned with much snow. The slopes were green and dotted with trees like a park. To the N. W. the Portage Cliffs were in full view. To the north high cedar-covered mountains cut off our view. To the East we could look over the Devonian sandstones to the Carboniferous cliffs, then away beyond to Jurassic and away over the Flaming Gorge cliffs to the Tertiary beyond camp No. 6. Through a gap in the Carboniferous and Tertiary we could see the river. To the east, mountains covered with cedars and pinons intercepted the view partially, but between their peaks we caught glimpses of the lateral valleys of Brown's Hole. [Brown's Park.] The yellow river rolled 1200 feet below. The roar of the rapids was softened by distance to a gentle murmur. The wind breathed softly through the cedars and pines, and taken together the scene was so quiet, lovely, and grand that for the moment I forgot that we were on the treacherous, perilous river and that the mountains so lovely and grand, were only in the distance. A glance at the river at our feet dispelled the illusion. There lay on the slope, half buried in the sand, a boat, which once belonged to a party of prospectors who two years ago tried to descend from Green River City to Brown's Hole in boats. They got as far as just above our camp when one of their number was drowned. The party disbanded, abandoning their boats and made the rest of their way overland to their place of destination. We have found old sacks, ropes, oars, and other mementos of their trip. Tall pines and spruce grow near our camp, willows and alders in the bottoms, box elder and mountain maple up the valleys of the streams, cacti and sage on the large slopes. The mountain silty phlox, a species of pink, and Vita Orgonis are the flowers. When we got back the Major read "The Lay of the Last Minstrel" aloud. It has been a most enjoyable Sunday.

Monday, June 5th. Camp No. 12. Left camp at 7:30. After a run of a mile landed to take some pictures; went with the Major to select plants, then with Beaman to show him. Went up two little streams. One was not a very good view, but the other was. The water tumbled down over the rocks some 16 feet. Was closed in by high mountains. The spruce, pinons, willow-leafed cotton-woods, mountain maple, thorn, cherry, and alder grow in great luxuriance on the banks. The waters come from the distant mountains, cold from the melting snows. The mountain sides are lined with pines and spruce, with bare cliffs of red sandstone rising 1200 feet. The Emma Dean left dinner camp at 2:00 P. M. to run down to Ashley's Falls [in Red Canyon] and look out a place for portage. As soon as Beaman finished his picture we started, and after a rapid ride of an hour came on the fall. We landed just above the falls in comparatively still water. The falls were originally only rapids such as we have run a half a dozen of; but the cliff on the left has fallen within perhaps 50 years and filled in the left bank, narrowing the river ⅓ and thrown high blocks across the stream, damming it so that the river is quiet for half a mile above. One high block of sandstone 25 feet square is in the center and divides the waters into two channels. We take the one on the left. Land just at the edge of the fall. Take everything out of the boats and carry them around eight rods to quiet water below. By 5:00 o'clock this was done. Then we took the Emma Dean on the rocks, carried her part way, and let her down in the water and pulled her round a point of rocks where the rations and I were. We then attached ropes to the bow and stern of the Canonita and let her run over the fall. She went safely but got two or three hard knocks. Thought it best not to risk the Nellie over the fall so took her over the rocks as we did the Emma Dean. When we got the boats over it was supper time and sunset. All were tired and glad to rest. Slept above the fall. We built a campfire and sitting around it read Hiawatha. The falls talk in tunes like thunder. We sleep tonight in the music of their roar. We went to look at the waters. Above they are glassy and smooth, then divide at the rock, plunge in unbroken sheets for a short distance, then boil and foam for a few feet, then plunge and shoot in a perfect sheet of foam into the canon below. The water on the right is narrower and more broken. Right under the lee of the rock is a little rainbow—in the twilight the waters seem to dash with the rapidity of an arrow.

Tuesday, June 6th. Camp No. 12. Left Ashley's Falls, after loading the boats, at about 9:00 o'clock. The E. D. first. After running through a rapid river for perhaps a mile we saw that the E. D. had landed at the mouth of a small creek; pulled in. Beaman went up the creek to get pictures; I went up another. Found a pretty cascade; Beaman took it. The pine, spruce, willow-leafed cotton-wood, aspen, alder, &c. vegetation. Got dinner and left. The river was pretty rough. We ran some two miles, laid by for the Canon-ita to come up. Then we had a long, rough rapid fully a mile. I think the water ran 10 miles per hour. Waves that tossed our boats like feathers. We went through all right, and after another mile came to Ashley Park, a little valley in the mountains. Camped under two large pine trees. Have run some bad rapids. The worst by far that we have seen. The rapids where we let down were not as bad. The canon this afternoon has often had perpendicular walls on both sides, but usually one only. The river has an average width of 250 feet. Current for the first four days has not been less than 4 miles per hour, often 6 or 8, and in a few places 10 or 12.

Wednesday, June 7th. Camp No. 13. Left camp at 7:00 to climb Dead Timber Mountain. The ascent is easy; top 4½ miles in straight line. Country cut up by small creeks, the principal of which is Ashleys. Ate a lunch on creek. From the top view is magnificent. To the north we look away over to the snowy ridge in which F. S. ridge is lost. To the N. W. we could trace Henry's Fork until it turns to the right within ten miles of F. S. ridges. [?] Away further we could see the Wasatch Mountains covered with snow. To the N. the valley of Green River can be traced for 50 miles an elevated plateau through which the river has cut a deep channel. It is a broken river. Right north Pilot Butte stands like a giant sentinel, and away beyond like white clouds in the horizon are the Wind River Mountains, 200 miles away. To the northeast we look over miles of red Devonian sandstones, then the gray ridges of Carboniferous, then Triassic ridges, then Jurassic flaming red. Then gray rolling hills of Cretaceous, then the Eocene and Plio-cene Tertiary. The general dip of all is a few degrees west of north, the trend of a few degrees south of west and east of north. The south face is generally abrupt, the northern slopes more gentle. Often the top of a ridge is a plateau covered with pine and cedar and occasionally grassy slopes. The whole geology and topography of the country is open before us. To the west we look into Brown's Hole. To the southeast we can see the river-bend to the south and enter the canon of Ladore, can trace it through the canon to Split Mountain Canon beyond, then to the south we look up a beautiful elevated *plateau valley*, over into the Uintah beyond. The Uintahs are broken down to low mountains less than 4000 feet, and when the river cuts through them to the south they rise higher beyond until lost in the main range.

Thursday, June 8th. Camp No. 14. Left camp at 7:00. River canons in about a mile. Cuts through sandstone. Cliffs often rising to river rapids. Current average 4 miles, in some places 10. We ran 4 rapids in which the waves were as large as any that we have seen. Got through all right. After running 8 miles came to Brown's

Hole. [Brown's Park.]   Found there Harrell had a large (2200) herd of cattle. He had mail for us. They are going to Green River in a few days and we can send to the Officer. The boys are glad. The valley seems to have been at one time a lake and afterward the river cut its present course. The geologists say that the present exposed strata of the valley. . . . . (Sentence incomplete).

Friday, June 9th. Camp No. 14. Still in camp. Busy all day with observations and writing. Richardson has decided to go home. Saturday, June 10th. Camp No. 14. Still in camp. Taking obser- vation all day.

Sunday, June 11th. Camp No. 15. Richardson started for home. Sent by Mr. Harrell to get letters from Salt Lake. Left camp at 8:00. The country through which we passed for an hour was a rolling plain 30 feet above the river. Then we came to a short little canon, about half a mile long, then came Swallow Canon about 2 miles long. Cliffs about 300 feet often vertical on both sides. Red sandstones. Seem like a ridge of the sandstone elevation from the general level of the valley. Had dinner in the lower part of the canon, then pulled out, passing Willow Creek and Beaver on the left before 2:00 o'clock. Stopped at the latter to take a picture. The valley so far seems to be a rolling plateau of recent origin with islands of older red sandstones in it. The river has cut a channel varying in depth 3 feet to 6 feet opposite our camp. The river since the foot of Swallow Canon has been full of islands—some a mile long. River often ¼ mile wide. Current perhaps 2 miles per hour. We are camped under some large cottonwoods. Valley 3 miles wide. River in Swallow Canon often 10 feet deep close to bank. Some large islands. Willows along shore.

Monday, June 12th. In camp No. 15 all day. Went to the top of Mt. Sunnerston. [?]   Had a long hard climb. Got to the top at 1:00 P. M. Took an observation. Came down, reached camp at 5:00 P. M. dry and tired. Got a good many bumps.

Tuesday, June 13th. Camp No. 16. Left camp at 7:30. Floated down the river; boats lashed together and the Major reading "Scott". River 600 feet wide; current 2½ miles. Broad valley on either side. Beautiful groves of cottonwoods along the banks, often covering 100 acres. Saw a wolf trotting along the bank. Camped for dinner at some cabins used last winter by Harrell Bros. After dinner ran down perhaps 1½ miles by river to the "Gate of Lodore." Camped in a grove of box elders. Mosquitoes so thick, went up on a bluff to sleep. Passed mouth of Vermilion Creek just before dinner. A tiny little stream.

Wednesday, June 14th. In camp No. 16. Took observations in morning and until through in afternoon. Then climbed left post of "Gate of Lodore". Thursday, June 15th. Camp 16. In camp taking observations. Comparing barometer all day. The Major and Jones climbed Turtle Creek [?] for observations. Bishop went to mouth of Vermilion Creek. Steward and Sandy got in just after dinner. Worked up time observations.

Friday, June 16th. Camp No. 16. In camp writing and copying observations. About 2:00 P. M. Mr. Bacon came and said Mr. Harrell brought no mail, but made arrangements to have it come tomorrow.

Saturday, June 17th. Camp No. 16. In camp until 4:00 P. M. Letters came from wife and Emma about noon. Sent two letters to wife. At 4:00 P. M. entered Lodore. Almost immediately came to a rapid; ran it and then another, and another, and another in quick succession. Four, one bad. Cliffs from 1500 to 2000 feet high on either side. River 300 feet. Current in places 10 to 12 miles per hour. Beaman stopped for pictures at ¾ mile below camp 16. Ran 1½ miles, then camped just above a bad rapid, one in which if we go 10 feet to right or left too far we shall wreck. If we go *just right* shall go through first rate. Cliffs on either side 2000 feet. On the right is a lovely grotto carved by the water from the red sandstone. The entrance is narrow, 20 feet, but walls 1500 feet. As you go up it widens until at 15 rods it stops in an amphitheatre 100 feet across. Water is trickling out drop by drop from the sides. Moss and a balsam were growing in the crevices. Above is a little ribband of blue sky. Down to the mouth is the yellow river, and over across a cliff 2500 feet high of bright red sandstone.

Sunday, June 18th. Camp No. 17. Left camp No. 16 at 10:00. Beaman taking pictures earlier. Ran the first bad rapid successfully. It was by far one of the most dangerous rapids run, but one of the easiest as we took it. Rocks in the middle, on both sides and all about. Not over ten feet of channel. After that we ran through more rapids, then camped for dinner. The rapids were rough, the worst in fact that we have run, but got through all right. Came very near running into the Emma Dean in the last. She had been caught in the eddy and was coming up stream in our path. Threw our boat out on the heaviest waves and just around her we had a hard pull to land but made it, and then caught the other boat below us, they not succeeding in getting up. After dinner ran a rapid, landed in an eddy and went below to examine one, started up 11 sheep; went back to the boats; got gun but did not get a shot. Found the first rapid could be run but just below were "Disaster Falls"[2] where the boat was lost. The Major went first. The river comes from the east, then winds south, then west, and just at the western bend plunges off over rocks in falls, then rapid and full for ¾ of a mile. We had to land at 2:00. At 1:00 the river seems to "ooze" towards the falls. We landed just at the first of trend all right. The

[2]As recorded on map made in 1922 by the United States Geological Survey, "Upper Disaster Falls" and "Lower Disaster Falls" are features of the Canyon of Lodore. "Where the boat was lost" seems to refer to some previous expedition.

Major had landed below half way down. The Canonita went too far tonight and came very near going over. I had signalled her above, still she did not get in the right place. Its alright though. We sleep on the *Sami*, but the Major slept on *giurs ajo*. Portage down now. Scenery good. Cliffs 2000 feet.

Monday, June 19th. Camp No. 18. Commenced portage early and nearly half way at noon. Made the other half with rations and one boat at 5:00 o'clock. Stopped for night. Cliffs on right bank 2000 feet, almost perpendicular. Little valley covered with cottonwoods on left. Pines on very summit of cliffs. Cedars on mountain tops. Rocks, red sandstone. Gulches frequently wooded. The cottonwood is mostly "briar laurel." Beaman has taken some fine pictures. Call the falls Disaster Falls. The gulch up which the ship escaped the Gate of Lodore. Let one boat down this afternoon. It is by far the worst rapid yet seen. I think the river falls——feet in ¾ of a mile. No boat could go through it.

Tuesday, June 20th. Camp No. 19. Let the other boat down this A. M. Loaded then let down with lines to the next bad place. Unloaded and made a short portage. Had dinner. After dinner pulled out and ran 3 rapids, bad ones, where the other party made portages. In No. 3 the Emma Dean shipped so much water that they landed to bail out. The Canonita was about half full. We had but very little. After bailing out ran another rapid and stopped to recondition. Concluded to go on. Ran one rapid, then I avoiding a rock, the Emma Dean ran into an eddy and turned round so we landed, rested a few minutes, then ran another rapid and camped, just above a place that we cannot run. Shall let down. Camp in a grove of old cedars, knotted and gnarled, on right bank. "Wheat stack" [topographic feature] ¼ mile north. Cliff just opposite on left bank vertical to the height of 2500 feet, red as flame. Red sandstone all above. Caught a glimpse of Serratus Ridge [?] today. Current 12 to 15 miles per hour in places. Have made one portage and ran six rapids. Read Marmion tonight.

Wednesday, June 21st. Camp No. 20. Stayed in camp while Beaman took pictures until about 10:00 o'clock. Then let the boats down past the rapid. Dinner. Ran one rapid, then let down past two bad ones, then ran one bad one, then smooth water for ¾ mile until we came to as much of a fall as Disaster. Camped on left bank. Scenery grand all day. Cliff after cliff 2000 feet high. River 300 to 400 feet wide. Current very rapid. Good many box elder trees on bank. Cottonwoods, cedars up the cliffs whenever a foothold is found. Pines on summit. Camped under cliff of Serratus Ridge crowned with Carboniferous. Boulders of grey limestone at falls and along bank.

Thursday, June 22d. Camp No. 21. Left camp for a climb at 8:45. Took gulch and climbed Serratus Ridge. Observations from highest N. E. point. Climb very pleasant. Looking north we could see over into Brown's Hole, through the Gate of Lodore. To the east Mt. Dawes shuts off the view. To the south we can see the canon of Bear River. [Yampa River.]

Friday, June 23rd. Camp No. 22. Made portage around Triplet Falls. Took until 2:00 P. M. Ran ½ mile, came to Boulder Falls. The river above the falls is 200 feet, current 3½ miles, then plunges down, down, for half a mile a sheet of foam. Rocks all around. Call the rapid "Hell's Half Mile".[3] Got the Dean around before night. Fine view of Dunn's Cliff and Boulder Gulch. Getting closer to the Carboniferous. It and the "transition beds'" crown most of the cliffs.

Saturday, June 24th. Camp No. 23. Finished portage around "Hell's Half Mile". Had dinner at lower end. Pulled out at 2:00 P. M. We just shaved two rocks in this run. Came one mile, two rapids run. Camped at foot of gulch of Leaping Brook (Rippling Brook) River, 350 feet. Cannot average 5 miles. Cliffs high and nearly vertical. Red sandstone at base but crowned with either limestone or transition rocks. Went up Leaping Brook Gulch with the Major. Climbed perhaps 800 feet when the gulch divides into two banches, right and left. The view up either is grand. The gulch is thickly grown with pines, cottonwoods, firs, and cedars. A little stream of clear cold water trickles down, often leaping 20 to 30 feet or sliding down moss covered rocks. The base is red sandstone the upper 1000 feet gray limestone, with firs and cedars growing from crevices. Up the left hand gulch is seen a grand crag 800 feet high isolated gray. Looking like a gem to grace the lovely glen. I have seen no more beautiful scenery on the trip.

Sunday, June 25th. Camp No. 24. Beaman took three pictures of "Leaping Brook Crags" today. After dinner let boats down rapid, then ran two, which we came to, one a bad one. Got out, looked it over and concluded to try it. Ran it alright. Rapid water for one mile when we came to Alcove Creek. Stopped while Beaman took two negatives. Ran a rapid just below landing, then another, when we found the Dean waiting (she having started first). We went ahead and ran about three miles very fast to mouth of Bear River. [Yampa.] We were in red sandstone at Alcove Creek, but soon came to Carboniferous limestone with fossils, then to Carboniferous sandstone buff colored, so colored to the mouth of Yampah. The sandstone is buff homogeneous,

[3]Dellenbaugh records his impression of Green River near the mouth of the Yampa:
"Just below us were three sharp rapids which received the name of Triplet Falls. A great deal of work was required to pass these, and then we ran three or four in good style, which brought us, in the late afternoon, to where the whole river spread out amongst innumerable rocks and for more than half a mile the water was a solid sheet of milky foam, sending up the usual wild roar, which echoed and echoed again and again amongst the cliffs around and above us. Some one proposed the name of "Hell's Half Mile" for this terrible place and the idea was at once adopted, so appropriate did it seem. We were at the mouth of Yampa River. From a wonderful echo which repeated a sentence of ten words, we called the place Echo Park. Such an echo in Europe would be worth a fortune."

heavily bedded and——feet thick worn by water into butte like cliffs. Yampah River is nearly as large as the Green but does not now apparently flow as much water. Is thought to be low. Green has been 400 feet wide. Current four miles. Must be very deep in places, for could not estimate actual width of river more than 75 feet, at at least two points. We are through Lodore with its rapids, its reminisences of disaster, its hard work and danger. It is as a tale that is past. We fear it no more, we rejoice; nine days only to run it. Three portages. No disaster. Are camped in Echo Park [Pat's Hole] a little "Valley like valley" cut from the buff sandstone by the hand of the waters. Near the river and on the islands are the beautiful groves of box elder. In drier parts of the park, cedars, underbrush of willow, rose sage, and buffalo berry. The park includes perhaps 500 acres. On the west across the Green the walls are 800 feet vertical, forming a short tongue of rock [Steamboat Rock] round which the river turns. Across the Yampah cliffs as high on south and east. On east and north are butte like towers 1500 feet high and away beyond to the north are seen the high Carboniferous cliffs 300 feet. The echo is fine. Eight words came back distinctly at some points—at others three distinct repetitions are heard.

Monday, June 26th. Camp No. 24. In camp all day. Took observations. Work them up, &c. Latitude of camp 40 degrees —35. Doubtful longitude 7.3 hours = 109 degrees.

Tuesday, June 27th. Camp No. 24. In camp all day. Took observations. The Major and part of party went up Yampah River this A. M. Steward and Clem went back to Alcove Brook to measure. They were gone until 10:00 P. M. Coming back they concluded to try the river on a cedar log. Came alright until they struck an eddy which took the log down. Steward found that the log would not sustain both, so he let go his hold, leaving Clem on it. The log dipped and tumbled over two or three times, but Clem kept hold of it and finally passed out of the eddy. Meanwhile Steward was taken down three times but being a good swimmer managed to come to the surface and at last got out. Rejoining Clem on the log they came to camp without further adventure, the only loss being Steward's hat and papers.

Wednesday, June 28th. Camp No. 24. In camp half sick. Did but very little except take observations. Thursday, June 29th. Camp No. 24. Climbed Tabernacle Butte 1000 feet this morning. In camp this P. M.

Friday, June 30th. Left camp at 9:30 to climb. Tried to get up river with boat, but after working an hour found that we could not get up until too late for a long climb so went down stream to Steward's' Creek[4] ¾ mile below camp. Landed. Followed up the

———
[4]Steward Creek, now Pool Creek, was named for J. F. Steward, assistant geologist of the expedition, who narrowly escaped drowning.

creek and bottom and canon to plateau, then climbed Folded Strata Cliff ——feet. Had a hard climb. In many places we had to go along the edge of the upturned strata. After getting half way up we came to the edge of the cliff overlooking the river, and looking down a perpendicular cliff of perhaps 800 feet. Along the very edge of this we climbed until we reached the limestone which here ran in vertical butts. We looked along for a place to climb until at last I found a crag that we thought would let us up. Tried it and found that we were above the vertical wall and ten or fifteen minutes of hard climbing put us where the remainder of the ascent was easy. From the crest we can see nearly all of Whirlpool Canon. Think we shall have two portages only. One with a bad landing place, the other good. A good many rapids. We can see the "Gate of Lodore". To the north Dunn's Cliff and Mt. Dawes. Peaks of Sierra Escalante in full view. Perhaps the monument we saw on Dunn's Cliff was erected by Escalante. Can see the Yampah for 20 miles. The river has cut a channel on the side of a long ridge, the valley to the south being many feet lower than the river. The sandstone of the valley is cut up into buttes and canons up the stream. Echo Wall is a long narrow ridge of sandstone. A ridge or range of mountains to the south with a general trend east and west; to north the general trend is the same, but the water has cut what was once a broad plateau into many almost distinct mountains. East, the Yampah Valley west of the ledge cuts off vision. After observations, went out on long narrow ridge towards river. I think the ridge is 20 rods long and in no place more than 20 feet wide and often not half that; at one point it is not 4; tumbled and broken by the weather. On the right or north the cliff is fully 1000 feet down vertical. On the left, south, 1500, but not fully perpendicular, still a misstep or stumble on either side would be fatal. When on the extreme point the view of the river is good. Whirlpool Canon with its rapids is beneath us. Work and danger are there. Can see a good place to climb out. While on this ledge we saw the Emma Dean creeping down Yampah River. With a glass the regular movement of the oars was distinctly seen. Bishop discharged his pistol. The report was loud, the echo rolled from hill to hill like thunder, the boys on the boat heard it. Down the cliff side now. Leaping from rock to rock, sliding down loose soil full of life. Excited, exhilarated, we were but a short time in passing over what had cost us three hours of toil. On reaching the plateau we went down a little dry canon. Sliding down rocks, running along like lizards we were soon at the boat, and soon in camp.

Saturday, July 1, 1871. Camp No. 24. In camp plotting map, &c. Sunday, July 2d. Camp No. 24. In camp all day. Lazy. Copied notes &c. Getting ready to enter Whirlpool Canon. About ¾ mile above our camp we came to a fold in the strata. It is apparently a "depressed fold"; that is, the crust of the earth fell down so that the rock that composes the walls of Echo Park is 2000 feet lower than it ought to be. The formation is Carboniferous. At the "break" the strata stood at an angle of 80 degrees. This sharp angle continues only for perhaps 200 feet, then gradually assumes the dip of the red sandstone.

Monday, July 3rd. Camp No. 25. Left camp 24 at 8:00 o'clock. We ran south for half a mile, then whirl round sharp to north into the red sandstone again. Keep in the sandstone for two and a half miles then striking it $3\frac{1}{2}$ from camp. The sandstone dips below the river, then at what we call Red Sandstone Falls. Ran two little rapids before the falls. Let over the falls by rope, before noon. We see occassional crags of red sandstone left in the general erosion and forming islands in the "transition beds". The limestone stands in crags above the sandstone. Beaman who had stayed at camp 24 to take some pictures, got in at 2:00 P. M. and we started. Ran three rapids without trouble, and camped at the mouth of Brush Creek.[5] Made 7 miles, ran 5 rapids, and let down just one. The river since noon has been in sand and limestones. The Ribbon Buttes are above us. Went down to look at next rapid. Can run it.

Tuesday, July 4th. Camp No. 25. Left camp at 8:30 for a climb. Three of us went up Brush Creek three miles, then climbed out to point "G" on maps. Got to the first cliff, then went along ridge for three miles. Point "G" is very high. Ran the barometer down 3.03 inches. Found that we were just back of Leaping Brook camp. Could see the valley of Cascade Creek [?] as well as Brush. We had the minal [usual?] vegetation on mountains, but found the laurel that only grows at an altitude of about 4000 feet above the river. In some other forms of vegetation could see evidences of great altitude. Got observations and started for camp at 3:45. Tried a new way of getting down. Failed and had a hard climb to get an old track. Made it. Got to camp at 7:30. Had a Fourth of July supper.

Wednesday, July 5th. Camp No. 26. Left camp 25 at 8:00. Ran 5 rapids, three bad, before dinner and let down past one with ropes. At dinner camp I saw sheep on opposite side of river. Three of the boys went over after them. After dinner ran a rapid, then let down past another, then ran two more and came out into "Island Park"[6] and "Whirlpool" was past. Island Park is a broken valley

<hr/>

[5]The record of nomenclature is here incomplete. Dellenbaugh states that, afterwards it was discovered that the stream called "Brush Creek" was not the one long "known by that name in the back country", the name was changed to Bishop Creek after Captain Bishop, and so appears on some maps. The present Brush Creek enters Green River near the village of Jensen.

[6]The entrance to Island Park at the end of Whirlpool Rapids is described by Dellenbaugh:

"Our second day's run was uneventful through a superb gorge about twenty-four hundred feet deep, and at a late hour in the afternoon, just after we had run our worst rapid in fine style, we perceived the great walls breaking away, and they soon melted off into rounded hills, exquisitely colored, as if painted by nature in imitation of the rainbow. The river spread out, between and around a large number of pretty islands bearing thick cottonwood groves. The shallowness of the water caused out keels to touch occasionally, but the current was comparatively slow and we were not disturbed over it. Powell hesitated as to calling this place Rainbow or Island Park, the choice eventually falling to the latter."

crossed by a fold in the strata. The islands in the river are large and covered with a heavy growth of cottonwoods. The "upland" is barren with small cedars and lots of sage. The fold seems to have involved the Carboniferous, Triassic, Jurassic, and Cretaceous, the strata often standing vertical. Camp in a grove of box elders on right bank.

Thursday, July 6th. Camp No. 26. In the morning went out with the Major and took bearings &c. for topography. In the afternoon we went out geologizing. Found Jurassic fossil. The Major has decided to go on ahead to Uintah as he says, but to Salt Lake as I believe.[7] Will go by river. Takes Bishop in his boat in place of Fred. We shall follow in a few days.

Friday, July 7th. Camp No. 26. Got up at 3:00 o'clock. The Major started at daylight. We started to climb the mountain at the same time. Had a long hard climb, getting Beaman's instruments up. Saw the Emma Dean in the rapids. Watched them for a long time. Came down the mountain in 34 minutes. Slept this P. M., wrote &c.

Saturday, July 8th. Camp No. 26. Beaman went up mountain to take pictures. Worked in camp mending &c. Got ready to start but on account of pictures did not. It rained a little last night and this P. M. has rained quite heavily for this country.

Sunday, July 9th. Camp No. 27. Left camp at 8:00 A. M., ran ½ mile when we saw a flock of mountain sheep. Shot at them but failed to hit. Had quite an engagement. Ran a rapid, then let Steward go up a gulch for geology while we let boats down part of the rapid by lines. Lifted boats over a very bad place, then let down by lines for half a mile. Had dinner, then let down another half mile, then ran half a mile, then let down past as bad a rapid as we have seen on the trip. Left our dinner camp after repairing the Canonita at 3:00 and went into camp at 5:00 P. M. Beaman took two pictures. Went down the river to reconnoiter. Saw the cave. Have made 2¾ miles today. Ran one bad rapid and let down with lines a mile and a half, but have not worked in all more than four hours.

Monday, July 10th. Camp No. 28. Beaman took pictures all forenoon. Took crags and cave. Left camp at 1:00 P. M. Let down past two rapids this P. M., and ran six, four bad ones. Struck three times on rocks. Sun in our faces and wind made it very bad running. The canon through which we are passing is Carboniferous and abounding in peaks and crags. The crags until the lower end limestone, there sandstone. Lose the "Ribbon Beds" at the lower end. Walls are often vertical for 1000 or more feet.

----

[7]On July 7 Powell, in the *Dean*, left the party at Island Park and without stops went to the mouth of the Duchesne, where a wagon trail to the Uintah Indian Agency reached the river. At the Agency he had expected to obtain mail, supplies, repairs for boats and return to the party, which in the meantime had been mapping the river and adjoining country. Learning that his wife was ill, he proceeded to Salt Lake City, leaving instructions for Thompson to wait for him.

It is as bad a canon as we have had. More rocks in the stream.
Have passed three places, one, one mile; two, half mile each, that
were full of rocks; the river wide and shallow, current not strong
enough to make bad falls but bad enough to break a boat. Think
we shall get through tomorrow.

Tuesday, July 11th. Camp No. 29. Left camp at 2:00 P. M.
Let boats over the fall before dinner. Beaman made some pictures. Good. Ran three rapids and let down past one. Ran out of
the canon at 5:00 P. M. Camped at the foot of canon. Found
pictures on rock.

Wednesday, July 12th. Camp No. 30. Beaman photographed
pictures this morning. Left camp at 9:00. The foot of Craig
Canon[8] is one of the most desolate, barren looking places that can
be well imagined. Naked sandstone rock composes the mountain-
side. Triassic. Against it lie beds of Triassic and Jurassic. We
are camped in a grove of cottonwoods.[9] The country to the west
is low hils and ridges. To the east for one mile the same. Then
higher to the "Bear River Range."[10] Ran down the river 12 miles
when we were within 2½ miles from morning's camp. Steward
went on hills this P. M. with Fred.

Thursday, July 13th. Camp No. 31. Last night was one of
excitement in our camp. There were several "wick-e-ups" about
one mile southeast of camp. The boys got to talking about Indians
and Steward got to protesting that "he did not like to have the
party divided". Beaman "did not either." Fred hatched up a
dozen ways in which the Major might have met with misfortune.
Of course they were somewhat excited, especially Steward and
Fred. Well, after we had gone to bed, except Fred, he awoke
Steward to show him a light in the west. Beaman and Hattan
awoke in season to see it. I did not. Clem slept. Beaman said it
was Venus setting. Hattan was silent. Steward and Fred were
sure it was a fire and Steward was full of forebodings of ill. Croak-
ed for an hour. Thought perhaps it was some of the Dean's crew
and at that I went to sleep. About 3:00 A. M. we were awakened
by a cracking in the trees. Steward calling to Beaman that perhaps
there might be some wild animal in the tree preparing to leap upon
them. I dozed for a minute when crash down came a big limb, but
fortunately not near us. Beaman and Hattan jumped and ran; I
did the same. Fred caught up his gun, but all was over before any
one stirred. Of course we had a big laugh and all who could went

---

[8]"Crag Canyon" or "Craggy Canyon" appears on the map accompanying the report by J. W.
Powell on the Lands of the Arid Region of the United States as Split Mountain Canyon, the
name now in use.

[9]The general site of Camps 30 and 31 in groves of cottonwood seems to have long been a
favorite camping place for both the Uinta Utes and White River Utes, who here found a favorable
crossing of the river. North of the present town of Jensen and about 2 miles above the mouth of
Brush Creek, Escalante crossed the river in 1776 (September 13)—also others later.

[10]Perhaps Yampa Plateau. By some scouts and fur traders Yampa River was called Bear
River.

to sleep. Steward couldn't, but tossed and fretted all night. In the morning while we were at breakfast talking and laughing over the matter of the night "How! How!" came to our ears, and down the hill rode an Indian in full costume except gun. Went out to meet him, shook hands all round, gave him something to eat and all that. Tried to talk with him, but he did not or could not speak "Americato" so we made poor work of talking. Finally he left us saying "Squaw Squaw" and down the river he went, coming back soon with a young squaw very well dressed and good looking for an Indian. They viewed the boat, we gave them some tobacco and sugar, and went down the river. About two miles down we saw them again on the bank. Went ashore and visited Mr. Lo in his summer wick-e-up. Tried more talk and made out that he was "Douglass Boy" and a White River Ute on his way to visit the Uintah Utes and wanted us to ferry him across the river. We did so, swimming his ponies, one a fine American horse, the other a poor pony. Went on our way and about the middle of the afternoon came to another camp. The men were away, but two squaws and a lot of pappooses were at home. Left some tobacco for the chief. Camped in a poor place after making about 20 miles southwest. Tertiary all day.

Friday, July 14th. Camp No. 32. Left camp 31 at 7:00 A. M. Made a nice run without anything of special interest until noon. After dinner found we could reach Uintah [Duchesne][11] river by hard work so pulled out for it. Ran nicely until about 4:00 P. M. when we encountered a storm that delayed us an hour or so. At sundown we reached the mouth of a river which looked as though it might be the Uintah, but was in the wrong place on the map. Down a mile we could see what seemed to be another river. Ran down to it, fired signal gun and all that, but no reply. Ran down half a mile further and camped. The croakers as usual are full of forebodings. The boys are killed. Everything bad has happened. We ought to start in the morning for Uintah and all that. I am going to sleep. Shall find traces of them in morning I think.

Saturday, July 15th. Camp No. 32. Got up early this morning and went down the river. Found mouth of White River ½ mile below. Then went up river until I came to the old ferry crossing.[12] On opposite side looked like tracks and traces of the boys. Decided to come up after breakfast and cross river to look for word. After breakfast we rowed up. Found that the boys had been here,

[11]On early maps and in descriptions by trappers and others the Uinta is shown as a tributary to Green River, and the smaller Duchesne as tributary to the Uinta.

[12]Camp 32 at the mouth of the Duchesne, which served as a base for Thompson's party from July 14 to August 5, was at the crossing most used by trappers and prospectors on the route from Colorado to Utah. Fort Robidoux (now White Rocks) was established about 1830 or 1832 about 30 miles up the Duchesne and Uinta Rivers; in 1871 the only building on or near the Green-Colorado in Utah north of Lee's Ferry. A ferry crossing at Camp 32 was part of the route from Golden, Colo., to Provo, Utah. The route, including a ferry at the present village of Ouray, is still in use.

and after long search found an old oyster can with note from
Major in it saying he had gone to Uintah. Went to camp. Spent
the day in visiting. At 7:00 P. M. while we were at supper heard
three shots and soon yells and saw two horesmen riding towards
our camp like Indians. Soon made them out to be Bishop and
Jones. Shook hands, got mail and learned that the Major had gone
to Salt Lake on account of his wife's sickness, that Hiller was at
the Agency, and the "Dean" up the river; that they had brought
two horses for Beaman and myself to go up to the Agency on.
We spent two or three hours talking over trip, then went to bed.

Sunday, July 16th. Camp No. 32. In camp getting ready to
go to Uintah. Monday, July 17th. Worked getting ready for a
start all the morning. Left camp at 3:00 P. M. Made 10 miles and
camped.

Tuesday, July 18th. Started at sunrise for agency. Got there
at 5:00 P. M. [Present day White Rocks.] Found "Heap Indians"
and some "White Men". Gave us use of Major Critchlow's office
and are disposed to accommodate all they can. Apparently, I am
not very much impressed with the success of the attempt to civilize
the Indian. The employees at the Agency plough the land, furnish seed, dig the irrigating ditches, cut the grains; in fact do all
the work that requires the use of tools. The Indians irrigate a little.
The "bucks" make the squaws do the work while they race horses
or loaf around the Agency. It is costly, the appropriations being
$30,000 for present year. Mr. Basor tells me there are not to ex-
ceed 200 Utes on both this and the White River Agency. Employees say that the Uintah Utes go over to the White River, pass
themselves off as belonging to that band, get presents, then come
back to Uintah and White River Utes do the same. The employees, all without exception, state that the Indians will steal
from Mormons at every chance, especially horses and cattle. The
employees do not seem to care how much stealing is done by the
Indians, provided the Mormons are the sufferers. An Indian called
Tyank started out some two months ago on a horse stealing expedition. Said he was going to "get ponies from Mormons." Went
over into the valley and got eight or ten horses and started for
Uintah; was followed, shot at and wounded in leg and forced to
abandon all but three horses and one mule. "Leg much sick," he
said. He has just got well. No notice was taken of the offense.
Others have been known to steal and get blankets. Two or three
months ago a trapper was killed by some Utes. The agent presented the mean doers with presents "to teach them to do so no
more."[13]

Wednesday, July 19th. Still at Agency. Have examined the

---
[13]Thompson's description of his experience at the Uintah Agency (Fort Robidoux or White
Rocks) gives a clear view of the relations of Government officials to the Mormons and to the
Indians and the difficulties of administration in isolated reservations.

rations. Shall start Basor tomorrow. Talked pictures with Table Antro and other "big Indians." Will photograph them tomorrow. The men at Agency have some fine wheat *in spots.* Corn is small and poor, potatoes look well. Garden vegetables ditto. The valley seems to be fertile wherever water can be used to irrigate.[14] The Indian is "heap lazy" I think. The white man could better afford to board him in Illionis than keep up a reservation here. Major Critchlow has gone to Salt Lake to buy a sawmill for the place. It seems to be that a grist mill would be much better. More real use. Major Critchlow seems to be very much disliked by both employees and Indians. "Kutch wano," not good, they say. He has, if the truth is told, altogether too strict notions to please, but I think I can see that he is much better than they are willing to allow.

Thursday, July 20th. At Agency. Sent rations today. Seargin went to camp. Beaman took pictures of several chiefs &c. Tried to make talk but guess I made an ass of myself. Friday, July 21st—Uintah. Second day. Heap lazy, as red man says. Saturday, July 22d. Waiting for the Major is slow work. Basor got back today.

Sunday, July 23d. Went with Leighton and Campbell to see the Indians. Rode mile. Went to Lo-ke-wa-na's wick-e-up first. He has a lodge of canvas and a summer house of boughs. Was lying on a buffalo robe. Squaw was smoking an elk skin. Fire in middle of wick-e-up. The boys sat in a ring and smoked with the host, and a visitor. He seemed to be the most industrious, best dispositioned Indian among them. Has perhaps two acres wheat, one of potatoes, one of corn that he has done most of the work on. Has it fenced with a sort of brush fence to keep out the goats and stock. His squaw looks old but seems to enjoy life better than most of them, that is, is not abused as much. We then went to Toby's wick-e-up. Not at home. Then to the "Doctors" where we found Toby and his squaw. Had quite a talk. The Doctor is a foul mouthed Indian. Asked when the Major would be back. Told him in two sleeps maybe three. Maybe one "Kutch" said he. "Kutch pike" one moon, maybe two. "Maybe one snow." Doctor asked me if I had a squaw. Told him yes. "Where?" said he. "Salt Lake." "Mormon, Mormon," said he. "Kutch Mormon," said I. "No Mormon. Squaw Mormon. Wick-e-up pretty soon come Pappoose," said he. "Kutch," said I. "How many moons pappoose," said he. "Kutch moons," said I. "Pappoose got one. Uh," said he.

––––

[14]Using the reconnaissance maps made by Thompson, Powell (Lands of the Arid Region of the United States) estimated the irrigable lands in the Uintah Basin, chiefly Uinta and Duchesne Valleys extending eastward along White River, as 280,320 acres. He described the Uinta-White Basin as "one of the most favored districts of the West"—an estimate justified by later development of the region about Duchesne, Roosevelt, and Vernal.

Saw some old worn out Moquis mills, so said. It seems
that the Utes have a tradition that the valley was once inhabited
by another race of men called "Sinob," men who cut the inscriptions on rocks made the old mills, built the old houses, but died because they knew too much. Indians' corn does not look well.
Planted late. Rode to find some old Moquis ruins. Unsuccessful.
Saw remains of Robedous trading post. Crossed a good many
nice little streams. To the Agency at 12:00. Wrote this P. M.
and read in novels.

Monday, July 24th. Waiting for the Major. Beaman having
box fixed. Tuesday, July 25th. Beaman's box not done. Wednesday, July 26th. Went to wigwams this A. M. and got three negatives. The Major came at 7:00 P. M. tonight.[15] Mr. Shelton, an
interpreter, came with him. Got letters from wife and others.

Thursday, July 27th. The Major thinks that he ought to go
to the mouth of the Dirty Devil by land. It seems that Mr. Hamblin has found a way into the river. The river that he thought was
the Dirty Devil proves to be the San Rafael, and it is extremely
doubtful if he can get in even there. The Major has employed
Mr. Dodds to go with Jacob and will go himself with Mr. Shelton
if an Indian can be induced to go along. Have talked all day with
Indians, but with no success so far. Have sent letters to Salt Lake
to Basor.

Friday, July 28th. Decided to kill a steer for beef and risk
Dodds, or Indian as the case may be. So in the morning the Major
and myself went out to hunt cattle. After some search we sep-
arated. The Major was unsuccessful. I found a lot and drove
them to corral. One red, glaring steer that I selected the Indians
said was Dodds, so Shelton shot it. We dressed and divided with
the Agency people and Indians. Built a little fire and dried it partially, to enable us to pack it down. Shall go to camp tomorrow
without fail. Tyank's brother goes with us to bring back the horses.
I think the Major takes this trip not because he is tired of the
river. That he isn't tired, but thinks the work can be as well done
without him. He would not own that this is the case of course,
but it is and thus determines his decision. He proposes to meet us
at Gunnison's Crossing before the 3rd of September, but I have
no idea that he will. The only thing I regret is that I have agreed
to wait until the 3rd of September. I think the Major will go to
Salt Lake before his return. Will be this way. He will go with
Hamblin and find a way to the D. D. then will have two weeks
spare time. Will think he can go there and meet us at D. D. so

---

[15]After Thompson had waited eight days, Powell returned from Salt Lake with the report
that attempts to bring supplies to the mouth of the Fremont had failed and that he must return
to Salt Lake to make other plans. Thompson was instructed to continue the river exploration 150
miles farther and to await Powell a month later at the end of Gray Canyon, near Green River,
Utah. If he failed to return, Thompson was to continue the river trip to the mouth of the Paria
on the provisions received at Uintah.

we will be idle at Gunnison's Crossing two or three weeks waiting for him, then have hard work and half do the work to the D. D.

Saturday, July 29th. This morning got up early and worked hard for three hours to get ready. Left the Agency at 8:00 A.M. Made good time to dinner at 12:00. Then good time to camp No. 32 at 7:00 P. M. The Indian rode on ahead and got the boys across the river to meet us. They seemed to be glad that we were back. The Indian was quite talkative today. Gave very graphic descriptions of his visits to [Fort] Bridger and Denver. Saw the cars. Saw white people, saw "heap store" "heap wick-e-up," "heap whiskey, vwano whiskey." My impressions of the Indians, the Agency, are unchanged. The Agency as at present conducted is a cheat, a swindle. The Indians do not make good agriculturalists. The attempt to raise grain &c fails. It seems as though something ought to be done in the way of stock raising. Some of them, as Antro, for instance, have quite a number of cattle. Tom has a large lot of goats and so on.

Sunday, July 29th. In camp. Spent the Sabbath quietly. Our Indian whom we ferried across the river came into camp today, was hungry. He is camped the other side of the river. Squaw with him, of course. At the Agency we were told that he had run away with the squaw betrothed to another. It looks like a love affair and romantic. Monday, July 30th. In camp. Bishop working on maps. Tuesday, July 31st. In camp. Working on maps, etc. Wednesday, August 1, 1871. In camp. Thursday, August 2d. In camp. All ready to start when maps are completed. Friday, August 4th. In camp. Ready this P. M. to leave the valley.

Saturday, August 5th. Camp No. 32. Took a "Lunar" this morning. Broke camp at 8:00 A. M. Ran 8⅛ miles to Dinner Camp at 11:30. On the right side near a bluff of sandstone 200 feet the "Turtle Beds" of White River. Climbed out. The country is a low broken desert plateau as nearly barren as any I have seen. It is elevated about 200 feet above the river. The streams in spring have cut the cliffs in many places into alcoves or rather it looks as though water had run over the top of the cliffs and falling worn alcoves. In any depression or valley a stream flows in units at times and coming to the cliff has often broken the walls down. Along the river are frequent groves of cottonwoods. The upland has only a small quantity of sage and an egilobium. The very sage looks dead. We passed the mouths of Uintah [Duchesne] and White Rivers.[16] The first is 6 rods wide, 6 feet deep, current 3 miles. The latter 8 rods wide and 8 feet deep, current 3 miles. The Green has been from 200 to 600 feet wide. Current averages two miles. In a few places I think the river has narrowed

---

[16]From Dellenbaugh's Journal it appears that during the absence of Thompson at the Uintah Agency a party led by Bishop made a five-day exploration of White River, including the fantastic erosion feature of "Goblin City."

to 100 feet. The water has generally been deep. Pulled out at 2:15. Landed to hunt deer. Beaman shot a badger. No deer. Ran until 5:30—7⅞ miles, making 16¾ in all. We have made 26 miles by our map, but it is wrong. Camp on island on right.

Sunday, August 6th. Camp No. 33. In camp all day. Beaman sick. Climbed the plateau this forenoon. The general level of the country is about 350 feet above the river. Very barren and desolate. Not even sage. Very few cacti. I think it merits the name of "Desolation."[17] The walls of the cliffs when they come to the river are cut by side streams in spring into gulches up one of which we climbed. Could see the mountains in the south. Buttes occasionally reared their heads all about us. The sandstone is broken into long posts, indeed all the strata exposed show a tendency to break into parallel separation. Some posts are 8 feet by 6 inches by 4 inches, often smaller. Strata dip N. W. at an angle of about one degree. We are camped in a cottonwood grove. The trees are not large and many of them are leaning to N. W. On the other side the river the trees are about the same size, but lean S. E. It seems as though a whirlwind just passed down the river not long ago. Our island, as are all islands in the river, is a bed of sand. The bed of the river seems to be clay. Read "Scott" this P. M. Am reading "Emerson" to the boys on the boat as we go along.

Monday, August 7th. Camp No. 34. Made 16¼ miles today. Left camp at 7:30. The river was very shallow this A. M. Wound many times. Ran until 10:45, then stopped and climbed out. Climbed the same butte that the Major and party climbed [in 1869.] The walls, or rather the plateau, is getting higher, cliffs along the river sometimes 500 feet. Since leaving camp 33 the banks have risen from the river in terraces. The first cliff or terrace at our camp seems to be about 450 feet, then back say a mile, the second rising to 1000 feet. The terraces rise usually above them. Their faces seem fluted or cut in immense alcoves, not very deep, but increasing. Often the whole face of the cliff will be buttressed at regular intervals like some Gothic church. At a distance it reminds one of pictures of some old castle. The present cap of the first terrace is a very hard, compact, clayey limestone, and projects like a *true* cap from the top. The view from the top of the Butte we climbed was peculiar. The country is still desolate. Cut by side gulches until it looks like pictures of canons in "Iris". Shot a beaver this P. M., killed and got one. Bishop skinned it and we shall try it tomorrow for breakfast.

————

[17]For about 90 miles south of the present Uteland Mine, Green River runs through a region of scant vegetation, where the bare rocks exposed along the river and in side gulches are eroded into picturesque "bad land" features, "the ruggedest gully that can be conceived." On modern maps this stretch of river through the north slopes of Tavaputs Plateau is termed Desolation Canyon.

Tuesday, August 8th. Camp No. 34. Beaver fried for break-fast. The taste is much like beef. Left camp at 7:30. Rowed down a mile when we came to a good view. Stopped for pictures and geology until noon. Got an indifferent negative. Beaman sick. Broke camp at 1:00 P. M. Ran a little rapid at first turn. Seemed like old times. Ran two miles, then came to a vast amphi-theatre. Stopped for pictures. Got one but were too near. Did not show an amphitheatre, but only cliffs. Decided to stop until morning and ascend the hill back of camp. Climbed the hill. The river has nearly cut through the cliff. Is within 500 feet after a circuit of a mile and a half.

Wednesday, August 9th. Camp No. 35. Went up with Beaman on the hill to take pictures. Got one, but it being very cloudy, it was not sharp. Decided to stop and try the afternoon and tomorrow, if necessary. Left camera &c on top. In afternoon went across the river to a side canon. The side canons are pic-tures. Often do not reach back more than ½ a mile. Such a one we were in. On either side rose castellated towers as gate posts to the height of 800 feet, fluted and pinnacled like some gigantic columning fit for the Temple of Nature. The way between these "sentinels" is perhaps 200 feet wide. You enter. Rock loose in your path. Crags hundreds of feet high around. Above a narrow way or path leads on for perhaps a hundred feet, then loses itself behind a bastion from the mighty wall. You follow up. The lines of a spring torrent afford foothold. Soon you reach the spot where a leap has been taken. It may be ten or it may be fifty feet. No matter. If the sides do not afford a place for footing we make detour, climb over loose gravel, dig foothold in the shale until we get above. Sometimes the walls narrow to perhaps two feet. In one the cleft is not more than two feet and yet turns at right angles. We went up with varying ease until within 200 feet of the top when the "crack" we were following widened out into an am-phitheatre with overhanging walls. No ascent possible, so down we go. We are camped under box-elder trees. In the valley cotton-woods are the only trees. In the canons are box-elders and some cottonwoods.

Thursday, August 10th. Camp No. 36. This morning went on the mountain with Beaman for pictures. He took seven good ones. Had dinner at 11:30 and dropped down half a mile and stopped while another view was taken. Ran down 12 miles and camped on left bank. The walls of the canon are becoming more vertical and closer to the river. Walls very rough and craggy from 1000 to 1400 feet. Side canyons every half mile. Groves box-elder and willow along the river. Bottom on one side or the other about ¼ of a mile wide. Canon ¾ of a mile wide at top Small cedars on the top of the canon walls. Passed one weak rapid. The walls are in rough arcs with Gothic buttresses at the extremities.

Friday, August 11th. Camp No. 37. This morning Captain Steward and myself climbed the right wall of canon. In about an hour and a half after a hard climb up a gulch, and along talus under high cliff reached the top. We are not in a mountain range, but the river has cut its way down 2500 feet into a Tertiary plateau. The general dip of the plateau is 5 degrees nearly north. So "Little Mountains" of our map are but a gentle slope or sloping plateau. [North slope of Tavaputs Plateau.] Ten or fifteen miles to the south the plateau appears more elevated, and a ridge extending in an easterly and westerly direction, seems to exist. This may be but an optical illusion, however. Found on the summit pinon, cedar and arborvitae. Greasewood and cedar growing on slope. The bituminous shale forms the top stratum. The canon is from five to eight miles wide at the summit on an average. Near the river the walls rise nearly vertical for 1200 to 1800 feet. At that height the walls are not usually more than $\frac{1}{4}$ mile abroad and quite rugged from the side canons. They then break back irregularly to the above mentioned width. Imagine the ruggedest gully that can be conceived—in fact a great crack; and you have the canon. Huge columns 500 feet high. Flanked by pinnacles, sectors of arcs with Gothic Buttresses. Sharp crags with their feet in the river and heads in the clouds. Wide slides of loose earth or talus. Valley is filled up with debris, through which the spring torrents have cut deep narrow channels or sometimes tunnels and all looking like the work of a madman, and you have the canons as seen from our highest point. Away in the distance to the north we could look back to the mountains forming Craggy Canon, [Split Mountain Canyon], and the Uintah Range. To the east White River Tertiary hills, and the valley called "fine and fertile" but which is in truth a desolate rough country with the tops of the ridges covered by stunted cedars and pinons. No water except spring torrents. To the south the ridge mentioned seems to have some pine timber on the very summit. We reached camp at 10:30. Beaman has taken five pictures. Left camp at 1:00 P. M. Ran about three miles when we came to a rapid. Examined and ran it. Came to another that looked so easy that we tried it without examination. We struck our keel on a rock but went through alright. The Dean followed, but struck on the same rock and stuck fast. The rock had about 12 inches of water on it, and could not be seen from above. While the Dean was on the rock the Canonita came along. Beaman tried a new experiment, or got scared, or something else, and steered his boat straight for a sunken rock out of the channel. Struck it bow-on, swung around, and drifted side-ways on a rock; stove a hole on her side, got off and floated down to a landing. The Dean soon got off without damage. We hauled the Canonita up and repaired her. (She had broken a rib and plank.) At 3:00 P. M. started again. The river has many shallow rocky places that are hard to run and somewhat dangerous. Have been very lucky so far, and have got through them alright, but the other boats have grounded several times. We are camped almost on the spot where the party camped before. Five miles ran four rapids.

Saturday, August 12th. Camp No. 38. Left camp at 7:45. Made 6¼ miles passing eight rapids and camped at 11:15 on the same ground that the party of two years ago did. They called the distance we have made 12½ miles. Think that so far the low water has been an advantage to us in the rapids. Have lain in camp this P. M. reading. The Sergeant and Fred climbed the mountain and got some pitch. There are at least three fine views from our camp. I do not like the lazy way we are traveling, but it is better than reaching the crossing before the 23rd inst. We are booked for a long wait, I am thinking.

Sunday, August 13th. Camp No. 38. This morning Jones, Steward and myself left camp at 8:00 o'clock to climb the wall of the canon south of camp. Had sharp work for an hour and a half when we got to the top, 2578 feet. We were not on the general level of the plateau by some 300 feet, estimated. On the bank of the river are some fine large cottonwoods, then comes a bench of greasewood and sage, then as you rise the hills, cedars; a little further up, pinon pine, and when 1500 feet, spruce trees often 15 to 18 inches in diameter are met. Stunted pines and cedars on the summits. The slopes of all the ridges are much heavier wooded than the very crests. In the gulches at the foot of the cliff we found water seeping out from a stratum of sandstone, and gathering into a little thread-like stream winding down through willows and coarse reed-like grass, leaping over falls of 20 feet and losing themselves in the gravel below. The view from the summit was of the same character as already described: a great gorge worn by water rough and ragged in the extreme. To the south the ridge spoken of before seems higher than the rest of the plateau, and appears more like the axis. Took bearings. Reached camp at 1:00 P. M. Worked up observation for height this afternoon.

Monday, August 14th. Camp No. 39. Left camp 38 at 8:30. Pushed and pulled our boats over the first rapid. Then ran one, then let down over two and camped for dinner. After dinner ran one bad rapid, then a little one. Then let down over a bad one, and camped under some cottonwoods on left bank. Made 5¼ miles, 7 rapids, by our estimate, but 8½ by two years ago. Beaman got a picture of the rapids just above dinner camp. We call it "Fretwater Falls." It makes a nice view. Stopped at 3:00 P. M. so that he might take others, but his chemicals not working well, he only got one. Boys are in good spirits tonight. We are getting along nicely, and my only anxiety is to "spin out" the distance between here and White River so as not to get there before the 23rd inst. Not over 40 miles and ten days. Country very barren of interest. The Tertiary still dipping at a small angle. The plateau still the same, and a great sameness in the scenery. I believe that I have not mentioned that it is the northern slopes of the mountains that are usually covered with timber, and the slopes, while the crests have only stunted cedars and pinons. No birds in the canon. Bats are quite plentiful and have been in Desolation.

Tuesday, August 15th. Camp No. 40. Beaman took four views this morning. Left camp 39 at 9:30. Ran three rapids or rather let down with ropes over one and kicked through two. Camped for dinner at 12:00. Left dinner camp at 2.15. Let down past two rapids and camped at 5:30. Made four miles. The river seems to be low. At our first "let-down" the river is not over 60 feet and the fall at least 10 in 200 yards, and 30 in half a mile. The rapids seem to be either very bad or very shallow. Rapids that could be run with perfect ease and safety with two feet more water are now well nigh impassable without a portage on account of rocks exposed. We have adopted a new style of portage. Two men go along with the boat, feet hanging over, then when the boat comes near a rock, push her off or jump into the water and guide her through the channel. Another holds by the rope from the rock or shore as a safeguard in case of accident. It is easier for the boats but harder for men. We have so far found a valley from ¼ to ¾ of a mile wide, usually covered with sage, greasewood, and latterly cedars.

Wednesday, August 16th. Camp No. 40. In camp. This A. M. Jones and myself crossed the river and went down the left bank two or three miles. Think we are at the beginning of the mountains put down on the map. The Captain and Jones have finished plotting their maps. Steward has copied his notes. It has been very hazy so much that I did not take the climb that I wished to this P. M. There are two or three good views from this camp. Beaman thought the atmosphere too hazy, so did not get them. This P. M. Captain Bishop and myself went up the river a mile or so, then up a gulch. Found a spring flowing from a stratum 300 feet above the river. It has formed quite a mass of travertine-like incrustations. The water is strongly alkaline.

Thursday, August 17th. Camp No. 41. This A. M. Jones, Steward and myself climbed the cliff west of camp. It is the highest point yet climbed, about 3100 feet, and I think the highest point in the plateau, though there may be others to the southwest as high. It was quite hazy so that our view was limited, yet we could see that the character of the canon changes below our camp. The ridges seem to start in the plateau six or eight miles away, and come down as a ridge to the river. Walls of canon evidently getting lower. In fact the ridges present the appearance of the beginning of a valley—i. e. the second stage when lateral erosion begins to over-balance vertical. Some good timber, such as spruce, pine, and cedar. Saw a few bushes of mountain maple. We find the bituminous shales on the very summit, but lose them below. Heavy bedded sandstone is the base. Dip N. 1 degree. At 2:20 P. M. we left camp. Ran 3¼ miles passing five rapids over three of which we had to let down with ropes. Camped at 5:30 on right bank in sandy valley in grove of cottonwoods. Left Beaman ¾ of a mile up the river to take views. He got some fine ones. Left him at the mouth of Nine Mile Creek, a beautiful little clear stream about a rod wide, coming in from the west. It has considerable water now, showing that it must be fed by springs. Indeed, the whole country seems to be much more favored in the way of springs than since Red Canon, though all the water is strongly alkaline. Beaman got a view of what I think is the highest nearly vertical cliff that we have seen. It is nearly 2800 feet above river. Called it Log Cabin Cliff on account of some shales that present the appearance of a Log Cabin. Dreamed of Pennell's folks last night. Record it to see if there is any coincidence. I seemed to be impressed with the presence of some member of the family and I have been unable to shake off the feeling today. Am trying Bruce Sage's theories.

Friday, August 18th. Camp No. 42. Beaman took two views this morning. Left camp at 10:30. Ran three rapids and let down first one before dinner, making two miles. Left dinner camp at 2:15 and ran three rapids and let down past one very bad one, making 2⅝ miles and camp 42 at 5:30, 4⅝ miles 8 rapids. Our map does not correspond with the map made two years ago, so we are uncertain where we are, but think about 20 miles from White River. The rapids have been rather better today than yesterday or the day before. Still sunken rocks make them dangerous. We got on a rock in the middle of the river today, but got off easily. Have found a valley of perhaps ¼ mile wide on one or the other side of the river all day. Sand-hills are frequent in these valleys, apparently formed by the wind. One that I noticed today was at least 20 feet higher than the valley.

Saturday, August 19th. Camp No. 43. Left camp at 7:30. Ran four rapids and let down past three in 4⅝ miles before dinner. Camped at 11:30. Let down past one and ran one mile after dinner, making 5⅝, and 8 rapids in all. Beaman took a view of the rapid, or fall, after dinner while we were letting the boats down. Called the fall "Chandler's Falls,"[18] and a little brook that comes in form the left, near the head of the Falls "Chandler's Creek." Stopped after half an hour's run this afternoon that Beaman might

---

[18]Chandler was the maiden name of the wife of J. F. Steward, assistant geologist of the expedition.

get views. Up a gulch on the right is a natural bridge of at least 300 feet span. It is 1500 feet above the river and 150 feet high. The walls of the canon are becoming more broken, lower, and the gulches broader. Dunes along the river. Angular masses of rock are becoming quite a feature in the valleys. They are the heavy bedded sandstone that here are the top of the cliffs.

Sunday, August 20th. Camp No. 44. This morning Beaman went over the river to get a view. While gone we ran the other boats down past one rapid and ran another in ¾ mile to a better camp, then went back and helped him over. Read "Emerson" aloud until noon. This P. M. climbed the wall of canon 1200 feet. Could see down the river two or three miles. Same general features. Ridges running from the plateau five miles back down to the river. More abrupt on the southern slope. Wooded on northern. On the north or right of the river the ridges seem longer than south, and more broken. Could see five ridges on the right, that seemed to be grand features in the topography, the first north of Camp 43, the other lower down. We are camped in a little valley under some old cottonwoods. The valley perhaps is a quarter of a mile wide, on the right bank is covered with cedars and greasewood, then the canon wall rises abruptly 500 feet, then back and up and impassable for 2000 feet. Looking up the river the canon wall checks the view at a bend half a mile above. Across the river a butte-like peak has its feet in the water and its head 1200 feet above. A little lower down the valley crosses the stream, and widens as on this. To the south the walls are lower and we look out to what seems like the opening of a valley. The outlines of beautiful scenery are here but want the adorning. Desolate now, and for years to come it must remain. It seems like geologically the first stages of a valley.

Monday, August 21st. Camp No. 45. Left camp at 7:30. Ran 4⅛ miles with 7 rapids over 6 of which we let down with ropes. Dinner Camp at 11:00. Left dinner Camp at 3:30. Ran 2¼ miles with four rapids letting over one, making 6⅜ miles, 11 rapids. The walls of canon often present more the appearance of isolated cliffs. The valleys are becoming wider, but those changes are gradual. Had a row with Beaman this morning. While letting down the first rapid he steered his boat out into the strong current where there was every probability of rocks, and ran through. I had told him where to go before starting. We had a few sharp words, and I told him plainly that he could not run his boat where I told him not to, that he must and should run it as I told him. Said some foolish things, but did him good, I think. He has taken three negatives today. Fine views. Much might be "gushed" on the scenery, ruined castles, turrets, minarets, natural bridges, &c. but I cannot gush. I leave this writing to read "Miles Standish."

Tuesday, August 22d. Camp No. 46. Left camp at 7:45.

Ran 2⅛ miles, passing five rapids, letting down past four of them before dinner. Camp at 11:00. Left dinner camp at 3:00 and ran 2⅛ miles with four rapids, making 5¼ miles, 8 rapids. Our first rapid this morning was a beautiful one. Swift, long, and no rocks. We swept along it gayly. The next one was a bad one. Think it was the one described by Jack Sumner as where they let down under an overhanging cliff by stages, the last man swimming after the boats had passed. If so, it has improved by low water. We had no trouble. Came to two peculiar rapids just below a digression in the river. The river suddenly narrowed to 75 feet and shot down a fall of four to six feet in ten rods. Then a sharp turn to the left and over rocks. We ran the shorts and landed in the eddy. Had another very peculiar one. The main channel of the river narrowed to less than 50 feet and fell 8 feet in ten rods. The first fall must have been five feet. The waters were higher than we have been in. Ran it alright, but is was exciting. While down examining a rapid I saw a horse feeding on the hillside on the opposite side of the river. Thought it might be the Major. After dinner took the field glass and examined the horse and locality. Nothing in sight. Ran the boats down to the spot under some excitement. The boys saw the horse before landing, and there was a "buggy." Went in rapidly so that if any "friendless" were encamped they might "shoot over". Landed. I ran up the bank, gave three or four whoops to alarm anybody. No answer. Went to the horse and found him dead lame. Examined the valley. No sign that anybody had been there for weeks. We finally concluded that the horse belonged to Indians who were encamped there in the spring, had fallen lame and been left. Ran down half a mile further, landed to look at a rapid when I found a stratum of sandstone containing fresh water fossils. We were just at a good camp, so landed.

Wednesday, August 23rd. Camp No. 47. Left camp 46 at 1:30 P. M. Let boats down past a bad rapid, then waited while Beaman got two views. Then pulled out and ran a rapid, then a long stretch of rapid river, and we made 2¾ miles, 2 rapids and Camp 47 at 5:00 P. M. Climbed up the cliffs this A. M. The walls of the canon, or rather the plateau have dropped at once from 2500 to 1600 feet, leaving the edge of the high plateau very abrupt —ridges projecting into the plain and needle-like cliffs about 500 feet high on the edge.[19] Everything rough and rugged. Camp 46 was just at the "breakdown." From our point of view, the plateau seems to rise again toward the south until it reaches nearly the original height. It seems as though the stratum above the needle cliffs had formed a protecting cap for the brown sandstone that

———

[19]The canyon traversed August 23-26 is now known as Gray Canyon. It cuts across the lofty Tavaputs Plateau. Its southern face is Book Cliffs. Because of numerous coal outcrops it is called also Coal Canyon.

breaks easily under regular fragment, and thus disintegrates rapidly—this stratum or strata have been graded from the south up to the point of breaking down. The dip has increased rapidly for the last two days—is now 5°—and being another protecting stratum in the surface about 15 miles long. We followed the bed of a dry gulch for two or three miles, working on a bed of lime-stone very hard, and apparently difficult to erode. It may be that this is the cap or "meridian" below. Beaman took several fine views. Steward has collected some fine fossils, twins caladunae milunae. Think it a ——————but very short and glossy. The rapid im-mediately below camp 46, falls 15 feet in 30 rods. Half a mile below the stream the river divides into four channels. We took a middle one, but it was shallow and we struck many times so I signalled the other boats to take the right channel. The Dean tried it, ran on a fallen, sunken tree, broke an oarlock but did no other damage. The Canonita tried our channel and came through alright. Rained a little this P. M.

Thursday, August 24th. Camp No. 48. Left camp 47 at 7:20. Ran 6½ miles, 5 rapids, letting down twice. Dinner camp at 12:00. Pulled out at 2:15, ran 5⅞ miles, 6 rapids, letting down just one —making 12⅜ miles, 11 rapids with bad "let downs". I think I was mistaken yesterday about the bad portage spoken of by Sum-ner. It was undoubtedly our last let down. The canon has been about ½ mile wide at top today, often not more than ¼. The wall on one or the other side nearly vertical for 300 feet. Composed largely of buff sandstone. Soon after leaving Camp 46 this morn-ing the dip increased 7 or 8 degrees, and soon seams of impure coal or lignite just below, found a stratum containing silver pectin &c, Cretaceous fossils, showing that we had passed from fresh to salt water. Found a salty incrustation on the rock and many places in the last three miles. We have evidently passed the di-vision between formations. The walls in the canon are about ½ mile apart, 500 feet vertical height, then avert back until perhaps five miles at top of plateau. The sandstone wall is worn in many places into grottoes and alcoves. One near our camp is entered by a narrow channel which widens and winds for 6 or 8 rods, then expands into a rotunda 200 feet across, vertical at top for 200 feet. The voice echoes and reverberates as in a canon. Went up again in the bed of a spring torrent. The very narrow abut at every turn; the view above, ahead and below cut off and only a rugged rift of sky above, is a complete representation of contour canons given by Dana.

Friday, August 25th. Camp No. 49. Left camp 48 at 12:20, ran 5¾ miles, leaving 6...... two and reached camp at the mouth of ....River at 3:15. ....Jones................out. Went to top of ...., is elevated about 2000 feet, but cut into............ ragged gulches, gullies, and peaks. There are pinons and cedars on .... mountains and little bunch grass on the plateau; it has a most desolate appearance. Quite a valley has been washed out at this point of observation and the needle cliffs. Left camp 48 at 12:15. Have seen some very nice views this afternoon. Have observed for several days that wherever we camp is an island composed of small necks, usually swift current in the river—all them are land pointing downward like shoals. Came to Little White [Price River] at 3:15. Camped The [Little] White has been 60 feet wide sometime, but it is dry now. Went up the stream two miles. The stream is very crooked; valley usually ¾ mile wide, box-elder and cottonwoods along the banks; some walls of canon 1000 feet, half the time vertical. No climbing out for miles. Sheep and deer in valley. Think Indians came down it.

Saturday, August 26th. Camp No. 50. Left camp 49 at 7:20. Ran 8¼ miles, running 8 rapids, letting down once near w. end of canon, and camped at .... We are getting along well, but a week's waiting will be hard. The country from [Little] White River is about the same as above. Have made 122⅝ miles with 94 rapids since leaving Uintah. Have let down just 32 of the rapids with ropes, but made no portage. The party two years ago estimated the same distance at 157 miles. Have run 18 days in all, but generally only part of the day. We have run only three days all day and slow then. Have been 21 days from Uintah, thus averaging about 6 miles a day or 7¼ running days. Jones and myself went down the river two miles—no sign of the Major. Will discuss the country another time.

Sunday, August 27th. Camp No. 50. In camp. Steward and myself went down the river five miles. Went below what I suppose is the old Spanish Crossing and poor country. Camped. Took a rough observation for latitude 37°-12-1. Sent Fred and Jack to put up the flag on the end of the island. We had the boats hauled up on the sand today for repair. Saw the Indians wick-e-ups down the valley, but they seemed to have been built more than two years. The valley is desolate, a barren waste of sand. Along the river are groves of cottonwoods. From our camp it merges out and apparently extends south for 20 miles. It is an eroded valley with cliffs all around, castellated in fairy turrets, pinnacles, towers, and bastions. One butte opposite our camp is like a Gothic church, spire on one end and buttresses along the side. [Cathedral Butte; Gunnison Buttes.] We are now in the upper beds of Cretaceous worn by water into great circular crenulations.

Monday, August 29th. Camp No. 51.[20] Work this forenoon.

[20]Camp 51 among the cottonwoods along the river near the present village of Green River, Utah, was in 1871 the best known place on the Green-Colorado between the Uinta Mountains and the mouth of Virgin River. The crossing here much used by the Indians was part of the "Old Spanish trail" from Santa Fe, N. Mex., to Los Angeles, Calif., used by William Wolfskill in 1830. Its latitude and longitude were fixed by the ill-fated Captain Gunnison on his route through Colorado into Utah in 1853. The crossing since known as Gunnison Crossing was used by the Fremont Expedition of 1854 and by the Mormon colonists who settled Moab (1855). It was selected as the site of the bridge built by the Denver & Rio Grande Railroad in 1883, and has become a link in the most-used highway in eastern Utah.

After dinner as we were commencing work, three shots were heard. Major sent all. We answered and I sent Fred and Clem down to the flag while we watched the bank. In about half an hour we had the pleasure of ferrying the Major and a Fred Hamblin across the river. They were just from Manti, bringing 300 lbs. of flour and a little meat and 20 lbs. sugar. It seems as near as I can make out, that Mr. Hamblin was not joined by Captain Dodds, and has gone to Kanab, whether to fit up to come to the Dirty Devil or not, no one knows. I cannot learn that the Major made any serious effort to get in and do not believe he did. Mr. Hamblin probably made a slight effort to rush the Dirty Devil or some attempt. It seems that he (the Major) concluded to go to Salt Lake, so took the stage. Went up, stayed three days, and then back to Manti. Bought a few supplies and came in. I do not care a cuss whether he comes with us or not on the river, but it makes one mad to wait and then have him come in and report a failure. We shall have some time, I see, before we get through; but "the Devil"—I knew how things would be before starting, so ought not to grumble. We moved camp this P. M. Ran four miles, two rapids, to a place where the pack train is encamped.

Wednesday, August 30th. Camp No. 51. In camp reading letters and writing. I worked on Lunar. Thursday, August 31st. Camp No. 51. Rode out on the hills this A. M. Wrote to wife this P. M. after working up observation made at Uintah. We shall fool away time, I see, until it gets mighty cold and unpleasant working in water.

Friday, September 1, 1871. Camp No. 52. Left camp 51 at 5:00 P. M. Ran down about ½ mile and one rapid. The Hamblins left us today for Kanab. Wrote to wife this morning—a long letter, 10 pages.

Saturday, September 2d. Camp No. 52. Ran 18 miles, one rapid today. Are camped near old camp of two years ago. River has been pretty shallow. Saw several places where the riverbed had been crossed by various parties; Gunnison's, the Old Spanish Crossing, and Indian Creek. Saw at one point some stone walls laid up by Indians, either for shelter or some other purpose. Walls about two feet high enclosing a sphere 10 x 5 feet. Saw stone piled up on hill about a mile south of these walls, evidently the conduit of some post-tertiary warm spring. But about 100 feet were ½ mile long, and in some places 50 feet; think has extended across the river at no remote period. A sort of headland projected into the river two years ago, but it is now an island. The mineral is in acicular crystals, globular form incrustations &c. The strata body dips north 10° west angle of dip. Cretaceous. The hills or cliffs are from 25 to 100 feet high. Irregular, with some exceptions. Opposite our camp are black shales.

Sunday, September 3rd. Camp No. 53. In camp taking observations for time and latitude. Major and Jones went west to the upheaval ridge, found it Jurassic. Got a fine lot of [Cretaceous] fossils. In many places west the country is a desert; on thousands of acres not a living thing. Trend of ridge N. and S. Steward and Bishop went out for topography and to visit the Arajondi [?] bed. Found that the country due east was cut and worn by water. Found a cave two or three hundred feet long in the Arajondi.

Monday, September 4th. Camp No. 54. Left camp 53 at 9:00 A. M. Ran 14 miles, passing one rapid. The country is very desolate. Saw hills rising at some points in buttes 600 feet. Have passed down through Cretaceous, perhaps all the Jurassic, and are now camped at Triassic. Some of the walls and buttes have been very beautiful, banded with different colored strata, worn in fantastic forms. Near the close of the day we came to springs boiling up in a branch of the river. At one point a stream at least six inches in diameter boils up through water about two feet deep. It flows with great force after spouting six or eight inches above the surface of the river. The water is alkaline—effervesces with acids. We counted as many as 75 places in which the water boiled up in a space eight rods long by three rods wide. Named the place Undine Springs. Came to the mouth of San Rafael River at 5:00 o'clock. It is now a stream 25 feet wide, 6 or 8 inches deep. Water not very good. Camped near its mouth. The valley at the mouth of S. R. is evidently quite a resort of Indians and seems easily accessible from east and west. Saw Sierra LaSal in the distance today, east.

Tuesday, September 5th. Camp No. 54. In camp all day taking observations &c. Major and Jones started for a two day trip up the San Rafael. Got lunars, and circumeridians on sun for Lat.

Wednesday, September 6th. Camp No. 54. In camp all day. Cloudy, so could get no observations except one for Lat. Major and Jones got in about 10:00 A. M. Have traced the San Rafael for 25 miles. Captain Bishop and Clem started for the "Red Cliffs" this morning. At this time, 7:15 P. M. have not returned, so we have built a big fire on a headland as a signal. Worked up observations all spare time today. Sun 110-45-24 approximate Lat. The Major describes the country of the San Rafael as very desolate. Saw ridges and hills following the general trend of strata 15° south of east with an approximation to system. They saw mountains south of Dirty Devil. Saw also the crater of an extinct volcano.[21] To the north and east across Green River the country is very rough, rising sometimes into precipitous buttes 5 to 500 feet

---

[21]The reference to an "extinct volcano" is not understood. Surveyors of the United States Land Office and other Government bureaus record no volcanic rocks in San Rafael Valley.

high.   One called Dellenbaugh butte[22] is largely composed of gypsum in strata from ⅓ to 12 inches thick.   Others, evidently the
red Triassic sandstone, to the east, seen over a long mountain-like
ridge of the latter is Sierra LaSal or Salt Mountains; two clusters
of beautifully rounded peaks 40 to 60 miles from us, and on the
east of Grand River.   Looking to the east we can see large patches
of grayish white sandstone.   No trees or shrubs.   Cottonwoods
plentiful along the rim in groves.   A little shrubby oak has made
its appearance along the San Rafael.   We are camped on an ancient
camping ground of the Indians, and evidently a great resort of their
arrow-makers.   Sage, quantities of broken arrow-heads and chips
lie scattered near the remains of old wick-e-ups.   The boys have
gathered several quarts of the most beautiful chalcedony, agate,
and jasper fragments.   Some are so clear and brilliant that they
ought to be called gems.   Found the very place where the arrow-
makers worked and their tools of stone with which they pounded
out their wares.   The material was obtained from a stratum
100 feet above the river.

Thursday, Sept. 7th. Camp No. 55. Ran 6⅞ miles today—
Cloudy and rainy.   Had breakfast before daylight this morning.
As soon as fairly light the Major and Hillers went across the
river to take the trail of Bishop and find him.   Went prepared
with food, water, &c.   At 7:00 o'clock Steward, Fred, and myself
dropped down the river with our boat, and taking more food and
the vinegar keg full of water, started on the tracks of both parties
as a sort of reserve force.   We had gone perhaps a mile when we
heard three shots.   Answered, and with glass soon discovered our
lost boys with the Major some two miles in advance of us.   The
boys were evidently paying their respects to the rations.   After
waiting a long time they signalled us to come farther down the
river with boats, and off they started.   Sent Fred to come for
their boats and we dropped down until we met them 2-⅛ miles
from camp, through what ought to be called the head of Labyrinth
Canon.   The walls are the maroon colored Triassic which we
called in Uintah Valley "Inscription" sandstone, rising vertically
on one or the other side 200 to 400 feet, and always on the "back"
of the bend.   In many places where the river has infringed sharply
on the cliff the wall is cut under 10, 12, and 20 feet in some places.
Where so cut near the water the rock is covered with a beautiful
moss.   Ran ashore and climbed the walls to get compass bearings.
The landscape is peculiar.   Acres, yes miles are nothing but bare
rock.   Buttes rise in towers, castles, churches, and capitols all
around.   Tom-fin con la-rup, stone-house-land, the Indians call
it; Castle Valley, the Whites, sage and greasewood in small

––– –
   [22]Dellenbaugh writes: "Opposite our dinner camp was one [butte] surprisingly symmertical,
resembling an artificial structure. I thought it looked like an art gallery, and the Major said it
ought to be named after the artist, so he called it 'Dellenbaugh's Butte.' "

quantities. A little grass in bunches. Just as I reached the top it commenced raining. Got under a sheltering cliff and enjoyed it. Down every little gulch came a stream of water, growing larger and larger. As I was obliged to climb gulches, getting up saw that I must get down soon or swim. Started, and in a few minutes was at the boat. Found the others there before me. Partially protected by overhanging cliffs we waited. Soon little clear rills came pouring over falling sometimes 300 feet to the bottom at one leap, increasing in size in a short time and changing their character. Instead of the clear rills they became torrents of red mud. From the point where we stood we saw three immense streams of bright red pouring over. Just below came one with a noise like Niagara pouring in a volume greater than the San Rafael river. Soon the green of the river changed to dirty yellow, rose three or four inches, and was in all respects metamorphosed, backing a little; we built a fire, made some coffee and had dinner. About 12:00 the other boats came down. Left at 2:15. Rained all the afternoon; camped in a grove of oak, a scrubby white oak, built large fires of oak, and had in all respects an oak camp. Rain by spells all night.

Friday, September 8th. Camp Oak. [Camp 56.] Clear this A. M. but we stayed in camp all day getting pictures. Went on the mountain back of camp after breakfast. Looking to the north we can see away to the "Needle Cliffs"[23] at the foot of Desolation Canon, over bare rock valley and through cliffs. The atmosphere cleared by the rain was transparent, the clouds magnificent, and I thought I had never witnessed a finer sight. Great depths before us—bare rock for foreground, river on the right with valley and mountains in distance. In the afternoon the Major and myself went up to Trin Alcove Canon. [?] Went up the main canon, and off into lateral ones. The latter often open out into amphitheatres—four branches. Sent for Beaman and had views.

Saturday, September 9th. Camp No. 56. Rained last night. Left camp at 9:45. Ran down 15⅛ miles. At noon we had a heavy shower. In afternoon a very heavy one. During the most of the shower the sun was shining brightly, forming a rainbow with its feet between us and the cliffs. Soon the little streams came pouring over the cliffs, and our rainbow soon stood in cascades. We are camped in the "Bows" of Labyrinth Canon.

Sunday, September 10th. Camp No. 57. Ran 5⅛ miles. Left camp at 10:45, ran until 12:15. Ran around the south bow of the "Knot". [Bow Knot Bend.] Ran 5⅛ miles to get 1000 feet. Beaman took views from ridge and did not come around with us. The walls of canon 500 to 700 feet; the upper half vertical; home of geneous sandstone, a maroon color. The upper member

---

[23] "Needle Cliffs" seems to refer to some particular prominence on Tavaputs Plateau seen through openings in Book Cliffs. For most of this area of mesas "needles" is an inappropriate term.

of the Triassic, the lower half beds of limestone—conglomerate and shaly rocks often into each other.   Steward found two fossils.   One apparently a spine of fish, and the other a conchifer. Decided to camp and hunt for more, so Jones and myself climbed out. A few cedars on summit and up ascent.   We climbed over rock curiously worn by water into caverns and holes, then along a ledge until at last Jones got up and drew me up by his revolver strap. The cap rock is a buff gray sandstone, but where not exposed covered with red sand.   Either the result of the weathering of red rock now gone from above or blown here from the southwest where the Vermilion cliff rock forms the upper stratum, probably the latter, we could see away to North Gunnison, Butte Cathedral, and the foot of Grey Canon, then the seven Buttes, the valley between and in the southeast Sally Butte and others.   East grey buttes rose like towers above the red sand.   Further away Sierra LaSal lay like blue clouds in the horizon.   South towerlike buttes and long ridge marked the course of Grand river, and just in the gap and formed at the junction a blue mountain rose.   [Abajo Mountains.]   Southwest a cluster of blue peaks [Henry Mountains], said by the Major to be volcanic (with doubt) and round to west the Wasatch cliffs with their castles of sandstone and intermediate crags of strata gave a variety and beauty to the scene.   Weird and wild, barren and ghost-like, it seemed like an unknown world.   The river is sunk.   No appearance of gorge or canon a mile away.   All is level to the eye, so abruptly has the river cut its channel.   The country is a plateau rising gradually from the foot of Grey Canon until now it is 1000 feet above the river, with occasional higher buttes.   A few cedars on summit. Two or three unknown shrubs in gulches, and along river banks, willows, cottonwoods and oaks.   Of the latter there are either two distinct species or well marked varieties, differing in acorns, cups, and leaves.   Very heavy dew last night.

Monday, September 11th.   Camp No. 58.   Ran 15⅛ miles. Left camp at 8:00 o'clock.   Ran until 11:00 when stopped for dinner and pictures.   I came on with our boat until 6:00 o'clock, when camped on left bank.   At 4:00 P. M. had a heavy shower lasting an hour.   The river seems to be rising, current stronger. We ran today with maroon sandstone for cap rock and shaly beds beneath, conglomeration, etc.   At our camp is quite a valley with high walls surrounding and a little creek winding through.   The capping sandstone is worn in many places into towers with vertical walls, in other places, cliffs.   It looks well nigh impossible to scale the walls.

Tuesday, September 12th.   Camp No. 59.   Ran 10¼ miles, leaving camp at 7:20, running until 11:00; stopping for pictures, etc.   Got view of Stonehead Cross. [Butte of the Cross.]   Stone, sand, and six continuous views of cliff.   Ran down three miles after dinner to a bend in the river called Bonita Bend. Here the river once ran around a thin wall of rock perhaps ¾ of a mile long. After a time short comparatively, but absolutely long, it cut through the wall, leaving a thin ½ mile long butte standing isolated in a semi-circular valley with walls of vertical rock 150 feet high, these walls worn into alcoves and buttresses. I am on a rock half way up the cliff at the bend of the river, taking in at one glance the valley with its trees, quiet stream, curious buttes, and encircling wall, while beyond a mile or two away rises another encircling wall 800 feet high, the orange or maroon sandstone worn into castellated towers, sharp pinnacles, and plateau walls. It is quiet as primeval earth. No animal life, yet once this valley was the home of man. Broken fragments of pottery show evidence of the presence of "Moquis" at some very remote period, and also disprove the inaccessibility of the river. Steward found an arrow-head just begun, on the bluffs, showing the presence of Indians. Found a curious half shrubby plant on the walls of canon, apparently a "Leguminose." It hangs in masses, sometimes 2 feet long, from some crevice where it obtains a little moisture. We decided today to use up all our photographic material between here and the mouth of Dirty Devil, then leave one boat there, go to the Paria with two, and come up next spring and run through with the boat left, taking views at pleasure. Soon after leaving camp 58, we ran up a bed of buff sandstone where 100 feet of it was under-laid by a stratum of red, which is our base at camp 59. In sight then we leave the orange sandstone 700 feet, then the red shales 300 feet, then the buff sandstone 75 feet and then red sandstone 50 feet, making the plateau rise 1150 feet above the river. The orange and red shale form what might be called the walls of the river valley, the buff and red, the canon walls.

Wednesday, September 13th. Camp No. 60. Ran 12 miles, leaving camp 59 at 11:00, running until 12:30, then from 2:00 to 3:00 and from 4:00 to 6:00. River very quiet. Ran through the "buff" sandstone and red shale underneath, raising stratum after stratum until at least a mile above camp a reddish buff sand-stone with fossils of carboniferous period made its appearance. Canon at camp is 400 feet wide at top, walls coming very close to river vertical for 250 feet on both sides. In the morning before leaving Bonita Bend, Beaman took two negatives and the Major and myself climbed the isolated cliff. In the afternoon while Beaman was taking view, climbed again to see if we could get out. Found that the buff sandstone above the red shales that composed the canon walls at that point was vertical for 140 feet at all points, often overhanging;—above this the orange sandstone stood in verti-cal walls 500 feet; not a break in either as far as we could see. The shales are curiously cut up at that point. Huge gulches are torn in every direction.

Thursday, September 14th. Camp No. 61. Ran 4½ miles, leaving camp at 1:00 P. M. Found a good many Carboniferous fossils this morning and decided that the whole of this canon below Labyrinth²⁴ is Carboniferous. Walls have usually been vertical on both sides today and not more than 600 feet apart. Measured the walls at one point, 900 feet above river to top of buff sandstone. Plateau probably 1500. Camped in a little valley on the right bank. Tried to climb out but did not succeed. Found ruins of Moquis houses, pieces of pottery, and a corn cob (10 rowed). Found where they had climbed out up the cliff by piling stones and using a cottonwood pole. Think it could not have been more than 50 years since the last ascent was made, probably not half that. Found at least the ruins of three houses, one with walls still standing at least six feet high. The place where the corn cob was found was under an overhanging cliff. Two little pen-like places were enclosed by stone walls. The corn cob was found six inches under the surface.

Friday, September 15th. Camp Junction 62.—1871. Ran 7½ miles this A. M. Left camp at 7:20. That is the Nell, and her crew left at that time to run to the junction, in time to get observations for time. Made the point at 9:10 and got observations alright. The canon has been about 450 feet wide at top. Walls vertical on both sides, and usually coming down to within 25 to 50 feet of water on one side and to water on the other. Walls 500 feet, current 2½ miles and a few willows occassionally along the bank.

The junction of Green and Grand Rivers is in a canon with walls on all sides 800 feet, nearly vertical. On the right is a little bench perhaps ⅓ of a mile long, and 5 rods wide. Between the Green and Grand is a tongue of perhaps two acres and a narrow strip of two rods width on the farther side of the Grand and Colorado. We are camped on the west side of the Colorado. I think a prettier joining of two streams to form a third was never seen. Neither absorbs or flows into the other, but like two forces of equal strength they mingle and unite. The Grand seems to contain the more water—is about 400 feet wide, current two miles per hour. The Green is 250 feet wide, current two miles.

The party that stayed behind²⁵ climbed out at the "Moquis trail". The river is described as magnificent. They found a good many broken arrowheads and the chips from their making, pieces of

---

²⁵During the four days spent at the junction of the Green and Colorado the expedition was divided into two parties. One, led by Powell, went a few miles up Colorado River and, scaling the walls, made geological observations. The other, under Thompson, remained at the junction, taking latitude and longitude observations. Notes and specimens collected constitute the first reliable record of basket-maker and pueblo peoples north of the San Juan River. The plan of Powell to explore Grand River through its course in Utah was abandoned by the 1871 expedition. The canyon of the Grand was not mapped until a half century later.

²⁴On maps resulting from the river traverse Labyrinth Canyon lies between the mouth of San Rafael and (the present) Barrie Creek. Below it and extending to the junction of the Green and Colorado the map shows "Stillwater Canyon" bordered by "Orange Cliffs."

pottery, and under a shelving rock carefully covered by a thin flat rock, Andy found a whole jar. It will hold about four gallons and was partially filled with split willows, such as are used by them in making trays. The willow splints were tied up by hemp from the nettle or bark. From all appearances the jar had not been disturbed for many years, probably not since the Moquis left the valley. All evidence so far points to a date of not over 100 years as that period.

Saturday, September 16th. Camp Junction 62. In camp all day taking observations for latitude and time. The Major and most of party climbed out. Got some fine pictures and saw magnificent views. The Major decided not to go up the Grand.

Sunday, September 17th. Camp No. 62—Junction. Climbed today the cliff west of camp. The view is strange, at once weird and enchanting. The top of the cliffs is buff sandstone worn into gullies and fissures, sometimes 300 feet deep and not more than two feet wide. Over these we leaped, an operation requiring nerve. At some points this stone is worn into crags, pinnacles, towers, etc. To the north we could overlook all Stillwater Canon, to the orange cliff at the breaking down of Labyrinth. These cliffs break into almost basaltic forms in many instances, leaving huge isolated buttes standing like sentinels to guard the land. To the northeast we could see the cliffs on the Canon of the Grand. Then more to the east the Sierra LaSal towers aloft with its grey gulches and forest covered sides. Southeast and south near at hand were the "Crags" and away beyond them the Sierra Abajo, blue in the distance. To the west was "Sinar-too weep", or "Ghost Land" composed of columns of grey and red sandstones, [Land of Standing Rocks] often 300 feet high with a base for 170 feet of grey, then 100 of red, then orange, and a cap sometimes of red, sometimes of grey, sometimes sharp pinnacles, sometimes round towers. Got to camp at 6:00 P. M.

Monday, September 18th. Camp No. 62. In camp all day taking observations, helping plot map, etc. Major and Jones climbed out south side of Grand River and got bearings on God knows what.

Tuesday, September 19th. Camp No. 63. Left camp at 1:00. Ran 9 miles, passing 8 rapids. Let past 7 of them with rope. Some of our rapids were very bad. We are camped ½ mile above the second day's camp of two years ago. Tried to put in the bearings taken by the Major yesterday, but they are a confused mess. Not worth anything.

Wednesday, September 20th. Camp No. 64. Ran ¾ mile letting past two rapids. To camp on north side of river. Major and Fred climbed out. While letting down the Nell, she got the start of us, pulled away and ran through the rapid on her own notion to the eddy below. We ran down the bank, and Jack swam out to her, passed an oar to us and we pulled her in. It was a narrow escape for her and lucky for us, as we could hardly spare any rations. Got observations today.

Thursday, September 21st. Camp No. 65. Left camp at 8:30 Ran 6⅞ miles with 14 rapids, letting down just 5 and running 9. All our "Let-downs" have been very bad and taking all hands. Some that we ran were as bad as any we have seen. The peculiar feature of this canon seems to be the huge boulders detached from the cliffs and strewn along the bank. In most of the canons, rapids are caused by washing in of debris from the gulches; here by the falling in of masses from cliffs. From Grand Junction nearly every point has presented strata, dipping at all degrees from 1 to 80. This peculiar dip often extends back only a short distance. Often the tilted strata shows a fault. These points or sides have evidently broken from the main body. On our first day's run we found a slight seam of coal. At camp 63 a bed of gypsum 30 feet thick crystalline in structure and bluish color. It was just above the river bed. Springs along the bank are sulphurous. The walls of the canon are about 1500 feet high, the country back rising to 1800 or 2000 feet in three miles. The top has usually been a buffish grey limestone, changing toward the bottom to blue almost, and very hard and crystalline in texture. It is full of fossils and these too are crystalline, almost calcite. Where we are camped the cliff on the north rises vertically 1600 feet. On the south, the same and not over ⅓ mile apart at the top. Very craggy at top. But few gulches compared with other canons. River up today, usually 250 feet; today not over 200 feet; today we found a good many cottonwoods and hackberry trees. One of the latter at our yesterday's camp was 18 inches in diameter and 80 feet high. Today we have seen only scrubby hackberries. Our camp is among rock on the north side, bed on sand.

Friday, September 22d. Camp No. 66. Ran 1¼ miles, letting down over three rapids, bad ones. Damaged two boats, so that we stopped at 3:00 o'clock to repair. Worked the rest of the day on them and camped at the head of the worst rapid we have seen or as bad. One rapid that we passed had at least 20 ft. fall in 600 feet. Canon about the same as yesterday. Two or three hackberry trees in sight. Cliff vertical near river 2000 feet. We can see opposite at least 3000 feet altitude. Craggy and rough.

Saturday, September 23rd. Camp No. 67. Ran 3⅝ miles today, passing six rapids, letting down past four. One rapid ½ mile long. Not as many huge sharp boulders above the bank. Ran one rapid with at least 12 ft. fall in 400 feet. Waves high. Walls of Canon craggy, cut in towers and pinnacles. They are true castles, dangerous. Opposite camp is a cliff 2000 feet high. Limestone stained reddish. Rapids made by cliff falling in.

Sunday, September 24th. Camp No. 68. Made 4½ miles,

ten rapids, nearly all rapids today. We seem just at the turning point of the canon; that is, where the dip is the other way south. Walls as yesterday. A few scrubby hackberry bushes or small trees along the bank. Cliffs appeared little more broken. Valley widens on the left where we are camped to ½ mile and perhaps ⅔ as long. Gulch up which is said to be fine scenery comes in from the east. Cliff opposite 1600 feet high, willows along valley. We have found much driftwood so far in the canon, often 50 feet above the water, and we saw a huge sandstone boulder that would weigh 500 tons, resting on limestone boulders which had worn into at least two feet. The sandstone is 20x20x20 feet and must be completely covered with water in floods, and by their action moved it enough to grind in the bed of harder rock on which it rests. Got to our present camp at 12:00.

Monday, September 25th. Camp No. 68. This morning helped repair our boat, then went up a gulch four miles north, Steward Gulch,[26] an eroded one. Gypsum, lime and sandstone walls. Found a bed of fossil coral 12 feet thick, that in two miles changed to fine gypsum. Beds of bituminous shale along the walls. Scenery grand. Walls 2000 feet wide. Cool, beautiful pools of water in it, formed by water trickling over cliffs and percolating through the shales. Saw mountain sheep. Camped at 5:00 P. M.

Tuesday, September 26th. Camp No. 69. Left camp at 8:30. Ran 6⅝ miles, passing 9 rapids, letting down over two of them. Ran some very bad ones. In one we filled the forward rowing space and came to shore in rather a crest-fallen condition. One we ran almost ashore on the left to avoid a rock on the right. Was a very risky place. Have been in a grand canon today. Not over ¼ mile wide at top and walls at least 2500 feet, often 3000. That grandeur must be seen to be appreciated. Got some very fine views. Camped near the head of a rapid. Just below our camp is a gulch or fissure in the right wall, perhaps 20 feet wide with gates 1500 feet high, 300 feet at top. As you go up it opens wider until you reach a little pool of water that has tumbled over a shelf 30 feet high. Climbing up this shelf it still widens for a few rods, having a solid limestone floor with pools of water standing on or in it, then rising a few feet, it rounds out into a valley having a little stream of water flowing along it almost 400 feet wide with cottonwood, pine, cedar, ash, willow, and spice bush also. Grass grows in bunches. Flowers are blooming, mosses growing on wet rocks. Ferns, a beautiful adiantum wave from the moist rocks. The soft subdued roar of the river lulls the ear, and "how lovely" is the involuntary expression. Then looking at the walls 2000 feet high, and showing only a narrow belt of sky "how grand" springs involuntarily. We have had

grand scenes and beautiful scenes, but none where beauty, grandeur, and sublimity were so combined in one glance. And if we
add to this beauty, a bird is singing merrily from some tree, and the
fragrance of a strange "composite" fills the air. It would be a wond-
rous beautiful glen anywhere, but it is doubly so in this almost barren region. The yucca grows in a curious shape—tall, with the
leaves running up a foot or more on the stem. We find the shrub
belonging to the "Rosaceae" (thought to be potentilla) the "sweet
scented" shrub, and a shrub with fine and thorny leaves. The
beautiful almost bluish cactus is frequently found. Golden-rods
all along. The fragrant Compositae and two species of "aster"
comprise most of the flowers. Going further up, the path winds
under a shelving, overhanging rock. The little brook cools its
waters in the shade and irresistibly one feels the impulse to rest.
Further up high boulders block the way. Butterflies, a "Vanessa";
birds, woodpeckers.

Wednesday, September 27th. Camp No. 70. Ran 9 miles,
passing 5 rapids, letting down past 3. The character of the canon
is changing. The walls are becoming lower and more broken. Just
above camp the dip changes to S. W. and has been increasing on
the whole. All day we run under about 350 feet of Carboniferous.

Thursday, September 28th. Camp No. 71. Ran ...... miles,
passing 6 rapids. Let down just one very bad one and part of another when we came to a place where we could let no further. River
turned short to left and dashed against the cliff, then turned to
right, making two right angles. Got aboard, ran as close to rocks
as we dared and then pulled. Made it alright. Left camp 71 at
9:30, ran one half hour, then camped where river turns to right
and Major and myself tried to climb out by going up the bed of a
beautiful little running creek. Went up a mile and a half and tried
the side; climbed until about 2:00 o'clock, when we found that it was
impossible to get over the sandstone forming the top of the cliff
at that part. Came back to the bed of creek and as it was too late
for another, decided to run for Mill Creek [Mille Crag][27] point
and be there tomorrow. Called the creek "Failure Creek" in re-
membrance of our failure. It is a clear, sweet, stream tumbling over
rocks and forming pools. Clear as crystal and often several feet
deep. The canon is very narrow and walls very high—3000 feet.
Views of startling grandeur appear at every turn. It is cut for
2000 feet at the base in mostly limestone, then 1000 feet up a buff
homogeneous sandstone. A few trees along its valley, but not
often, as in high water the stream completely fills the canon. Found
a rare, "circus" [Cereus?] today—quite plentiful—found it in

[27]Millecrag point and Millecrag bend are names suggested by the innumerable pinnacles into
which the canyon walls are carved. For some reason Dark Canyon, the largest tributary of the
Colorado between its junction with the Green and the mouth of the Fremont. is not mentioned
by Thompson. Its mouth is near the lower end of Cataract Canyon and the beginning of the
short Narrow Canyon.

flower and seed. Evidently the late rains have stimulated a few blossom buds to anticipate next year's work. We camped at 5:00 P. M., and after running two miles camped among rocks, making our beds on drifts of sand. Just after getting in camp a little shower visited us, blowing sand and wetting shirts. Then the moon arose directly in the east end of the canon (We are on an east and west stretch of perhaps 3½ miles). The finest moonrise I ever saw. First the clouds became edged with silver while their marrow was black and dark, then the cliff tops, while all was night around us and the canon seemed a bottomless abyss. Then the clouds shifted and more and more of their shapes became illumined, the light crept down the cliffs, a little crescent of bright silver hung in the end of the canon above a black depth of darkness. It then grew larger and larger and we and the canon were flooded in the light of a full moon. The effect on the rapid below us was startling. Every drip of water glistened as it sprang in air. Every wave caught a glow and the whole river seemed one dancing sea of light. There the light fell on cliff, every crevice and crag was shown with startling distinctiveness, rendering the shadows more intense.

Friday, September 29th. Camp No. 72. Ran 4 miles, running five rapids. Rain this morning. Left camp 71 at 8:30. Made camp 72 at 10:00. Got ready and climbed out at 1500 ft. elevation. Had fine view. Saw ridge of mountains to west with snow on summits. The surface of plateau was buff gray sandstone, and in all directions except north the orange sandstone of Triassic formation stood in cliffs and buttes. Evidently the Carboniferous is exposed in a sort of oval basin with its longer axis in a northern and southern direction. Found near our camp evidences of the Shiremos [Shinumo] occupation, such as corn and cobs with fragments of pottery and part of a wall of masonry, partially closing up an aperture. Not quite a cavern in the sandstone. Found the corn, etc. in this cavern.

Saturday, September 30th. Camp No. 73. Ran ...... miles, passing rapids. Left camp early. Ran to north of Dirty Devil Creek, passing through Narrow Canon. This canon in the upper part has limestone walls 1200 feet high, rapidly dipping under until they disappear at about two miles. Then the Triassic sandstone, walls about ⅓ mile apart in upper jutting, gradually closing in till not more than 400 feet and 600 feet high. River current 3½. Passed several springs pouring out from the bank into the river. Most of them were sulphurous and warm. One that we listed was 91° when atmosphere was 50°. On reaching D. D. Major and myself went across the creek and found an old Indian trail which we followed down the river two miles, then up a gulch to right for four miles. Found no place to climb out but abundant evidence that Indians have been in with horses within a few years. Found old Moquis trace, such as pottery in pieces.

Sunday, October 1, 1871. Camp No. 74. Ran 1⅝ miles. Cached the Canonita this morning.[28] Then Captain Bishop and myself with Steward dropped down 1⅝ miles to gulch on right where Indian trail is and went up some 6 miles and then climbed out. Found water in the gulch running in a pretty little stream, and that the "trail" still continued up toward the mountains. Saw that the gulch drained the northern mountains of the volcanic range. Got back to camp at dark.

Monday, October 2d. Camp No. 75.[29] [30] Ran 16 miles, passing ten rapids, running all. Found an old Moquis house on a point. House was 22x12, outside walls 15 inches thick and 15 feet high at one point. One end is much broken down. The house was evidently two or three stories. The stones were very nicely laid, joints broken, corners square—held up with long and short stones. Under the cliffs were also ruins; or rather they were on a ledge or bench 8 or 10 feet wide along the cliff. On the smooth face of the cliff were many inscriptions or figures. Fred sketched them. At the house were several figures on a smooth flat rock. Found pieces of pottery and arrowheads, at our camp and also in ruins— one house 20x30 feet but very old and worn down. Also saw a "kiver" or underground "clan room." Climbed out this evening. Was up 1215 feet above the river. The country seems covered with a red sand, some brush; in many places bare rock. The "orange" cliffs here almost left us, and from our observation point can be discerned running eastward. To the south looms up Mount Seneca Howland.[31] To the northwest the "Unknown" Mountains[32] lift their craggy heads. To west of the river the bare sandstone is exposed for miles. River 350 feet wide, current 2 miles, canon ⅓ mile wide.

[28]The failure of the supporting land party to reach the mouth of the Fremont River and the inadequate supplies brought to Gunnison Crossing made it necessary to avoid delay in reaching the Crossing of the Fathers, where provisions were presumably waiting. Dellenbaugh writes: "Our long stretch (nearly 600 miles) on short rations made the small amount we could allow ourselves at each meal seem almost like nothing at all." The plan was to travel rapidly, then next season use the *Canonita* for a leisurely traverse that permitted adequate scientific observations.

[29]The location of Camp 75 is not easy to determine from the meager information given. Ruins appear along the river from Crescent Wash to Red Canyon. Conditions for landing and climbing cliffs are especially favorable at the mouth of Trachyte Creek, the site of Dandy Crossing and of the cabins built by Cass Hite (1880?). As a comment on the state of knowledge of Utah geography in 1871 it is interesting to note that this place, the most easily accessible of all points on the river between Gunnison Crossing and Virgin River, was completely unknown. Supplies for the river party could have been brought in by pack train or even wagon.

[30]The stretch of river from the mouth of the Fremont to the mouth of Trachyte Creek was first called Mound Canyon by Powell and its extension to the mouth of the Paria, Monument Canyon. On published maps the two are combined as Glen Canyon.

[31]Mount Seneca Howland was named for Seneca Howland, member of Powell's 1869 river party who was killed by the Indians on Shivwits Plateau. To pioneer scouts it was known as Navajo Mountain, the name it now bears.

[32]The group of five peaks mentioned in the diary and elsewhere as "Unknown Mountains", "Our Mountains", "Dirty Devil Mountains", were later named Henry Mountains. In 1875 Powell (Exploration of the Colorado River) wrote:

"Professor Joseph Henry, the Secretary of the Smithsonian Institution, under whose direction the work was performed, prior to the 1st of July, 1874, has contributed greatly to any success which we may have had, by his instructions and advice, and by his most earnest sympathy; and I have taken the liberty to express my gratitude for his kindness, and reverence for his profound attainments, by attaching his name to a group of lofty mountains."

Tuesday, October 3rd. Camp No. 76. Ran 27 miles, passing 11 small rapids. River 400 feet, current 1½ or 2 miles, walls of canon often close in to 1000 feet at top, from 200 to 600 feet high, often vertical. Climbed out at dinner and came here. In all directions naked orange sandstone, and with pockets or wells often 30 or 40 feet deep and frequently containing water. One at least 40 feet deep had 5 feet of water.[33] Great many round concretions like marbles in the hollows. Saw "our mountains" in the N. W. and Mt. Seneca Howland in the south. To the west is a long upheaved ridge which we shall cross in a day or two. Climbed out at camp at night 712 feet. Country covered with orange sand with a sort of greasewood. Got back after dark.

Wednesday, October 4th. Camp No. 77. Ran 21 miles, passing 10 or 12 rapids or shallows. The shallows were very bad. A stratum of shale sandstone was the river-bed. The channel was 600 feet wide and the rock cut by currents in grooves. One moment we were aground and the next in water 10 feet deep. In one of these "riffles" we stove a hole in our boat, that let in water as fast as one could bail out. Ran on home in this condition when we camped for dinner. Repaired our boat and had a fine run this afternoon. Climbed up a gulch at camp into an amphitheatre set all round with terraces planted with cottonwoods, oaks, willows, shrubs of various species, springs of water, and above these terraces a cliff of 600 feet high overhanging orange sandstone.

Thursday, October 5th. Camp No. 78. Ran 25 miles today. River shallow and rapid in some places. Walls of canon are of orange sandstone, rounded on top and curiously worn by water. In many places deep gorges cut, not more in some cases than 20 feet wide, 200 deep, and winding back perhaps ¼ mile when they widen out into amphitheatres that would hold 10,000 people. Music Temple is one of these. The walls are often cut into alcoves in which are groves of trees, shrubs, etc. Hundreds of springs along the cliffs. Passed the mouth of the San Juan river at 11:30. It is a strong current, 8 rods wide. Water flows in it rapidly—is very muddy, shallow and crooked. Canon walls at the junction from 300 to 1200 feet high and impossible to climb. Camped for dinner at Music Temple.[34] Climbed up 800 feet. Bare rock all around, wonderfully worn. Mt. Seneca Howland full in sight.[35] It is a fine mountain covered for the most part by trees. To the west the

---

[33]The abundance of these "wells", in places the only source of water, is characteristic of the sandstone (Navajo formation) that walls in the Colorado between the mouth of Red Canyon and Lees Ferry. They are especially numerous in the ridge, later mapped by Thompson as the Water Pocket Fold.

[34]Dellenbaugh relates that in the overarched alcove named Music Temple were carved the names of Seneca Howland, O. G. Howland, and William Dunn, the three members of the Powell party of 1869 who lost their lives on Shivwits Plateau.

[35]The plan of Powell to ascend Mount Seneca Howland (Navajo Mountain) was frustrated by lack of supplies. Dellenbaugh writes: "We were near the last crust—the remaining food was divided into two portions, one for supper, the other for breakfast." It was essential to hurry on to the Crossing of the Fathers, where supplies awaited.

Jurassic is in sight. Cliffs like monuments are in sight down the river.

Friday, October 6th. Camp No. 79. Ran 20 miles today. Walls of canon almost vertical on both sides and from 200 to 1000 feet high. All the side streams come in by very narrow canons, often not more than 10 feet wide; these open out into alcoves, often of large extent. Occasionally a monument-like cliff appears near the river. Saw a place where there had been a recent fire in a little valley. Landed and found tracks of two men and horses. Evidently, we thought, Hamblin was up in the country looking for us. Ran 13½ miles before dinner, then about 6 after, when we came to a place where some white men were encamped.[36] Landed and found Captain Dodds with rations, mail, etc. He is accompanied by two prospectors. Hamblin has been here but is now gone to Fort Defiance. It seems that Captain Dodds succeeded in getting in to the mouth of the Dirty Devil, or so near that he saw the mouth and knew there was no travel, and went back for Hamblin when they received orders from the Major to go to "El Vado de las Padres" with the rations and to get there by the 25th of September. It is now apparent that if the Major had made any effort to carry out his original plans, it would have been done easily. They left Kanab early in September, so have no late news for us. Shall send out all our fossils, etc. from here.

Saturday, October 7th. Camp No. 79. In camp, taking observations, etc. Boys work on collections.——Sunday, October 8th. Camp No. 79. Taking observations today. Boys got all work done. Major starts early in the morning for Kanab.—— Monday, October 9th. The Major decided late last night to give the boys a chance to write today, so we are in camp, all busy.—— Tuesday, October 10th. Major started today for Kanab. He is to get a horse and saddle for Nell, [Mrs. Thompson] and bring her down with him if Emma [Mrs. Powell] does not come.

Wednesday, October 11th. Camp No. 79. This morning Bishop, Beaman, Clem and myself started in the Dean for up river. Got up six miles by 12:30. Were at the foot of rapids and could not get over. Landed, went up gulches, and found that we could not get out nor could we find views worth taking. Spent the afternoon trying to find a way to get out. Found that the valley was a resort for Indians and had been for Moquis. Found pieces of pottery, etc. Found two old camp fires and at last found the trail

---

[36]The week spent at the Crossing of the Fathers (October 6-13) was a "red letter" period in the life of the river party. The land party from Kanab, led by Jacob Hamblin and Capt. Pardyn Dodd, also two prospectors, George Riley and John Bonnemont, had been waiting for two weeks "beside a large pile of rations." There was food in plenty ("we could eat all we wanted"), also wearing apparel such as shoes and overalls to replace those worn to shreds. There was time to record data on maps and in note books, to pack specimens, write letters, and to study the local geology. Best of all, the men worn down by physical and mental strain had an opportunity to recuperate. Major Powell, who here joined the land party on its return to Kanab, made the first geological observations of the Kaiparowits Plateau, the "Wahweap Country," and Paria Valley.

by which they went up the cliff. They had piled up brush and stones until a trail was made for animals. The Moquis had cut steps in the solid sandstone rocks, and we went out by the old Moquis trail. In some places they were nearly worn out by age, in others quite good. Were large enough to put our toes in, and far enough apart to give us a good step. Think we climbed 50 feet this way. When at the top it was so late that we could not get an observation, so returned to camp.

Thursday, October 12th. Camp 79. Cold last night. Climbed up the Moquis' stairway and got the observations. Got back at 12:00. Had dinner and rowed to camp against a heavy head wind. Found that Steward had been sick ever since we left camp. Seems to be sort of fever. Friday, October 13th. Camp No. 79. Tried to climb out this A. M. Did not succeed. This P. M. Bishop and myself took hammer and chisel and cut "holds" in the sandstone; climbed up 850 feet. Got bearings.

Saturday, October 14th. Camp No. 80. Bishop and myself went out on the trail toward Kanab some five miles, but found no place to climb out. Got back to camp at 2:00 P. M. Found two Navajos in camp. A chief "Agna Grande" and his son. In about an hour seven more came in. They were very lavish in expressions of kindness, hugged us and made long speeches. One had a fine black mustache. They seem a smaller race than the Uintah Utes, but active and intelligent. Seemed to be going to Mormon settlements to trade. We ran down past the "Ford". It was indicated by a line of small piles of stone. Ran 3 miles, then camped on left bank.

Sunday, October 15th. Camp No. 80. In camp all day. Jones and myself crossed river this P. M. and climbed the bank, Got observations. Think we can see the Pahria and perhaps Kaibab Plateau. Saw what looks like a fold. ("El Vado de las Padres" comes down a rocky slope from the east, follows up a bar in middle of river for half a mile, then goes out west at a canon not more than 10 feet wide.) Monday, October 16th. Camp No. 81. Ran 10¾ miles. River 400 feet wide, walls 400 feet high, canon 800 feet across. Left camp at 10:00 A. M. Ran 5 miles, then dinner; then ran 5¾ miles to a creek coming in from left. Called the Creek Navajo Creek.

Tuesday, October 17th. Camp No. 82. Ran 6¼ miles. Climbed out this morning and got bearings. Found evidences of former occupancy of the creek valley in the shape of pieces of pottery and arrowheads. The country to south and west rises in cliffs within 10 miles. To the east and south it is more open with isolated buttes. Plateau is 875 feet above the river. Passed Warm Springs. The cliffs or canon walls are perhaps 450 feet high, then rising gradually for a mile or so to 800 or 900 feet. The sand is usually covered with a little shrub about a foot high. The canon walls in the run today have been closer, not over 600 feet average. Current in river 3½ miles.

Wednesday, October 18th. Camp No. 83. Ran 1 mile and came to a creek coming in on right.[37] Camped and Beaman took views while Fred and I tried to climb out. Tried three places but could not get up. Find creek 8 feet wide, 6 inches deep. Very clear; walls of creek canon 8 to 80 feet apart, 800 feet high. Thursday, October 19th. Camp No. 84. Ran 6-⅝ miles. Got six pictures today. Canon walls from 400 to 800 feet. Vertical or so nearly, that it has been impossible to climb out. Walls ¼ mile apart. River 400 feet. Current 3 miles. We are in the sandstone yet. Found it cut by a thin bit of limestone at camp. Dip west of north and very gentle. Friday, October 20th. Camp No. 85. Ran 5¾ miles. Canon walls getting higher; are now 1000 feet; not over ⅜ mile apart at top. Plateau 1700 feet, current 3 miles, river average 400 feet. Camped in valley. Indians have been in not long ago. Found Moquis pottery, etc.

Saturday, October 21st. Camp No. 85. Climbed "Echo Peaks[38] today, 2400 feet. Saw mouth Pahria and Marble Canon for 20 miles. "Kaibab Plateau" in distance. To the north can look over all the country as far as cliffs beyond "El Vado de las Padres." Saw Navajo Mountain; to N. W. saw high cliffs. [Edge of Paunsaugunt Plateau.] Just below our camp is a *small* fold involving only the "Triassic", apparently. It raises up the "Chocolate" Beds. Could not determine either extent or direction. Sunday, October 22d. Camp No. 85. In camp. Beaman took three views. Monday, October 23rd. Camp No. 86. Ran 3 miles to the mouth of Pahria. Camped, made "wick-e-ups" and commenced work. Tuesday, October 24th. Camp No. 86. Took observations, and helped on map. Wednesday, October 25th. Camp No. 86. Took observations.

Thursday, October 26th. Camp No. 86. Climbed the right wall of canon. Height 2000 feet. Got bearings. Between the mouth of Pahria and "El Vado" the country is broken, but lower than at either; much cut by canons. There seems to be three well defined lines of cliffs or terraces. The first is near the river, highest near "El Vado" and trending to the north about four miles below the "Ford," gradually getting lower until they run into the second

[37]This creek is shown on Thompson's map as Sentinel Rock, so named from "the Sentinels", a lofty sandstone tower at its mouth. It is now known by its Piute name, Wahweap.

[38]Dellenbaugh (Romance of the Colorado River, pp. 292-293) writes:

"I took it into my head to try to shoot from there [Echo Peaks] into the water of Glen Canyon beneath us, and borrowed Bishop's 44-calibre Remington revolver for the purpose. When I pulled the trigger I was positively startled by the violence of the report, a deafening shock like a thousand thunder claps in one; then dead silence. Next, from far away there was a rattle of musketry, and peal after peal of echoing shot came back to us. The interval of silence was timed on another trial and was found to be exactly twenty seconds. The result was always the same, and from the unusual echo we named the place Echo Peaks."

line some six miles north of camp 86. The second line seems to start from north of "El Vado" and runs out back of the first. The third line seems to be the line that comes to river above "El Vado" and joins with the first and second lines at the place above mentioned, or rather they seem to join together. Back of these lines to the north of camp 86 seems to be some higher cliffs composed of light colored sandstone. To the left of the river are some buttes six or seven hundred feet high. The plateau is 2000 feet high. The cliffs above the river are from 800 to 1200 feet high, then back of this is a lower terrace from which the plateau rises to the above mentioned height. From the point of observation of October 12th the cliffs extend in a line to the east for miles, then seem to trend southward. To the south and west can see but little. The "Fold" at Echo Peaks trends 170 degrees, but north of the Colorado the fold seems to trend more to west. The "Fold" involves the strata to the top of Carboniferous and can be seen with the glass at the point where the lines of cliffs seem to meet. Could see that Navajo Mountain is upheaved. Could see the strata line against the north side of mountain.[39]

Friday, October 27th. Camp No. 86. Finished plotting map. Sick ones getting better. Saturday, October 28th. Camp No. 86. This morning went up river to look out for place for boats.[40] When I got back heard someone shouting to us from across the river. Went over and found that it was [Jacob] Hamblin's party, consisting of himself, Mr. [Isaac] Haight, Mr. [George] Adair, and Mr. [Joe] Mangin and two Navajo boys, a Navajo sub chief called "Coneco" with five warriors and an old Indian with his son belonging to another clan. We took them and their goods across in boats, then swam the horses across.[41] Some of the Indians have never seen as large a river and are greatly surprised. Others seem to take the big water as a matter of course. They acted like a party of girls in the boat. One fellow started to swim across, but the water was so cold that we picked him up in the boat. They, "the Indians", have blankets which they wish to trade for ponies

---

[39]The geology of the region north and east of Thompson's Camp 86 is described in "The Navajo Country" and "The Kaiparowits Region," publications issued by the United States Geological Survey.

[40]According to the plans adopted, the river traverse for 1871 ended at Lees Ferry. The boats were to be cached awaiting the continuation of the traverse in 1872. The party was to leave the river by pack train sent from Kanab.

Camp 86, where the river party remained 11 days, might be considered the beginning of settlements on Colorado River and of the development of a permanent route from Utah to Arizona. In the spring of 1872 the site was occupied by John Doyle Lee, who named it Lonely Dell, and since that time its fields irrigated by water from the Paria and its surrounding grazing lands have been utilized by a small population. Until the highway bridge was built across Marble Canyon (1929), Lees Ferry was the only established crossing of the Colorado between Green River, Utah and Needles, California.

[41]Hamblin was returning from the Hopi country to the Utah settlements over a route selected by him the previous year as a substitute for he more difficult trail through the Crossing of the Fathers, and the long round about trail across the Colorado at the mouth of the Virgin and over the Coconino Plateau. Dellenbaugh writes: "We were met by a slow moving, very quiet individual who said his name was Jacob Hamblin. His voice was so low, his manner so simple, his clothing so usual, that I could hardly believe that this was Utah's famous Indian fighter and manager."

or sheep. They are a very intelligent looking Indian, and exhibit a good deal of animation. We gave them some soup and bread tonight, and got them to sing and dance around the fire. The sing- ing seems to be sort of a repetition of the same word or syllables, but the tune possesses considerable scope, now it is low and soft, now high and harsh and with constantly varying volume. All those who joined used the same words and sung the same tune. The dance was simply a hop in a circle around the fire to a sort of chant. They would go around a few times, then back. We could ascertain the subject of only one song, a "Comanche" war song. The old Chief would neither dance nor sing, but beat on a camp kettle for them. Their blankets are very good. Mr. Hamblin has one that cost 70 days work. Will sell for $40.00—woven very tight and hard. Have made arrangements with Mr. Hamblin to send a wagon in as far as possible for our sick.

Sunday, October 29th. Camp No. 86. Mr. Hamblin and party left early this morning. Took observations. Monday, Octo- ber 30th. Camp No. 86. Cached the Dean on the east side of river. Made five caches of articles not wanted at Kanab. Tues- day, October 31st. Camp No. 86. Took observations.

Wednesday, November 1, 1871. Camp No. 86 Took ob- servations. Train looked for anxiously, but "no see it". Thurs- day, November 2d. Camp No. 86. This morning soon after breakfast a Mr. Mangin from Kanab rode into camp. It seems that "Agna Grande" got to Kanab before the Major left, and show- ed my letter to Fred Hamblin, so the train started on Monday, 23rd, but in charge of Mr. Riley, who thinking water might be scarce on the route, took the trail to "El Vado", intending to get to the mouth of Pahria down the cliffs. They had been hunting a place for several days. Yesterday morning Mr. Mangin left camp, got to the cliffs, came down the old Indian Trail, got into the valley last night, camped, and came in this morning. He had had nothing to eat since yesterday morning. Got breakfast and started back. This is his story. Says he wanted to come the regular trail, but Riley wouldn't. Says he blames Riley, and Riley blames him.

Friday, November 3rd. Camp No. 86. Fred, Clem, and I started up the river this morning. Went up about five miles, fol- lowing Mr. Mangin's trail until he struck up the mountain, then followed it up, winding around until at last we came out not half a mile from where we climbed up the other day. Followed his trail on to the edge of rocks, then stationed Clem on a high point while Fred and I took Mangin's trail (which had divided) and fol- lowed out, intending to follow until about 3:00 o'clock. It was now 12:30. Then if we did not find them, to go back to camp and start again in the morning. I had not followed my track half a mile when I heard three shots from Fred. He had met them.

Ran over to the train, shook hands all around, then took trail back. It was an awful way back. We got in camp about 5:00 o'clock. It seems that they started from Kanab the 23rd, and have been all this time coming. The mare that was bought at Uintah gave out and they were obliged to leave her. The stock looks about as it did at "El Vado". Shall try to start back day after tomorrow.

Saturday, November 4th. Camp No. 86. While we were getting ready to move tomorrow, who should ride into camp but Mr. Haight and Mr. Riggs from Kanab.[42] It seems that when they got there (Kanab) and learned that supplies had been in ten days, Hamblin started them back with 50 lbs. flour and some sugar for us, and to hunt up the lost ones. They got in a little before dinner. Brought in lost ones, except the "Chicago Five".

Sunday, November 5th. Camp No. 86. Snowy and cold all day, so no one started for Kanab. In camp, etc.

Monday, November 6th. Camp No. 1. Haight, Riggs, Mangin, and Joe Hamblin started for Kanab. We got off about 2:00 P. M. Came about 8 miles. Found a spring that afforded us enough water for bread and coffee but not for stock. Tuesday, November 7th. Camp No. 2. Got off about 9:00 o'clock. Found Sevier Creek [?] in about 2 miles and Spring Creek [Badger Creek] 6 miles further on. Went to Spring and camped. Dry country, not very much sagebrush. Snowing and wind all day—wind and cold. Two miles from Spring Creek the turn swings W.N.-N. W. Wednesday, November 8th. Camp No. 3. Stock much scattered so we could not get off before 11:00 A. M. Came to Jacob's Pool in two miles. Pushed on, made House Rock Springs[43] by 12:00. Went on until 5:00 P. M. Good camp. Thursday, November 9th. Camp No. 3. Went to Kaibab today. Saw Kanab and line of cliffs from Pipe Springs to El Vado. Friday, November 10th. Camp No. 3. Killed the steer. Saturday, November 11th. Left camp 3 for Kanab at 9:00 A. M. Made some 20 miles and camped among sagebrush camp. A little snow and rain today. Some snow on the Buckskin, but not bad travelling.

Sunday, November 12th. Kanab. Left camp at 9:00. Made Kanab at 3:00 P. M. Found that Hamblin was not at home, and that people were expecting the Major any day. He had told Mrs. Hamblin that he should take his wife to camp, but everybody laughed at the idea. Has told Bishop Stewart that he should spend a month on Buckskin Mountain before going to the Moquis,

[42]Knowing that the Thompson party were short of provisions and that the pack train sent from Kanab on October 23 had not reached the Paria on October 29 and fearing that it had met with disaster, Hamblin sent in provisions on a record trip of two days.

[43]Dellenbaugh describes in considerable detail the events from November 5 to December 4. Following the trail by way of Jacob Pools, headquarters were made at House Rock Spring, the name adopted from some camper who had labeled with charcoal two boulders under which he slept, "Rock House Hotel". On November 11 Thmopson left for Kanab with Jones and Steward who needed medical attention. He returned to the base camp on November 17 and left again on November 21. Finally, after the long delayed arrival of Major Powell, the entire party moved from House Rock to Eight Mile Spring east of Kanab.

and left word for Jacob to be on hand to start for the Moquis as soon as he gets back. Got several letters from wife. She says the Major says "he shall start the 5th of November," and be 12 or 15 days on the road, but he told the folks here that he should be but 9 days on the road. He has been gone 23 days from Kanab, 33 from leaving "El Vado de las Padres."

Monday, November 13th. Kanab. Have decided to stop until after the mail comes in Wednesday. Mr. Hamblin got home tonight. Says that a telegram went to St. George on Friday night, the 10th, that the Major left Salt Lake that day with an escort of cavalry. What for, the Lord knows,—I don't. Tuesday, November 14th. Kanab. Let Mr. Hamblin have 100 lbs. flour and ½ bushel potatoes. Mr. Crosly brought 92 lbs. corn. Got 47 lbs. meat of Mr. Hamblin. Heard today that the Major had engaged a cabin at the Fort, 2 rooms of Farnsworth. Wednesday, November 15th. Bought three blankets of Mr. Hamblin for $16.00. Engaged him to get three bushel apples, 25 lbs. dried grapes, and 25 lbs. figs for me at St. George. Mail not in.

Thursday, November 16th. Nothing in mail for any of us. Left Kanab at 3:00 P. M. Camped at "Eight Mile Springs." Friday, the 17th. Camp No. 3. Left "Eight Mile Springs" at 9:00. Made camp at dark. Saturday, November 18th. In camp. Climbed out on north to get view. Sunday, November 19th. Captain Bishop and myself went on Kaibab plateau to locate points of observation. Monday, November 20th. Climbed the mountain north of camp to locate points of observation. Tuesday, November 21st. Kanab. Left camp at 8:00 A. M. Captain and Fred came up with me on the Kaibab. Got to Kanab at 8:00 P. M. Wednesday, November 22nd. In Kanab. Beaman moved to a room in the Fort. Thursday, November 23rd. In Kanab. Friday, November 24th. Hunted for Kit today. She came up after dark. Saturday, November 25th. At Kanab. Sunday, the 26th. At Kanab. Riley came in. Monday, November 27. At Kanab. Hamblin came in. Tuesday, November 28th. Got dried grapes, peaches, apples, etc. of Jacob, 50 lbs. dried grapes, 18c, 1 bushel apples, $3.00, 4 lbs. figs, @ 40c, 164 lbs. peaches, @ 10c, 56 lbs. peaches @ 12c. Wednesday, November 29th. Got word today that the Major was only 34 miles from here last Sunday; that he was going to camp on the "Scoomp pah",[44] that he personally was going to "House Rock" to bring out the rest of the party. Left Ranche Canyon. Have 13 lbs. coffee.

Thursday, November 30th. Left Kanab at 10:00 A. M. with Jacobson. Met the ambulance containing wife, Emma, Jack, Fuzz [Mrs. Thompson's dog], and a girl 3 miles above Johnson's ranch.

---

[44]Scoompah (Skumpah) (Clarkston) on Thompson Creek, a branch of Johnson Canyon was a group of ranches established in 1870 by two families, Clark and Lee. It was a way station on the old road to Kanab which passed through Upper Kanab (later Alton) and Johnson.

Came as far as Johnson and camped for the night. One wagon
got in at 12:00, the other is 20 miles behind, the driver having
killed a horse. Found that they had no flour so sent Jack to Kanab
to get some.

Friday, December 1, 1871. In camp. Steward came to see us,
met Jack and sent up to Captain Dodds to get the other wagon.
Saturday, December 2nd. Went to Kanab. Decided to camp at
Eight Mile Spring. Sunday, December 3rd. Moved camp to
Eight Mile Spring. All day job. Monday, December 4th. Horses
lost. Tuesday, December 5th. Camp. Went to Kanab. Boys
got in. [from House Rock Springs.] Wednesday, December 6th.
Horses lost so we could not move. Thursday, December 7th.
Moved my part of outfit to 3 miles south of Kanab. Am going to
find a place to measure a base line.[45] Friday, December 8th. Picked
out a camp to "fit up" for work. Saturday, the 9th. Went to
Kanab to get things made. Sunday, the 10th. Kept the Sabbath.
Monday, December 11th. Sent Mac to Eight Mile Spring for
Riley to come over and take care of our stock. They wander off
so far that it takes half a day to get them.

Tuesday, December 12th. Riley and Captain Dodds came
over, and with them the Major. They are expecting to go down
on the Buckskin Mountain. The Major proposed a ride. I acquiesced. He said that he had almost decided to go to Washington
this winter and try for another appropriation, either for the valleys
of Sevier and Virgin, or for publication of our reports. Asked
what I thought of it, I told him to go ahead. He said "If I fail, will
you work without salary next year to complete this work?" I replied, "Yes, but I must have enough to live on." "Of course", he
replied. After some further conversation on his part, I said to him,
"Make up your mind what you want to do, then come over and
talk with me, and I will tell you just what I will do. I am perfectly
willing to work until we can get this job finished, be it one or two
years". The Major will get the appropriation, without a doubt.

Wednesday, December 13th. In camp getting ready to work.
Captain Dodds and MacEntire, got a stone in place for end
of "base". Thursday, December 14th. Took the transit to "Gap"
to locate the meridian line. Sent Mac to some "buttes" down the
creek to put up a flag. Captain, Bishop, and Jones at Kanab getting
things ready. Friday, the 15th. Tried to locate meridian, but so
cloudy could not. Saturday, December 16th. Cloudy. Waiting.
Sunday, the 17th. Cloudy. Monday, December 18th. Major
came over and we decided to move his camp over to ours. I said

[45]Beginning with December 7 and extending to May 25, 1872, Thompson and assistants gave
their attention to the preparation of a topographic map. The brief entries in the Diary for this
period note chiefly the routine relating to personnel, equipment, methods of procedure, and areas
surveyed. The pleasures, hardships, disappointments, and dangers of work in an unexplored
country are minimized as features incident to all new scientific exploratory work. The survey
during winter and spring included Kaibab and Kanab Plateaus, the region between Paria and
Virgin Rivers, the Mt. Trumbull district, and areas west to the Nevada line.

to him again, "Make up your mind what you wish to do, and then talk with me." Cloudy.

Tuesday, December 19th. Moved camp to a point a mile below the "Gap" on the Kanab wash. Cloudy, no observations. Wednesday, the 20th. In camp, cloudy. Thursday, the 21st. Cloudy. Sent Jones and Mac to Pajo Spring to put up a monument on the cliff. Friday, December 22nd. Major, Captain Dodds and Riley, with John Stewart [son of Bishop Stewart] started today for the Buckskin Mountain to find a way to get rations in near the mouth of the Little Colorado next summer. Cloudy. Saturday, December 23rd. Got an observation early this morning, but before I could use it, it commenced snowing and raining. Drove two stakes, however, and shall commence work as soon as storm ceases. Joe Mangin commenced work at $20.00 a month. Jones got back about 6:00 tonight, Mac at 8:00 P. M.

Sunday, December 24th. Cloudy and snowy with some rain. Monday, the 25th. Christmas. Cloudy with little rain. Tuesday, the 26th. Commenced work, but a very poor day. Got line partly out. Cloudy. Wednesday, December 27th. Went out to work, but at 9:00 o'clock A. M. commenced raining and kept it up all day. Thursday, the 28th. Rain all day. Rained severely last night. Friday, the 29th. Rain by showers so we could not work. Saturday, December 30th. Worked, but it was a very bad day for measurements on account of wind. Almost impossible to keep robes on horses. Jones and myself went on "Cedar Ridge" and put up a flag. Sunday, December 31st, 1871. Kept the Sabbath by riding out. Got an observation that will enable us to locate our line tonight.

Monday, January 1, 1872. The "boys" did about half a day's work today on account of "New Years". Found by our observation last night that we were about correct the other time. John Stewart came in tonight and said that they had gone to the Colorado River down the Kanab wash. Found about 12 inches snow on the Kaibab so did not try to get down there. Major got in at 8:00 P. M. Tuesday, January 2d. Ranged out line below camp and placed a stone at north end. Major at Kanab. Captain Dodds and Riley got in at 12:00. Found gold in sand in Colorado. Wednesday, January 3rd. Went to Kanab with Major. Thursday, the 4th. Went over on line and then took angles. Friday, January 5th. Rather sagy. Indians in camp.

Saturday, January 6th. Went to Kanab. Decided to let Captain Dodds employ three men and measure the line. He tried to find men at Kanab, but did not succeed. Climbed the cliff north of Kanab with Major. Went to the Piute camp tonight to see dances. Sunday, January 7th. In camp. Indians here to trade. Monday, January 8th. Went wth Captain Dodds on the "line".

Charles Riggs and Thomas Stewart commenced work. We did well today. Jones, Mac and Boring collected silicified wood from "Terraces" for the Major. Fred went to Frank's camp to sketch. Bishop commenced on his map.

Tuesday, January 9th. Worked on line, went to Kanab and to Indian camp. Jones and Mac went to flag on "Cedar Ridge" to build monument. Wednesday, the 10th. Went with Jones and Mac to monument on ridge. Thursday, January 11th. Went to Kanab. Jones and Mac got stone and job. Friday, January 12th. Went to end of line. Located stone on south end of line. Went to dance at Kanab this evening. Dance was "S........" well conducted. Mrs. Olliphant, floor manager. Had supper. Dancing good.

Saturday, January 13th. Jones and Mac went to cliff west of Kanab, but did not get up. I went to Kanab. Sunday, January 14th. Jones and Bonnemont went to cliff west of Kanab. I took observations in camp. Monday, January 15th. We, that is Jones, Mac, Fred and I started on a ten days trip over the Kaibab. Went to Kanab to get supplies. Forgot sextant so the boys went to "Eight Mile Spring" to camp while two went to "Willow Camp" and shall join them in morning.

Tuesday, January 16th. Clem and Bonnemont started down Kanab wash today. I left camp at 10:20. Went to Eight Mile, found the boys gone. Followed the trail to Navajo Wells where I found them in camp. A cold windstorm sprang up at sundown, lasting three hours. It seems peculiar to country.

Wednesday, January 17th. Climbed the Kaibab. Built monument. Camp without water. The camp is 1620 feet above Kanab camp, 1025 above Navajo well. The rise of the mountain is quite gradual, not more than 20 degrees—much cut by valleys. From monument "D" we can see on the other side of the valley, first the Vermilion Cliffs-Triassic. They are 1500 feet above the valley, part of the distance vertical. Slope apparently averages 50 degrees. Then a terrace rising at an angle of five degrees, then white Cretaceous [Jurassic] cliffs with the same characteristics as the vermilion. Back of these are the Tertiary mountains, in many places cliff-like in character, often of a pink dark color. The Triassic cliffs end at Pipe Springs apparently, or topographically. The Cretaceous commence just above or to the right of Cottonwood Canon. The Tertiary over Johnson's canon. This description applied as far as Mollie's Nipple. [White Cone].

Thursday, January 18th. Took angles this morning. Broke camp at 12:00 noon, followed road and made House Rock Springs at 8:00 P. M. The road comes into the valley about 10 miles above H. R. Think the road was badly located for distance, though easy grade. Found considerable quartz on the north end of Kaibab. The dip of mountain seems to be east of north.

Friday, January 19th. Went up on cliff back of springs. Put up a flag. Station 2. Saturday, January 20th. Went up to Red Cliffs [Paria Plateau] above House Rock [Spring]. Found the distance was so great that we could not do our work and get back. Hunted around an old camp for water. Did not find any. Decided to go back to camp, take a pack animal and make a dry camp Sunday, January 21st. Left H. R. at 12:30. Got to our camp near the top of Red Cliff at 5:00. Camped under some cedars. Camp dry, but to compensate, plenty of wood. After dark the boys, Fred and Mac, set fire to some large dead cedars nearby. They burned all night. Cold, but pleasant.

Monday, January 22d. Climbed to top of cliff. Built monument. Took observations for time and latitude. The view from R. C. is fine. The Kaibab is lapped by the Triassic on the east, north, and west. Then the Jurassic and so on, all being in terraces until the Tertiary mountains, snow clad, end the view. The dip seems to be east of north at least 30 degrees. Think the Kaibab has an anticlinal axis. House Rock Valley is two miles wide at House Rock Springs and widens rapidly towards the S. E. dipping from a point 4 miles above H. R. S. towards the Colorado. At the divide a mile wide and gradually narrowing towards the north. Bearing of Colorado slope 334 (true), of the Paria slope 10 (true). The cliffs are terraced on the east, often vertical red sandstone. Several slope 15 degrees. On the west a slope to top of mountain like a bent bow, all limestone with occasional deep gorges. Slope 20 degrees. Lower end of Kaibab at least 2500 feet, decreasing to 1200 at upper, 1700 at H. R. above the valley. At the divide the red sandstone is 600 at Red Cliff, 1200 at H. R., 1230 and 1500 at lower end. Built monument. Took angles and went back to camp.

Tuesday, January 23rd. Sent Jones and Fred to put up monument at angle of Kaibab, but they did not succeed in finding an eligible joint. Mac and I went to signal station 2 to take angles. About sunset 13 Navajo Indians rode into camp. Their chief was "Ah lish kill," an Indian whom we had seen at "El Vado de las Padres". They had some good horses and two jacks, packed with blankets. Gave them flour and peaches.

Wednesday, January 24th. Snowed all day, but very light and dry. We moved our camp to Mount's Spring [?]. The Navajos left about 8:00 A. M. for Kanab. They had a curious ceremony about sunrise. They were all standing in a circle when at a signal they all sat down and sang for three or four minutes a low musical chant or song, then stood up again. It seemed a re-

ligious exercise. Very cold but every prospect of a clear day tomorrow.

Thursday, the 25th. At 9:35 A. M. Mac and I left camp.
Could not find a place on the east ridge of the Kaibab to put a flag.
Made signal station No. 3 on the west side, just on the crest above
Summit Valley. Left Signal Station 3 at 3:00 P. M. Camped on
the valley at foot of mountain. We found that the snow had fallen
on the east ridge of the mountain to the depth of 3 inches. De-
creased in depth after passing Summit Valley to ½ inch on the
west side. No snow in Kanab Valley.

Friday, January 26th. Climbed the Kaibab. Made Station 4
back from crest of ridge one mile. The mountain rises from valley
at slope of 25 degrees for 1000 feet, then slopes gently, say two
degrees back to Station 3. The mountain slopes from foot towards
valley for six miles at angle of two degrees. The contour of the
mountain is rounded on west side. No precipitous walls, etc.,
gulches deep in some places, but generally north of Station 4. Long
ridges run out towards valley, gradually sloping, mountain gradually becoming lower toward north; higher south and more abrupt.
Very cold. Left camp at 1:35 P. M. Got to camp Kanab at 7:30,
25 miles.

Saturday, January 27, went to Kanab. Sunday 28th. In
camp. Rode Kitty. Got back off at first, but finally rode. Monday,
the 29th. In camp. Took time. Tuesday, the 30th. Went to
Kanab. Got ready to start for Kaibab. Wednesday, January 31st.
Went to Kanab with the Major. He settled up with Beaman,
Jones. Went to Pipe Springs; Fred, Mac to Cottonwood canon.

Thursday, Febraury 1, 1872. Went to Kanab with Major.
Friday, the 2nd. Major started for Salt Lake today. Saturday,
February 3rd. Went to Kanab. Told Beaman that I could not
fit him out with horses and took all his instruments, chemicals, etc.,
and stored them at Hamblins. I do not think he wants to be fair
with me.

Sunday, February 4th. In Camp. Clem and Bonnemont
got in. Clem did not get pictures. For some reason his chemicals
would not work. He thinks it is in the bath. Broke his camera
all to bits. Horse fell off cliff and fell on it. Clem says the
pictures would spot and fog. Tried the water from the creek—
tried a good many times, but always with the same result.

Monday, February 5th. Settled with Bonnemont. Let him
have saddle and bridle for $15.00, knife $1.00, and gave check
for $84.00. Balance due. Got blanket, $20.00, of John Stewart
and a buckskin which I took to Mrs. Hatch. Got other camera,
chemicals and Beaman's bath for Clem. Gave Beaman an order
for Jass.

Tuesday, the 6th   Went to Kanab. S. Stewart and the

Riggs boys quit today. Paid them with check, also paid Chas. Riggs for trip to Colorado last fall, $12.00 and Mrs. Riggs $10.00 for butter and milk, making $82.50 in all. Clem tried pictures with his old bath. The pictures were spotted and fogged. Tried four pictures with Beaman's bath, but Clem's old chemicals. Picture all right. Captain Dodds went with me and I showed him where I wanted line remeasured.

Wednesday, February 7th. Worked with Clem. Tried all ways to find where the trouble was. It is in his bath. Made one attempt with the bath he took down the river, but with same result as before. Fogged and streaked. Took four or five good pictures with Beaman's bath.

Thursday, February 8th. Worked with Clem. Took 2 or 3 good pictures. Sent Clem to Kanab this P. M. to get tent, etc. Telegraphed the Major at Salt Lake to stop payment on Beaman's checks until he heard from me. Have tried six times in all to get pictures with Clem's old bath, but with same result every time. No picture. Have tried 13 times with Beaman's bath and same chemicals as at first and always a picture. It seems that Clem's bath worked well before he took it to Kanab, or day before he started. Beaman filtered it while there and it has not worked since, and Beaman has all the time said Clem would not get pictures. S. Hamblin and Farnsworth came to work at $1.50 per day. Wrote two letters to the Major. Wrote Bishop Windsor [Winsor], telling him we wanted a beef by Wednesday the 15th. Jones and Fred took observations on north end of line for Latitude.

Friday, February 9th. Jones and Fred located Arizona line. Loaned John Stewart a pack saddle. Went to Kanab. Got aneroid boxes made by Mr. Bunting, $1.00. Saturday, the 10th. Jones and Fred at Point "C" taking angles. Mac and I went to south end of line.—Sunday, the 11th. In camp. Let John Stewart have check for $50.00. Monday, February 12th. Sent Jones and Fred to get angles from S. Station 5, but they failed. Mac and I went to south end of line again. Paid Joe $17.00 and Mac $3.00.

Tuesday, February 13th. Mr. Jones and Fred went to S. S. 5, and I went to Kanab. Got telegram from Wes [Powell]. Telegraphed him "Deposit in my name. Have given written checks." Have paid the Bishop, Stewart, $2.00. Let Joseph Stewart have 22 lbs. coffee. Let Joseph and Mangin have shirt and pair overalls, also pair blankets, $4.00. Wednesday, the 14th and Thursday the 15th. Jones and Fred got back. Sent load of goods to Kanab. Got 600 lbs. of beef of Bishop W.

Friday, February 16th. Moved camp. Let Bishop Windsor have check $175.00. Signed check that the Major neglected to for Jacob Hamblin for $50.00. Camped at Eight Mile Spring. Got telegrams from this. Sent answer. Saturday, February 17th.

Went to Navajo well. Climbed to Point "B." Triangulated. Could see Points D and E and Signal Station 4 base to point "C". Sunday, February 18th. Climbed to Signal Station 6 on Triassic Cliffs. Back of Triassic Cliffs the White Jurassic rise, much broken by canons, covered with small cedars and pinons. They end in a sharp serrated ridge. Back of these are pink Tertiary, ending at a little greater angle than the Jurassic. Snow covered.

Monday, February 19th. Left camp at Eight Mile Spring at 9:00. Got to Kanab and got out rations for a two weeks' trip, then went to camp in Kanab Creek. Alfred Zenny commenced work at $25.00 per month. George Adair got back with rations as per memoranda made this day. Jack got in also. Clem made no pictures on this trip. Gave G. Adair check for $25.00.

Tuesday, Fbruary 20th. In camp part of day, mapping, etc., then went to Kanab. Settled with McEntire. Paid him by accepting order in favor of Bishop of $30.00.

Wednesday, the 21st. Went to Kanab to get mail and rations. No word from the Major or Eastern mail. Settled with and gave Joe Mangin check for $8.00, balence due him after I pay Bishop Windsor $14.00. Finished "Base Line". Paid Farnsworth for work of self and boy, together with pay for work done by him on Major's account. Paid Lyman, Hamblin, also gave written checks. Paid Lyman for Jones.

Thursday, February 22d. George Adair commenced work at $40.00 per month. Found all our stock for the first time for a month. I had had two men looking for them yesterday.

Friday, February 23rd. Broke Camp at 9:00. Went to camp on Buckskin at 5:00 P. M. Found water in Pockets some ten miles out. Camped in Gulch canon. Mountain rises very gradually 5 degrees for 15 miles from Camp Kanab. Think the Gulch is cut out of same sandstone at House Rock Valley, i. e., upper member of Carboniferous. After 15 miles mountain 10 degrees to foot of last rise; cut by side canyons which lead back frequently for 5 miles. Cedars at ten miles on salient ridge at 15 Pine put in an appearance. Pine and fir in canons, water three-fourths of mile up canon. Camp 2000 feet above camp Kanab.

Saturday, February 24th. Moved camp up to Stewart's Ranche [in Stewart or Jump Up Canyon]. Snow commenced falling at 2:00 P. M. Camp near springs [Big Spring] which bursts out of hill 200 feet above valley. A stream 15 inches in diameter, flowing down forms a small pond, then a little brook for ¼ mile before it sinks. Foundations of Moquis houses in valley; canon ⅛ mile wide, walls sloping 700 feet high. Many huge pines in valley. One that is fallen was at least 200 feet high and 5 feet through, another 150 feet high and 5 feet through. Some large pines.

Sunday, the 25th. Snowed by spells all day, 8 inches fallen in camp. Camp about 2400 feet above Camp Kanab. Monday, February 26th. Found the stock and climbed the mountain on east side of canon today. Could see but little on account of snowing. Climbed a pine 100 feet. Tree at least 125 feet high. Saw south wall of Colorado near Mt. Trumbull trail—was up 1000 feet above Stewart's Ranche. East wall of Canon 700 feet above valley, slope 25 degrees, slope of valley 5 degrees.

Tuesday, February 27th. Selected views. Plotted map or lines. Decided to send George to Kanab for rations and Jones with Captain Dodds to S.E. of Kaibab. Andy and Frank to S.W. angle. Wednesday, February 28th. Snowed all day. George started for Kanab. Only found 13 head of horses, though men were out all day. Snow 12 inches deep. Thursday, February 29th. Got horses in by 1:00 P. M., except Juitte and Buttons. Captain Dodds and Jones started to go as far on Kaibab as they could. Fred and Andy went to the farther breakdown of the Kaibab, there to build monument F.

Friday, March 1, 1872. Went up on the mountain to put up flag. Did not find a point. Rations from Kanab arrived. When George got to Kanab he received word that his wife was very ill at Beaver, so he hired Brigham S. Young to come with rations and he went to Beaver. Saturday, March 2nd. Captain Dodds and Jones got back. They did not go far on account of snow. Have not found Juitte or Buttons. Sunday, March 3rd. Climbed up the Kaibab. Had all hands hunting horses. Did not find. Fred and Andy got in, Cleve and Jack Stanton. They put up a monument on point F. Found the horses.

Monday, March 4th. Fred and I went up on Kaibab. Part of the horses could not be found, so we could not start today.— Tuesday, the 5th. Found the horses and moved to Oak Spring [on a tributary to Snake Gulch]. Cliffs at lower end of canon 1400 feet high. Wednesday, March 6th. Broke camp at 9:00 A. M. and passed down canon [Snake Gulch]. Walls 800 feet at upper end and 1200 feet at Junction with Kanab wash. Course of Canon S. W. Made 22 miles and camped a mile below the junction. Snowstorm this A. M. Snow P. M. Moquis inscription in upper end of canon. Saw a new species of cactus. Y———— starting. Wash is ½ as wide at camp. A great many caves and plants that indicate water in valley.

Thursday, March 7th. Broke camp at 9:00. Wash much obstructed by willows. Made about 18 miles and camped at "Pocket". Friday, March 8th. Broke camp at 9:00. Went up Pipe Spring wash. Canon walls 500 feet at Junction. Canon ⅛ mile wide. Followed it 7 miles when we climbed out and made Pipe in 7 more.

Saturday, March 9th. Jones, (our baby) wife, Captain Dodds, and myself went to Kanab. Brigham went also, as I did not wish to keep him longer. Paid him $10.00 for work. Got letters from Major, etc. Gave check to Cash $14.50 for corn— and $2.00 for Jones. Robertson $23.75 for blacksmithing, and L. Hamblin $10.00 for rations. Got 3 lbs. beef of Winsor. Sunday, March 10th. Got rations and came to Pipe Spring. Willie Johnson commenced work at $45.00 per month. Monday, March 11th. Jones, Johnson[46] and myself climbed cliff 1000 feet back of Pipe Spring and put up flag. Fred worked on map and copied bearings. Jack and Clem got in. Have taken 30 views, some of them good.

Tuesday, March 12th. Jones and Johnson went to Signal Station 5. I worked on map. Fred copied bearings. Captain Dodds went to Kanab to get tent for Photographer, the dark box being used up. Gave Jacob check for $85.00. Wednesday, March 13th. Clem went to Kanab for more chemicals. Jones and Johnson got home. Captain Dodds got back. Fred at work on bearings. Traded in old buckskin for a little mare. Thursday, March 14th. Johnson, Fred and myself went to Point H., built monument. Took bearings, etc. Jack on dark tent. Clem got back. Jones observing. Friday, March 15th. Let Stewart Bishop have check for $20.00. He says John says we owed him balance of $25.00. Boys, wash, etc. Jones to take observations. Wrote Major two letters.

Saturday, March 16th. Johnson, Fred and myself worked, plotting bearings. Jones on observations. Captain Dodds shoeing. Got telegram from Fan.

Sunday, March 17th. Plotted bearings with boys. Jones observing. Monday, the 18th. Plotted bearing part of day. Fred and Johnson worked on map the rest. Took dinner. Poor.

Tuesday, March 19th. Jones, Fred, Johnson and myself went to Point H. to identify bearings, and correspondence. Got back at 3:00 P. M., when Fred and I went to Pt. A. The east side of Kanab and other washes are the higher. Fennemore came.[7] Talked with Jack and Clem.

Wednesday, March 20th. Fred and Johnson on sketch. Finished it. Fennemore getting ready to take pictures. Clem talked with me and said he did not care to stay. Told him he had better come on the trip to Trumbull, learn what he could, and then should have a separate outfit if possible. He acquiesced, but I think reluctantly. Has not helped get ready, but little.

Thursday, March 21st. Left Pipe at 10:30 A. M. for Mt.

[46]George Johnson of Kanab was employed as topographic assistant. He was a member of the crew of the Canonita in 1872.

[47]Fennemore was employed as photographer. He replaced Beaman who resigned his position on account of illness. At the present time, June, 1939, James Fennemore, aged 90 years resides in Phoenix, Arizona. He is the only known living member of the Powell-Colorado survey parties.

Trumbull, etc.[48] Clem's horse, Buttons, got away from him and lost his gun, so he stopped to hunt it. Is to come up if he finds it. Camp at a "pocket", Wild Band. Saw three horses in the distance —wild ones probably. Country level—could take a wagon without difficulty. Route straight from Pipe to Trumbull, pocket a mile and a half south of direct line. Spring thought to be in canon nearly north. Distance 15 miles. Clem not up.

Friday, March 22d. Broke camp at 8:30. Made 20 miles at 4:00 P. M.—16 miles easy for wagon. Strike lava and rough country then, but not very bad. Think we are north of best route. Outlines of rounded hills. Are camped on a gulch. No water, grass poor. Think the basaltic lava has overflowed since the present hills were eroded. Lava in valley, hills apparently are Carboniferous. Many lava pebbles on the surface. Left Alfred to come up with Clem. Alfred waited at Wild Bench camp until 12:00, and then came on without him.

Saturday, March 23rd. Broke camp at 7:30 without breakfast. Took a moccasin trail and found a water pocket, "Rocky Pool" at 10:00 A. M. Camped for the day. Rough. Could not take wagon way we came. No trail between to the Whitmore Ranch between us and Mountain. Fennemore took two views. Sunday, March 24th. Captain Dodds and myself took a trail and followed it to Whitmore's ranch. It is at the old Patite Spring. Jones and Fred went to right of Mount Trumbull. Found a trail leading to Whitmore's Ranch. Johnson went down the wash after fossils and on geology.

Monday, March 25th. Climbed Mount Trumbull. Jones and Fred stayed on top to take observations. Jack and Fennemore to take views. Built monument 1. Tuesday, March 26th. Broke camp at 9:30 A. M. Went to camp near lava bed. Went to Whitmore's Ranch. Did not see him. Wednesday, March 27th. Captain Dodds and Jones took rations and went on trail to river.[49] Will be gone two days. Jack and Fennemore took three views of lava bed. Fred and I climbed a hill, got view of country, and then went to Whitmore's. Saw him. Says he has followed trail up river 12 miles. Goes down valley four or five miles, then turns to right. Is not the old trail of last year but is called the Ute crossing.

Thursday, March 28th. Fred and Johnson put up flag on Mt. Lucy [?]. Is signal station No. 7. Went up to the last crater of volcano. The cone is in two parts, composed of light, cellular slag. It was once a cone, or perhaps oblong form, say 500 feet high. The lava filled the interior, broke down the north

---

[48]Mount Trumbull, the most prominent among the volcanic peaks that constitute the Uinkaret Mountain (North Side Mountains of Ives, 1858), was named for Lyman Trumbull, U. S. Senator from Illinois, 1854-1873.

[49]One purpose of visits to points along Grand Canyon was to find favorable places where supplies could be brought to the river party who in 1872 were to use the boats cached at the mouth of the Fremont and at Lees Ferry for a traverse to the mouth of the Virgin.

and south walls and flowed a stream one mile wide and $1\frac{1}{2}$ miles long toward the north, $\frac{1}{4}$ mile wide at break on south, $1\frac{1}{2}$ miles long dividing the lower end around a hill into two branches. The end of these streams near the cone are of the same light slaggy, cellular, basalt as the cone bed increases in density toward the ends which are a solid basaltic lava, with few comparative cells. Trees on upper portion of streams. Pines 100 years old. Few trees on lower. Nothing about the crater indicates a lapse of more than 300 years since the outflow. The old volcano has a crater extending from Mount Trumbull on the east to Mount Lucy on the west and six miles from north to south. Friday, March 29th. Johnson examined lava bed for zeolitic minerals. Showed Fred where I wanted sketch of crater made. Jones and Captain Dodds not in.

Saturday, March 30th. Jones and Fennemore started for Kanab to get rations, materials, etc., with the wagon. Are to meet us at Ft. Pierce. If grass at Berry's Spring is good, will camp there and come to Ft. Pierce to tell us. Told Jones he need not hunt for Clem. Captain Dodds, Johnson and myself left camp at 10:00 A. M. to try the Indian trail from Whitmore's to river. Left it when 4 miles from Whitmore's and took a side trail; climbed out of valley and went some ten miles on the table. Trail played out. Came back to valley and camped.

Sunday, March 31st. Left our dry camp at 7:00 A. M. Went ten miles down the valley, or rather down the valley until two miles below Lava Ridge, crossing valley, then trail leads over a low, much broken divide. Followed it out to a point where we could tell that it ran to right of high butte, then decided that I would come back to camp, leaving Johnson and Captain Dodds to go on. Found water enough to water horses on rocks. Left the boys at 1:30 P. M. We were, where I left, 3,565 feet lower than "divide" near Whitmore's; 3,065 feet lower than camp Lava Spring. Many flowers in blossom. N............ shooting up. Found a single looking "smilex". Got to camp at 6:30 P. M. in a snow storm.

Monday, April 1, 1872. Sick. Jack and Andy went down the valley to make view from top of cliff. Stormy, so Fred could not work. Tuesday, April 2d. Snowing all day. Is at least 15 inches on level. Of course we can do nothing. Wednesday, April 3rd. Cleared off last night. Thawed a little. Clouds are running so low that distant points are enveloped. All the boys got in. Captain Dodds and Johnson did not get to river on the trail. Followed it out about five miles beyond where I left them. Found many trails but none that took the gulches, so they came back and went to river near the point where the Major went down. Captain thinks horses could be got to within 1000 to 1500 feet, perhaps all the way. Jack and Andy got in after dark. So cloudy they could do nothing with pictures. Snowing a little at night.

Thursday, April 4th. Clear. Went to Whitmore's and found out what I could about trail to St. George. Did not get stock together until afternoon so could not start. Friday, April 5th. Broke camp early. Ground soft, and snow on mountain 16 inches deep. No snow after we got out 6 miles, but very soft. Missed the right trail or rather there were so many that we took the wrong one, a stock trail that ran out. Finally struck an old faint one that we followed until camping time. Signs of storm tomorrow.

Saturday, April 6th. Very windy with little rain last night. So cloudy we could not see any distance so took course and pushed on. In half an hour commenced snowing. Came to a line of vertical cliffs running north and south. Snowing so hard we camped. Melted enough to fill our kegs. Let the animals have a good feed. Cleared enough so we started again at 2:30 P. M. Snow by spells, very soft. Camped at 5:00 P. M. Made perhaps 5 miles today. Snowing at this writing, 9:00 P. M. Sunday, April 7th. Bore to right and travelled 20 miles along line of cliff. Camped near a canon with water. Ate all our flour tonight.

Monday, April 8th Broke camp at 8:00. Breakfast of beans. Got to Hurricane Hill[50] at 2:00 P. M. Bought meal and milk, $5.00 worth, of Wakeman at Gould's Ranch. Got to Berry's Spring at dark. Found the wagon with Clem, Fennemore and George, Jones having gone to Ft. Pierce. He left Kanab on Wednesday the 3rd, at which time George commenced work again. Jones bought ———— lbs of corn of Winsor and got 5 lbs. of beef. Tuesday, April 9th. In camp waiting for Jones and letters. Got one from Beaman. Let Johnson have $5.00.

Wednesday, April 10th. Went to Toquerville. Got photographic material and Indian goods at Toquerville. Took dinner at Haights. Bought articles, $8.75 for expedition, and shoes, $3.75 for Alfred. Paid Harmon $15.00 for freight on goods from Toquer to Salt Lake. Gave him check for $50.00. Charge expedition with 18 yards calico 30c, 1 yard to 25, 1 tin dish 50c, 1 dozen eggs 25c. Paid $1.85 premium on gold. Borrowed $10.00 of Jack. Thursday, April 11th. In camp. Boys getting ready to start tomorrow.

Friday, April 12th. Captain Dodds and Fred, Jack and Fennemore, started for the Mingkard Mountains [Virgin Mountains] today with 12 days' provisions. Jones, Johnson and Andy started for Pine Valley Mountains with six days' rations. Saturday, April 13th. Went to St. George, taking George Adair with me to talk to Indians. Went to Mrs. Ivins. Went to theatre.

---

[50]Because snow storms in the Uinkaret Mountains made topographic work impracticable. Thompson decided to go to the lower country about St. George. Enroute he encountered a high westward-facing cliff down which he finally found a trail at Hurricane Hill near the present village of Hurricane. To the entire escarpment some 200 miles long he applied the name Hurricane Cliffs.

Sunday, April 14th. Talked with Indians a little. St. George is a very pretty town, 1500 population. Is watered by springs, large lots, well built. Seems to be considerable enterprise in town. Nice Court House of cut stone. A tabernacle of cut stone, school house, etc. People seem much above common run of Mormons. Have two taverns, three stores, a tanning, shoe, and harness shop. Are talking about bringing the Virgin into town. Many trees, mostly cottonwoods along the streets. Figs, apricots, peaches, apples, etc. grow in open air, almonds as well. Grapes are abundant; the black ham berry and mission flourish, but the Isabella is the most esteemed for wine making.

Monday, April 15th. Talked with Indians. The Santa Claras say the Mormons will do for them, that the Americans talk but do not do anything. The Shevwits are afraid. Think we want to kill them. Can hardly get an Indian to own himself a Urigkavit or Shevwit. They want to know what we will give them, if anything. Say they are very poor. Tuesday, April 16th. Back in camp. Talked with Shevwits' Chief. Have agreed to meet Thomas at Ft. Pierce in 7 days, by 24th inst. Paid $4.20 to Pymms for George Adair. Paid for keeping horses, $6.00, corn, $3.50 and George's board $5.50—$15.00. Got one dozen canteens made of C. S. Riding, $10.50 and $16.45 of Co-op store for expedition. Paid $1.50 for fixing Jack's gun at Washington. Wednesday, April 17th. In camp. Johnson and George got back from Washington.

Thursday, April 18th. Sent Clem to Kanab. Johnson went home today. Sent George to Rockville for corn and flour. Sent Alfred to Toquerville for mail. Clem is to take Prince from Goulds to Pipe, is to get Mormon Spy Roan moved, fit himself out for the photographing, get the mail, etc. Let Jones have $1.00. Let Alfred have 50c. Gave Johnson's check for $50.00. Alfred got mail matter. Four prospectors camped near us. One man claims to have picked White[51] up at Callville after his voyage through the Canon. Says White was poor, legs a scab—starved, was on San Juan river with Captain Baker and Mr._____ prospecting. The Indians fired on them, killed Baker. White and Mr._____ got a few pounds (14) of flour from Jack and made some ropes and flew down the river—made a raft of logs. The second day out White's companion was drowned. When White got through his raft was tied together by strips of clothing. He had one rope 15 feet long that he used to lash himself on to his raft of 3 logs. The tale may be true, but I doubt it. The same man said that in '57 a party of miners crossed the river from the south end of the Buckskin Mountain.

<hr/>

[51]This story that James White in 1867 descended the Colorado from Gunnison Crossing to Callville on a raft tied together with buckskin straps and pack ropes has so far remained without corroboration. To those familiar with the Colorado canyons, the reported traverse seems one of many mythical events. (But the reader may wish to consult "The Grand Canyon" Sen. Doc. No. 42, 65th Cong. 1st Session, May 25, 1917, an article by Thomas F. Dawson in support of White's claims.—J. C. A.)

Friday, April 19th. George got back from Rockville. No-
one could get checks cashed. Spent $2.00 for grain. Jones on ob-
servation. Saturday, April 20th. Sent George to Washington for
flour, etc. Got 200 lbs., $16.00, and 5 gallons sorghum, $6.25. Got
check for $30.00 cashed. Sunday, the 21st. In camp, keeping Sab-
bath. Monday, the 22nd. Sent George and Andy to Toquerville
for Indian goods. Clem got back from Kanab. No letters from
the Major.

Tuesday, April 23rd. Went to Washington to meet Indians.
Taking George and Jones, and goods. Wednesday, April 24th.
Distributing goods to 134 Indians counting squaws and children
—warriors, squaws, children. Paid $5.00 for flour, etc., $6.00 for
Burns and Jones. Went to St. George and bought 200 lbs. corn,
$14.00, 100 lbs. flour, $8.00. Paid $4.00 for hotel bill. Thursday,
April 25th. Went back to camp. Found Captain Dodds, Fred,
Jack and Fennemore in camp. Dodds had gone to visit at Saver
Falls. Saw springs on other side of Sage Valley; are large, flow
a great deal of water. Fennemore and Jones got 20 pictures—
good ones. Jack says Fennemore is a "bilk"; will not climb for
views.

Friday, April 26th. Getting ready for breaking camp. Johnson got in. Saturday, April 27th. Broke camp. Sent Jones and
Johnson to Pine Valley Mountains. Jack and Fennemore up the
valley of the Virgin for views. Captain Dodds and Andy are to
take goods to Kanab, then go to Paria to see about boats, etc.
Alfred is to go with them to Kanab, then come back to Toquer to
get balance of Indian goods. I take George, Fred, and Clem and
go to Sharp Mountain [Mount Bangs]. Made St. George. Bought
corn, $4.80. Saw Major C. F. Powell, Indian Agent. He had
distributed goods to Santa Clara and St. George Indians.

Sunday, April 28th. Lost horses. Could not get track of
two. Had two men hunting them. Clem got view of St. George.
Monday, April 29th. Horses were not found yesterday. Sent
Fred to Berry Spring and George on range. Fred got in at 5:00
P. M. met the strays. Bought $2.50 of corn to feed. Agreed to meet
at Kaibab in 8 days. Tuesday, April 30th. Broke camp. Made
20 miles and camped. Dry.

Wednesday, May 1, 1872. Broke camp at 7:30. Made 10
miles at 11:00 o'clock, finding no water, when concluded to stop
and rest an hour. Fred found a small alkali spring. Got a bite to
eat, watered horses and went on. At 6:00 P. M. found a pool.
Camped and climbed; could see nothing. Think I am too far to
south.

Saturday, May 4th. Climbed Mount K. or Mount Turner.
Very foggy. From Mount Trumbull comes the first line of cliffs;
is Hurricane. Large ravine almost N. and whirling around into
Mount Lucy. Twenty miles to west is the divide between Grand

Wash. The Wash seems to have many branches; reaches to Beaver Dam Mountains, drains east slope, and bears 10 degrees west of south to river. Several levels of country 2200 feet above camp No. 1. Much cut by canon. Beaver [Dam] Mountains are a continuation of Santa Clara. The Pine Valley, Santa Clara and Beaver Dam, and mountains below seem to be a continuous range in this form. The S. C. seems to be mountain ranges or rather two mountains much cut up. Several trend 10 west of N. N.W. from Mount L. across the Virgin west 12 miles is a lower range of mountains running east around S. C. and apparently are P. V. The high plateau of Grand Canon seems broken down at foot of Grand Wash. Left our camp at 9:00 A. M. Went down Sevier river at upper end of valley. Found water about 8 miles from camp which flowed quietly down the Wash, Saturday night.

Sunday, May 5th. Broke camp at 9:00. Travelled until dark. Found no water, camped five miles from river. Monday, May 6th. Broke camp at 8:00. Went down the valley. Camped and got dinner, then went to St. George. Bought bill of goods at Co-op. Paid shoemaker $16.50 for shoes. Paid $4.50 for corn, vinegar and sorghum, Andy $1.50 for canteen. Tuesday, May 7th. Left camp at 11:00. Made Ft. Pierce—16 miles.

Wednesday, May 8th. Rain in morning. Left Ft. Pierce at 11:00 A. M. Made a dry camp a few miles from Antelope Spring —15 miles. Thursday, May 9th. Broke camp at 8:00. Found a little water in rocks at 12:00 noon. Made Pipe at 7:00 P. M. Rain all the forenoon. Found the boys all at Pipe except Captain Dodds and Andy. Got a letter from the Major. Friday, May 10th. Broke camp and went to Kanab. Camped just below town. George went home.

Saturday, May 11th. In camp. Johnson went home. Alfred started for Toquer to get Indian goods. Made arrangements with Jacob to get 5 mules to pack. Sunday, May 12th. In camp. First day of rest for five weeks. Monday, May 13th. Wife went to Johnson Canon. Sent 12 horses by Johnson to the canon for feed. Put up tents and commenced work on map. Tuesday, May 14th. Worked on map. Sent Jones to Pipe Spring for rest of goods. Let George Adair have 215 lbs. flour. Traded Sis mule for Dinah.

Wednesday, May 15th. Worked on map. Captain Dodds and Andy got in. Report boats at Paria alright—no oars. Caches all torn up. Took ropes out to Lee's and left in house. Wrote Major. Fennemore and Jack printing pictures. Jones got in with stuff from Pipe. Snowing all day, but mild. Thursday, May 16th. Mountains white this morning. Worked on map. Gave Jack $1.00. Friday, May 17. Finished plotting map today. Will take Fred at least three days. Saturday, May 18th. In camp. Beef of Winsor, 868 lbs. Alfred got back from Toquerville. Brought Indian goods, together with boxes from Nebeker. 24 boxes, one with photographic material. Freight $5.00 and Exp. $15.40. Went to Johnson with Clem. Gave Windsor [Winsor] check for $100.00. Fennemore and Clem have had work done for their eyesight by Watson, Mrs. Mace and Robertsen.

Sunday, May 19th. In camp. Monday, May 20. Distributed goods to Indians. Jacob helped. George commenced work again. Tuesday, May 21st. Moved big tent up town. Let Jacob have a big tent to put up. Jones on observation. Wednesday, May 22. Worked fixing up tent, etc. Jones on observation. Thursday, May 23rd. In town and about camp. Paul Bishop finished map. Jones on observation. Friday, May 24th. George, Johnson and Fred put up stations. Captain Dodds fixed Jack's. Saturday, May 25. Moved to Eight Mile Spring. Found water dried up. Sent camp to Johnson while I came to Kanab.[52] Got 5 horses of Jacob. Sunday, May 26. Made report to Major Dodge of distribution Indian goods. Monday, May 27. Made out accounts. Jack came in. Sent George and Fennemore to camp. Tuesday, May 28th. Finished accounts and writing. Wrote to Major Brown. Wrote to Major Dodge. Did not go to camp, for did not get through until dark.

Wednesday, May 29th. Left Kanab at 5:00 A. M. Got to camp at 8:00, found that Fennemore got lost coming out Monday. Got in camp at noon yesterday. His mule got away from him and has gone back to Kanab. Sent Alfred for it. Johnson, Fred and myself climbed Point B. At Signal Station "E" the upper stratum is a calcarious sandstone. The dip is 25 degrees west of north. Back, say for 6 miles to north, the country dips, say, two degrees down from face of Vermilion Cliffs. The white Jurassic sandstone is the surface rock the last three miles. Country cut by canons like Kanab and Johnsons. The Vermilion cliffs seem to continue to the Paria, then strike a fold running down the Paria to the mouth, and crossing, forms Echo Cliffs. At about 6 miles distance north, and keeping a general parallelism with the Vermilions are "White" Cliffs. They commence at Point 1 and continue a long way east. Point 1 is where road turns to Long Valley. Below 1 is Virgin Temple—on the other side of the river and above Rockville. No. 2 is a bold salient. No. 3 also, and a little to left of a line from "B" to left point, Table Mountain. Back of White Cliffs rise the "Pink", described when I climb Eight Mile Cliffs, continuing parallel with the Vermilion to a point 5 miles above Point "B" when they approach the Vermilion, begin lower and run out. The Kaibab Plateau becomes lower toward the Paria river and finally stretches a level plain out by canons across the country this

----

[52]The dispatch of the reorganized party to the settlement of Johnson was the first step in the adventurous overland journey through unknown country from Kanab to the mouth of the Fremont. The Diary entries from May 30 to July 7 are reproduced as a continuous narrative in Powell's Report.

side of "Echo Falls." Section covered calc. sandstone. 74 feet Grey sandstone. Thin layer parallel with canon 6700-401 feet of heavily bedded sandstone, color varying. To Vermilion with occasional pockets of softer lighter colored sandstone with notches of clay. Elevation—300 feet rock similar in character to last, but less heavily bedded. Below this are the meshy variegated beds forming part of Triassic.

Thursday, May 30th. Broke camp at 11:00 A. M. Alfred did not get back from Kanab. Left word at Johnson that if he was going to continue work, to follow out; if he was going to quit, to take old Navajo back to Paugh. Employed Nephi Johnson to take care of Mormon. Came up from 6300 feet to 6920, first 200 feet red and light gray sandstone, next 200 often yellow stone with gray, next 200 white. Think we are likely in Jurassic. The valley is almost similar in form 20 miles across. Much growth of cedar and pine toward the "Pink Cliffs". The valley rises in foot hills to the mountains, cut by canons coming down from the mountains. Camp at Lee's or Clarkston." Fred, brother, sketches the valley.

Friday, May 31st. Broke camp at 8:00. Travelled 16 miles by 3:00, when we came to a beautiful valley with a fine cool spring in it, and we camped. About ¾ of a mile south is a lake 200 yards across [Swallow Park]. It is the mouth of a narrow canon [Kitchen Canyon] cut in sandstone and running to the Paria through the White Cliffs. Country over which we have passed rather rough. Course generally east, ridges running down from the Pink Cliffs, forming valleys with good grass. Timber cedar, with here and there a pine. Call the spring and valley where we are camped "Adair Spring and Adair Valley". Course nearly east 16 miles.

Saturday, June 1, 1872. Broke camp at 8:00 A. M. From camp started east over a low divide into another valley. Kept on a sort of bench for perhaps 5 miles, when we came to cedar and a canon running almost east and starting from the bench. Canon walls quite steep. A spring about 3 miles down. Sandstone. Followed the canon 4 miles, when we left it to left and came to another canon in ½ mile. Our Indian Tom, who had joined us at Clarkston, here did not understand the country, and said there was a canon further to north that he did "je-sue-ge-way". Told him to "figure" and on we went. After climbing in and out of two or three shallow gulches we came to a very deep rocky canon which was one Tom understood. Down into it we wound—through brush and brier. On reaching the bottom found a sandstone bottom with walls of softer stone (sand) of a yellowish white color. The lower part thinly bedded shale, almost slate. We went down a few rods when we came to where the sandstone was cut by a deep canon, often not more than 4 or 5 feet across. Captain Dodds recognized this as a canon which they had struck five miles further down and followed up to where we now were. Soon found their trail. Climbed out and on over a rough country going nearly north. A few miles brought us to a nice clear stream flowing in a narrow valley. Crossed and two miles on, came to Averetts Canon, named because Averett was here killed by Indians.[58] Saw the tree behind which the Indians were concealed when they fired on him, and the rock against which he rolled, not more than 20 yards distant. Two miles on came to Clear Creek [Willis Creek], a muddy branch of the Paria. Crossed. Its valley is narrow, walls rocky. Three miles further and down we go into the Paria Valley 800 feet lower than our camp at Adair's Spring. The Paria where we are camped is a muddy stream, flowing about as much water as at its mouth 75 miles below. The valley is ¾ of a mile wide, grass thick, small scrubby cedars on sides. Came about 18 miles today. Dip 20 degrees west of north.

Sunday, June 2d. Broke camp at 8:00. Followed up the Paria a mile to where it branches, then took left fork [Henrieville Creek], followed it up to its head 12 miles, the valley rising at least 75 feet to the mile. Walls on either side are steep. Passed two small creeks coming in from the right and three from the left. Valley narrow, streams clear. Found a seam of coal 2 feet wide in the cliffs [Pollock Mine]. An infuse lamp would perhaps burn well, but think not. Found an incrustation of alum on the same rock. At the head of the valley we climb a ridge 1000 feet. Trail very steep and narrow. While climbing, shower came on which made the trail very slippery. The whole country at the head of valley is worn into steep gulches and steep ridges. Think the coal was on Cretaceous, perhaps base of Tenham [Formation]. Table ridge [Table Cliff, southern edge of Aquarius Plateau] rises perhaps 3000 feet higher than summit of divide. Up the valley are pines, a few firs, and a good many cedars. Along the creek a good many birch of a species allied to the "spice birch." Bark peels easily and is tougher than "paper birch." Trees are only three or four inches in diameter. Crossing the divide a fine grassy valley commences [Upper Potato Valley]; springs seep out almost at summit. Pine trees grow in the valley and on the mountain slopes. On the west side the mountains rise to Table Mountain [Table Cliffs]. On the east to a mountain 1000 feet lower [Kaiparowits Peak]. Two miles down the valley is a fine spring. We are camped on a gravel ridge. Best grass I have seen. Dip I think 30 degrees east of north, which would indicate that the Paria flows in an anticlinal axis. Trail horribly steep. Shower came on us just as we commenced ascending. Hard work getting up.

---

[58]In 1866 Elijah Averett was killed while pursuing a band of marauding Piutes. A sandstone slab bearing the initials "E. A." marks the spot. In 1935 a new monument was erected.

Monday, June 3rd. Rain this morning. Indian Tom went back. Gave him an old blanket. Went down the valley 13 miles to where a large stream comes in [Birch-Escalante]. Could not ford it, or rather could not find a place where we could get down, and camped. The valley in the upper part is quite marshy. As soon as a little stream begins to run, it dries. Slope of valley averages 75 feet to mile. Walls often steep. Valley quite narrow in places, in others a mile. Rain tonight.

Tuesday, June 4th. In camp. Rain all day. Sick.

Wednesday, June 5th. Broke camp at 8:00 A. M. Made 12 miles and camped where the [Escalante] creek "canons."[54] This creek, two branches on left, with quite good bottoms, one small one on right. In lower part, flows through a deep channel. Is now 15 feet wide, swift and deep, swollen by rains. The valley is wider from last camp. Just below the mouth of canon a stream comes in from west; two pictures taken. To the east the valley widens, has a gentle slope up for a mile and a half, then slopes toward the west to broken cliffs, say ten miles. The valley has a line of cliffs on the southwest [Kaiparowits Plateau], being say, 30 degrees east of south that continue to Colorado river. On the north a gradual slope up to a broken ridge. Poor grass and few cedars. Captain Dodds and myself rode ten miles E. S. E., but could not see the Dirty Devil Mountains. Saw Navajo Mountain at the end of line of cliffs. Found water in a gulch. Shall move camp here tomorrow.

Thursday, June 6th. Broke camp at 8:00, and moved to Rocky Gulch [Harris Wash]. Captain Dodds and myself climbed to southeast, to a point from which we could overlook the whole country. To the north are the Wasatch Mountains, snow on summits and in drifts on south slope. Seem rough and lava-like on summit. As they slope down, the country is eroded until the white sand rock comes to summit. Thirty-five miles north of canon to summit, to the east and 40 miles away, are the Dirty Devil Mountains [Henry Mountains]. Can only see three, or counting the little one, four. East of them can just see the top of mountains thought to be Sierra La Sal, and further east the Sierra Abajo. From the mouth of the canon Potato Valley Creek [Escalante River], flows east, say 10 miles in a straight line, then turns 40 east of south to the Colorado at a point thought to be a little above the mouth of the San Juan. It drains the east slope of Wasatch, and the country from the cliffs south of valley spoken of yesterday to within ten miles west of the Dirty Devil mountains. *Is not the Dirty Devil* [Fremont River]. A great part of

[54]The topography in the vicinity of the present village of Escalante is confusing. Escalante Valley down which Thompson was travelling continues southeast as Escalante Desert at the base of Kaiparowits Plateau. The river, however, heads into a sandstone ridge and continues to the Colorado in a canyon. The failure of the land party of 1871 was caused by mistaking this then unknown river for the Fremont.

its valley from mouth of canon is white sand rock, cut into innumerable gulches. Cedars are scattered sparsely over patches, very little grass. We can see two large creeks flowing in from the north and one small one from south. Should think the valley ended to east in a line of cliffs ten miles west of Dirty Devil mountains. There is a high divide between Henry from the Wasatch to the D. D. No chance whatever for this stream to flow north around the D. D. mountains into the D. D. river. Captain Dodds says that the D. D. mountains were to his left and back all the time when he went down last September. Showed me a point where he climbed out. It is southwest of southern D. D. mountain. He, Captain Dodd, says that there was only one place where horses could cross and that only by going down the creek half a mile. It is utterly impossible to think of crossing. The creek is swimming high. Cannot pack down it. The only way possible to get to the river is to go round under the Wasatch Cliffs and cross to the D. D. on the divide spoken of and this looks much cut, through the glass. We are stopped. The Dirty Devil has not yet been reached. The boys got three good negatives of Rock Gulch.

Friday, June 7th. Captain Dodds, George, Clem and myself, went to cliff southeast of Rock Gulch this A. M. Sent camp back to head of canon. Looked over the country as well as I could under the Wasatch cliffs. We must keep above the White Sand rock. It is doubtful whether we ought to go to the long ridge running out toward the D. D. or down this side. Have decided to try to get to the D. D. mountains by going up Pine Creek, then northeast along under the summit of the Wasatch Cliffs to the "Salient Angle," then across the divide to the D. D. mountains, then down the creek to the river, the creek that Captain Bishop and myself went up. Shall send George, Jones and Clem back to Kanab for rations, to bring them in to the lower end of Potato Valley. Shall take six men and try to get into our boat. Shall send Jack, Fred, Johnson and Fennemore down in the boat while Captain Dodds, Andy and myself bring the horses back to the lower end of Potato, and meet the other boys there with rations. I do not think the chance of getting in is even.

Saturday, June 8th. Sent the boys to Kanab—sent 7 horses with them. We left camp at 10:00 A. M. Got to camp 18 miles, at 5:30 P. M. Went up the creek valley for 10 miles, then the creek turns to the right and enters a close, rocky canon. The trail goes up a dry wash to left and keeps the left hand wash for 5 miles, then climbs the mountain and goes down to a fine little creek. Camp is about 1800 feet higher than last night. The valley ascends about 75 feet to the mile. The creek is beautiful soft water, is 10 feet wide and runs over a rock bed. A great many fine trees along its banks—birch and cottonwood. The dip is 25 degrees west. The creek flows on the strike. I think the sandstone through which Birch Creek [?] has cut is Triassic. Think the "fold" we saw above Mount Navajo is the same as these cliffs. Struck igneous rock—think basalt; 800 feet below the highest point climbed. The top of the Wasatch is igneous basalt or trachyte. Think at least the upper 2000 feet is. We are camped by a little brook that leaps from rock to rock down the mountain side, its bank grassy and lined with aspen and birch [Boulder Creek ?]. The water is pure, clear and cold. Groves of aspen are scattered all over the mountain-side, and evidently many brooks. Grass good.

Sunday, June 9th. Broke camp at 8:00. Made 15 miles and camped at 4:00 P. M. near a beautiful little lake of perhaps 200 acres. Crossed four brooks today. Trail very rough. Climbed up and down a deep, steep canon in the sandstone. Country as described yesterday. Climbed a point where the barometer registered 10,910 feet, the upper thousand igneous. One creek that we followed for half a mile must have tumbled down 500 feet to the mile. Call the lake by which we are camped Aspen Lake. There are 5 lakes in sight from a point above camp. The aspens grow very thick. Pine and fir trees, also. Found the bear-berry in blossom. Strawberries just in bloom.

Monday, June 10th. Broke camp at 8:00 A. M. Traveled 10 miles by 12 M. over an open country with groves of aspen and pine [Aquarius Plateau]. Crossed three streams. Saw a lake as large as Aspen. Grass good. The surface has many trachyte boulders, though I think the foundation is sandstone nowhere exposed. Fennemore sick with sort of dysentery attack; not fit to travel, so concluded to rest this afternoon. Sent Jack to photograph the lake. Johnson helped him. The landscape from the divide which we came over is beautiful. The mountain slopes a little west of south from the mountain up to the sand rock, a distance of 20 miles, and is 20 miles wide. Slope quite easy. Creeks every mile or two. Often groves of aspen and pine and clear meadows. Is a perfect paradise for the ranchers. Indians have been in, but not for years. Have camped here for the winter. Cold enough to freeze last night. Boys report four lakes. Jack got two views.

Tuesday, June 11th. Broke camp at 9:00 A. M. Traveled 15 miles, crossed 7 creeks, two of them quite large. For ten miles the slope of the mountain is covered with bunch grass in groves of aspen and pine. We have turned an angle in the mountain tonight and traveled the last mile northwest. Can look over the country between the D. D. mountains and our camp. It is cut by deep canons and looks impassable. The plain is covered with

pine and cedar.   The D. D. mountains are 15 miles away.   Shall
hunt for trail to them tomorrow.

Wednesday, June 12th.   Captain Dodds and myself climbed
a high point N. W. of camp, this morning.   The main mountain
range breaks back toward the north.   Around a high point there
seems a low pass to the Sevier [Fremont Valley above Torrey].
We went down about 1800 feet to the valley.   Fine grass and
good pine timber.   Crossed two creeks in ten miles.   Saw fresh
horse sign, and an old trail.   Followed marks of horses to an old
camp.   We were in the sand rock.   I sent Johnson and Fred to
the S. E. to look for trail.   They found one leading toward mountain, old but lately traveled.   Jack and Fennemore got three views.

Thursday, June 13th.   Broke camp at 8:00.   Took the trail.
After descending 1000 feet we reached the sandstone of [like that
in] Mound Canon [Glen Canyon].   It is gulched and gullied.
Drainage to the Dirty Devil, trail in some places good, others
indited.   Very crooked.   Came to one place where the valley
is at least 1800 feet below.   We go down over bare sandstone
rock almost as steep as a horse can stand on.   Come to a fine
valley with a beautiful stream of water [Branch of Pleasant
Creek]. Trend N. and S.   Many Indian signs.   Saw smoke in
distance.   Made 20 miles by trail—12 in direct line.   Camped
in grove of cottonwoods.

Friday, June 14th.   Broke camp at 9:30.   Traveled three
miles towards the smoke we saw last night when we saw two
squaws gathering seeds.   They saw us and commenced calling
to someone in distance.   We kept on trail until we came to some
wick-e-ups on a hill.   We could see some Indians running to the
cedars, and as we came nearer one old man came down the hill
to meet us.   He was very much frightened—trembled like an
aspen leaf.   We told him "Tich-a-boo," "friendly," when he
cheered up a little.   Went to the wick-e-ups, stayed and gave
him some tobacco—smoked.   Soon two squaws came in and then
two young bucks.   We talked about trail, and one of the bucks
told us there was a trail to the river over the D. D. mountains
[Henry Mountains].   Went to creek and camped.   Three more
men have come into camp.   Have talked with the "Captain." He
points out a trail running east.   Says it goes between two mountains. We shall take it tomorrow. He says it will take three days.

Saturday, June 15th.   Broke camp at 6:00.   Indians all left
before we did.   Traveled S. E. 12 miles when we passed through
a narrow canon into a larger one.   Have had very heavy rains
so trail is completely washed out for miles.   Many cattle signs in
large canon.   Could not find trail so went up canon exploring
side canon.   Find trail out.   Have not found one yet.   Dip N.
about 10 degrees.   Tenting.   Johnson found fossils.   Cretaceous.

Sunday, June 16th. Broke camp at 6:00. Went up canon to end. Explored side canons, no trail at 12:00. Captain Dodds and Fred, Jack, and myself climbed the east wall 1000 feet and taking different directions of hunters for trail where it crosses above. Jack and I found old horse sign but no trail. Found the divide between the D. D. and Colorado. The plateau seems to extend to mountains. Found a way to get down a point to the canon. Packed up and in an hour and a half were on up. Went to a water pocket that Fred and the Captain found, for camp. Shall try the "divide" tomorrow. Dip seems decreasing. We are in a spot of grayish white sand rock.

Monday, June 17th. Broke camp at 8:30. Traveled the "divide" until 11:00 o'clock when we came to a valley, descended cliffs 600 feet. Were in valley next to D. D. mountains [Head of Pine Alcove Creek?]. The plateau we have just traversed seems to be horizontal until we reach the valley, then the dip is west and increasing until the sandstone lies against the mountains at an angle of 15 degrees. It now seems as though the sandstone we have passed over is the synclinal axis as the grey standstone of Mound [Upper Glen] Canon. After descending the cliffs, the dip is west, increasing, the strata lying against the side of the mountains. We climbed 1700 feet above the valley to a spring pouring out of the mountainside, second mountain [Mount Pennel]. Some fine groves of aspen and spruce, but generally the mountainside is bare. At 800 feet above valley the sedimentary rocks end and trachyte commences. The plateau over which we have passed is much cut by canons and gulches and ends in a line of cliffs with a S.W. and N.E. trend at lower end of second mountain; a valley near the mountains that drains the mountains.

Tuesday, June 18th. In camp. Very cold. Ice froze last night ½ inch thick. Snow by showers. Captain, Jack and myself climbed to top of second mountain about 3000 feet above camp. Saw the mouth of D.D. creek. Snow on mountain. Clouds soon obstructed view, so we came back. Sent Fred and Johnson to climb first mountain [Mount Ellen; named for Mrs. Thompson]. They got part way up and gave out. Johnson found some fossils. A nautilus I think, and perhaps a belemnite. We found an argillaceous sandstone 1000 feet above camp. The mountains are very steep, 35 degrees from valley. Very cold. (Professor says Tuesday the 18th, that Fred and Johnson got part way up and gave out. The fact was that Johnson kept objecting all the time to going on, and finally I yielded to his repeated urging to go back. He was a "quitter" every time there was any hard thing to do.)

Wednesday, June 19th. Broke camp at 9:00. Traveled 8 miles around north and second mountain to a creek by noon

[Trachyte Creek].   Camped and Captain Dodds and myself climbed third mountain [Mount Hillers], saw a creek that I think is the one Captain Bishop and myself came up.   Country rough. Found an old trail leading down creek.

Thursday, June 20th.   Broke camp at 9:00.   Horses lost. Traveled until 4:00, ten miles.   Had to prospect trail a good deal. Climbed at our camp and found that the creek is not the one I want but one that flows into Colorado, ten miles below D. D. Ricogenogen, a point three miles east is one on left creek I came up. Shall go to it in morning.   Have come down 1400 feet today. Think we would have no difficulty in going down its bed to the Colorado.

Friday, June 21st.   Climbed a high point.   Found the gulch I wish to go down on other side.   Sent Captain Dodds back for train while I prospect a trail.   Train up at 2:00 P. M.   Went down bare sand rock winding for a mile, then down steep bank to bed of creek [Crescent Wash].   Camped.   The country is higher from creek to D. D. river.   In fact the creek of last night's camp seems the lowest point.   I think the Sierra Abajo was the central point of upheaval with perhaps the LaSal, and the river has cut into their slopes.   The Sierra Abajo seems nearer the river than the LaSal.   The whole country from the low divide between San Rafael and Dirty Devil and the Salient point of Wasatch Cliffs [Aquarius Plateau] and first mountain of D. D. range is drained by the Dirty Devil.   The D. D. mountains are drained by creeks into the Colorado.   The plateau is 1600 feet above the Colorado, between the Dirty Devil River and the mountains and Colorado.   Is bare rock and sand.   Very few sage bushes.

Saturday, June 22d.   Broke camp at 7:00.   The "creek" is really a gulch, running 15 miles from river, is fed by springs, or rather made.   Got to Colorado at 11:30.   River high, at least 15 feet above what it was last September.   Went up to boat.   Found her all right.   Caulked her a little, launched and came to camp.

Sunday, June 23rd.   Fred sketched our trail since leaving Kanab.   Got it done at 5:00 P. M., when we started on our way back.   Went up the gulch 7 miles to a camp.   The boys worked on boat [the Canonita, left in 1871].   She is all right.   Will be as good as new.   River falling at the rate of a foot a day.

Monday, June 24th.[55]   Broke camp at 8:00.   Made Trachyte Creek at 2:00 and Aspen Grove at 7:00.   Have come at least 30 miles and up 4400 feet.   Shower this P. M.   I think that more

[55]As previously arranged, the party was divided at the mouth of the Fremont. Thompson, accompanied by Hatten and Dodds, returned to the foot of Potato Valley (Escalante) where they expected to meet Jones and George Adair with supplies from Kanab. Hillers, Dellenbaugh, Fennemore and Johnson put the Canonita in order and guided her down river to the mouth of the Paria (June 26-July 13) where they were hospitably received by John D. Lee. On July 15 Hatten and W. C. Powell arrived by wagon with stores of provisions.

of the strata are denuded from the valley than on the mountain-side, *perhaps not*. Made a section as far as tilted strata.

Tuesday, June 25th. Broke camp at 8:00. Went three miles to spring in divide between first and second mountain. At 11:30 started to climb first mountain [Mount Ellen]. A shower came up and we stopped until 2:00 P. M. Climbed to highest point by 4:00 P. M. From the mouth of D.D. a line of cliffs *facing east* breaks around in east of Navajo mountain. It continues to N.E. but much broken. The D.D. seems to flow southeast until near the mouth, when it winds south. The Wasatch Mountains seem at least 60 miles north. There is a nearer line of cliffs, say 40 miles. The D.D. seems to have a large valley; Pleasant Creek joins it N.E. of number 1. The highest point of Cataract Canon plateau is south of Abajo. Country N.E. is level and 4000 feet lower, rising to Wasatch cliffs. Country to the N.W. much gullied but in general, the Dirty Devil mountains stand in a valley of grass. The valley on the west is more cut by canons than east. Beyond the D.D. the country rises to the height of Cataract Plateau. Sierra La Sal—57, Sierra Abajo—89, Low Divide—270, Mouth D.D.—98, ˜Navajo—170, Aneroid F of mountain—11,950 feet, Wet bulb (thermometer)—48, Dry bulb (thermometer)—52 feet, Aneroid Camp—8600 feet. Do not think the needle of barometer indicated correct height. Seemed to stop at 11,950 feet.

Wednesday, June 26th. Broke camp at 8:30. Made 25 miles to pool in sandrock at fold. [North end of Waterpocket Fold]. Where we leave the bed of dry creek, four miles from mountain the strata are horizontal from that point the dip is N.W. or 25 degrees N. of west. Dip two degrees. At our camp is a fold or tilt crossing the general dip at right angles, trend 20 degrees E. of it, 20 W. of S. Think the white sand rock through which we have passed is Jurassic. The fold seems to have brought up Triassic upper beds. In the valley where we are camped the trail lies in piles [of boulders?] 18 inches deep covered by dirt washed down by shower of yesterday.

Thursday, June 27th. Broke camp at 8:00. Traveled until 7:00. Camped on Wasatch Mountain [Aquarius Plateau] 10,400 feet by aneroid. The fold spoken of yesterday dips 15 degrees and the dip is 30 degrees south of east. After passing through the gap and traveling N.W. three miles, found a bed of fossils, Cretaceous, I think. If I am correct, the fold commences in the Tertiary and has involved or rather brought to the surface the Triassic and perhaps the upper whitish buff Carboniferous. The strata through which we passed yesterday afternoon must rest un-conformably on the Tertiary. The same formations are involved in the upheaval around the mountains, as at the fold. Think the fold is narrower and more profound near the river, that is, fan-shaped north of river. I believe the Navajo Mountain is of same age and same formation.

Friday, June 28th. Broke camp at 7:30. Made creek at Steep Hill at 5:00 P. M. Was cold last night, barometer registered 10,500 feet, and top of mountain at least 1,500 feet higher. We came lower down than we went out and found much better traveling. The Triassic in valley below seems nearly horizontal. The lowest exposed stratum seems a light buff sandstone under the red. Think our camp is in Tertiary.

Saturday, June 29th. Broke camp at 7:00. Made 35 miles and camped in foot of Potato Valley [Escalante] at 8:00 P. M. Found that the men left there—had left and gone up to the mountains. We climbed up cliff at our camp. Had to build trail. The strata seem horizontal until we strike the "tilt" near North Creek, [fork] of Birch. Sunday, June 30th. In camp. Men got in. Thought we were in trouble and had started to help us.

Monday, July 1, 1872. Sent Captain Dodds, George [Adair] and Andy to Kanab with orders to take four horses and a wagon and go with a bill of rations, etc., to the Paria, and when there to fix boats until boys came. Told them to go to Windsor and get a beef, jerk it and take part. Jones, Clem and self came ten miles up valley and camped. S.N. observation for Latitude and time at point Potato Valley. Sent letter to Nellie and Major.

Tuesday, July 2d. Looked for fossils at camp. Found only fragments. Made 14 miles and camped at spring. The strata keep their general gentle up until within four miles of camp, then increase to 12 degrees. Dip westerly. Must see more before giving an opinion, but it now seems as though the fold at Colorado river spread fan shaped to N.W. with greater dip on outer limbs.

Wednesday, July 3rd. Climbed Table Mountain, Pt. V. 2,650 feet above camp, slope 30 degrees. East are the D.D. [Henry] mountains between the broken country. Potato Valley bears N.E. Walls on either side quite step. S.E. is Navajo Mountain. Country between broken. Cliff extends N. from N. mountain. Light line of cliffs also from N. mountain to Pt. P. and Table mountain. Country to south much broken cliffs and canons. Only two well defined lines of cliffs after disappearance of Triassic near Mollie's Nipple. The pink Tertiary cliffs back of Clarkston [Skumpah] seem to have a ridge breaking back to head of Paria Valley. The upper part of Paria Valley is open and covered with timber and grass. Think trail passes around Pt. 4 to left, then bears N. down an apparent wash to Sevier. Between first and second lines of cliffs, country broken in all ways. Table Mountain is limestone in upper part. Dip west. Thickness. The Paria seems to have eroded the mountain between Table and Pink Tertiary to form its valley. Table and Tertiary Pink are *spurs*.

Can see the outlines of Kaibab—No. 4 and 5 seem on a basaltic ridge.

Thursday, July 4th. Climbed to Point P. The magnetic bearing of Navajo mountain is the same as trend of cliffs of Colorado above "El Vado". The line of cliffs from Navajo Mountain seem to form a plateau [Kaiparowits Plateau] bordered on east by valley running from middle of Potato Valley, and on west by line from Navajo Mountain to Point P. for ten miles. S.E. of Point P. the country is very much broken. The general course of Paria seems to be 25 degrees west of south until 20 miles from mouth, then south. The upper end of 20 miles bears 180 from Point P. *true*. From Point N. the Pink Cliffs seem to circle to Point Q., getting lower where Paria breaks through. The summit of Point P. is a chalky limestone like No. 2 of Point Q. From Point O. to the northward the cliffs swing on the arc of a circle to the Salient we have taken. First is a Salient point of the Table Mount Cliff one mile from Point O, then one mile further and bearing as taken—44 degrees, then there are two Salients between that point and Salient taken first at Pine Creek, second at Boulder. The line of Pink Cliffs spoken of are high on left of where Paria breaks through.

Friday, July 5th. Broke camp at 8:00. Made 25 miles and camped on Buffalo Berry Creek [?]. Dip of Strata N.W. about 3 degrees. I think We have been in Tertiary all day. Passed a bed of gypsum 6 miles N.E. of camp, the level of country 600 feet above valley of Paria. Saturday, July 6th. Broke camp at 7:00. Made Clarkston and camp 25 miles at 5:00 P. M.

Sunday, July 7th. Left Clem and Jones at Clarkston to take views while I went to Kanab. Got in at 3:00 P. M. No word from the Major.[56] A man is here who represents himself as a Mr. Hansen traveling as near the 35th parallel as he can and getting information along proposed railroad route for a Cincinnati firm. He told wife however, that his name was "Beadle" author of the "Expose" of Mormonism. Says he took the Emma Dean from "Cache" and crossed the river but left her securely fastened on this side. I think he is a "humbug".

Monday, July 8th. At Kanab. Got beef, 808 lbs. of Windsor and 1200 lbs. flour, 6 lbs. cream tartar, and 10 lbs. soap from Jacob. Went to Point "B". Boys not there. Settled with "Alfred". Paid him check and money. Captain Dodds went to Short Creek for horse. Gave him $5.00 cash and a check.

Tuesday, July 9th. Jones and Clem got in. No word from

[56]Plans for field work in 1872 included the traverse of the Colorado below Lees Ferry in continuation of the traverse of 1871. The down river trip was to start as soon as practicable after the Canonita had been brought to Lees Ferry and Thompson had returned from his overland expedition to Fremont River. The Canonita reached its destination July 13 and Thompson arrived at Kanab July 7. Powell, who was to lead the party, did not arrive until August 2. In the meantime the party at Lees Ferry repaired the boats, and Thompson continued his map program in the region about base camp.

Major. Wednesday, July 10th. Rain all day. Got the boys ready to start for Paria, but could not start Captain Dodds. Thursday, July 11th. Went to Point B. with Jones and George. Clem and Andy started for Paria with rations. Have 1500 lbs. on wagon—four animals. Friday, July 12th. Climbed Point B. Can do nothing. Came back to Kanab. Captain Dodds back. Did not get Prince. Sent Jones to Johnson for horses. Saturday, July 13th. At Kanab. Jones got back with horses. Sunday, July 14th. At Kanab. Talking with Indians, etc.

Monday, July 15th. Left Kanab at 10:00. Make "Oak Spring" Kaibab Plateau at 7:00 P. M. George, Jones, and myself with Frank and Charley, Indians. Three other Indians, two squaws and one papoose, went along.

Tuesday, July 16th. Left "Oak Spring" at 8:00 A. M. Made 20 miles and camp at "Pine Spring" at 3:00 P. M. Think our camp is 5 degrees east of south from "Stewart's Ranch". Country not very rough. Heavy pine timber all the way. We go up the canon from Stewart's for 8 miles, then climb a hill between the forks of canon. Followed on trail until within four miles of spring. Heard a cry something like an Indian halloo while riding along. After we got in camp Frank asked George what he called that which lived after the body did. George replied "a spirit." "Well," said Frank, "that was what hallooed in the forest today. It was the spirit of a dead Indian. I have often heard it. Sometimes it is near, sometimes far away. When I was here with Beaman I heard it call near me. I answered, telling it to come to me. It did not come nor reply, and I felt very much ashamed to think I had called." Rain tonight.

Wednesday, July 17th. Left Pine Spring at 8:00. Traveled in west-southwest direction for five or six miles, when we came to the canon of the Colorado. At a point exactly west [east?] of Mount Trumbull we were at the bend of the river. On our right the river bore 247 degrees true for 45 miles or to the "Lava Falls". On the left 160 true for 10 miles. These bearings are of the "Upper Terrace". Valley of Upper Terrace 8 miles average width. The river swings from side to side of this valley. Mouth of Kanab Wash bears west, distant to river, 14 miles or 9 in straight line. The Pa Ute trail to river goes down the first or "Limestone Cliffs" to the right of where we stood and down the cliff to water at a point a little west of south of us. To our left and near where we first saw the canon is another old trail. Along the left wall of the valley before us are springs. We can take rations in without trouble at this point. Do not think we could get in for a good many miles up the river. Think we are 18 miles by trail, 15 in straight line from Stewart's. Direction 195 degrees. (true)? Camped at old ranch.

Thursday, July 18th. Broke camp at 7:00 A. M. Made Kanab, 35 miles at 6:00 P. M. No word from the Major. Captain Dodds started for Salt Lake Wednesday, 17th inst. Friday, July 19th. At Kanab. Saturday, July 20th. At Kanab. Johnson came to see me. The Canonita got to mouth of Paria alright Thursday, the 11th. Johnson came home, got there the 17th. I settled with him and paid him check of $70.00 accounts, etc. Think he will quit.

Sunday, July 21st. Went to Cave Canon today. Rained. Talked with Jacob. I am certain from Jacob's talk and Ives map, that the Cataract Creek of Ives and Coenina Canon of Frank are the same, and Ives has made a big mistake in placing the little Colorado as far west as he has. It is too far by 60 miles. Monday, July 22d. At Kanab. Worked on "data" a little. Tuesday, July 23rd. At Kanab. Got mail but no word from the Major.

Wednesday, July 24th. A great day with the Mormons. The anniversary of the advent of the "Pioneer Corps" into Salt Lake Valley 25 years ago (1847, July 24th). Celebrated all through Utah. Went to the speaking in the "Bowery". The speeches were a narration of the persecutions, trials, and sufferings of the Mormons. Thos. Kane's account of his visit to Nauvoo was read. Took dinner with Bishop Stewart. He told us about his dream at Murphysborough, Tenn. concerning plural marriage. Dance in evening.

Thursday, July 25th. Worked on triangulations. Friday, July 26th. Worked on plotting points. Saturday, July 27. Worked on plotting. Sunday, July 28. Worked on plotting. Monday, July 29th. Worked on plotting. Tuesday, July 30th. Worked on plotting. Got mail but no word from the Major. Saw in Deseret News that he arrived in Salt Lake the 17th. Sent Jones to Johnson for the horses that are there. He could not find Grey Billy. Wednesday, July 31st. Sent Jones and George to build a monument at Point 5. Call it "A" in place of one at Pipe.

Thursday, August 1, 1872. Jones went last night from Point 5 to Pipe Springs. George went to Point "C" and put up a flag, then to Johnson. Saw Professor DeMotte and Captain Bishop at Johnson with team of four mules for us. [They had] left Salt Lake City the 22nd ult. The Major was to leave next day. It seems that the Major's stop and work in Salt Lake was to get the telegraph in order so that we might ascertain the longitude of Kanab, and Professor DeMotte is to assist. If we can get the use of the line and Prof. DeMotte can leave us out of the transit, the plan will work.

Friday, August 2d. Prof. DeMotte[57] and Captain Bishop got

[57]Harvey C. DeMotte, Professor of Mathematics, Wesleyan University, Bloomington, Illinois, was a personal friend of Powell. His services as assistant to Thompson are recognized in the name DeMotte Park on Kaibab Plateau.

in . About $850.00 in team, $500.00 mules that are well worth over $600.00. Jones got in at 2:00 P. M. and about 4:00 P. M. the Major came. He left Salt Lake the . . . Magnetic Bearings— Cross Mt.—183°, [degrees] Bill Williams—151°, Little Butte (Red)—145°, San Francisco—137½°. Bearings *are not true;* N.E. variations not allowed for. Barometer stands at 8,500 on cliff—200 feet below the general level of Plateau. Observations taken on farthest point reached, 5 degrees of south from Stewart's. Got to camp at 3:00 P. M. Major and myself went ten miles south to the canon and back by dark. Did not see the view. The canon is deep. Side canon deep—red—the limestone being stained. We can see unconformable rocks at the base. See very near the whole depth of Carboniferous.

Saturday, August 10th. Went to "Kanav Spring" S.E. 10 miles from Rock Spring at 3:00 P. M., went to the river 7 miles south. Struck the river first 3 miles from camp in a direction 30 degrees south of west. Same side canon as we saw yesterday, but then we were on the west side, today on east, at last point. Canon does not seem as deep as where we struck it yesterday. Saw uncomformable rocks. The side canons reach back from 4 to 8 miles from the river. The upper canon is from 6 to 10 miles wide at the top.

Sunday, August 11th. This A. M. started on a S.E. course, for the river. Struck the canon in 5 miles; that is the head of a side canon; then went out 3 miles to a point about three miles from the river. At the next point to the east the river bends to north. We are at the angle of the bend. Back to camp and started for the Paria. Traveled 10 miles about N. Course up a canon across a ridge into a valley *in* the top of the mountain valley about one mile wide, ten miles long. Axis six degrees east of south. Depression 200 feet. Called it DeMotte's Park. Camp at a lake.

Monday, August 12th. Left camp at 7:30. Traveled E.N.E. Course 15 miles, when we came to the east slope of the plateau. The east side descends in two folds or rather one side of folds, each of 1000 feet. Slope 3½ miles divides thus—first slope ½ mile—an almost level of 2¼ miles, then second slope 3¼ miles. East slope of mountain cut by canons. Dip of first *drop* 25 degrees, second 15 degrees. Trend of east side, north. Went out in valley 8 miles direct N.E. to camp. Dry.

Tuesday, August 13th. Traveled N.E. four miles until we struck the old Paria trail near the point of cliffs. Valley 7 miles from crest to crest. There is another fold near cliff on east side of valley. Made camp at mouth of Paria—22 miles—at 4:00 P. M.

INTO GRAND CANYON

Wednesday, August 14th, 1872. Loaded boats and ran down a long rapid 1⅛ miles to camp. Thursday, August 15th. The wagons went home. Sent $75.00 to George; [with] rations [he was to] meet us by September 4th at the mouth of Kanab canyon. Friday, August 16th. In camp 87. Getting ready to embark. Saturday, August 17th. Camp No. 88. Left camp at 9:00 A. M.[58] Ran 4¾ miles to noon when we took pictures. Ran 5 miles P. M. making one portage of 300 yards. River narrow 100 feet; walls at camp 600 feet, base red thinly bedded sandstone. Not massive limestone. Ran two rapids and a . . . at the head of a fall of 25 feet in 200 yards. Gulches at rapids. The canon is not over . . . walls vertical at least part of the way down, in terraces.

Sunday, August 18th. Camp No. 89. Ran 11⅜ miles, making one portage in the morning and letting down two rapids and running 4 large. River narrow in many places not over 75 feet and hardly ever more than 200. Whirlpools all the way, often strong enough to turn the boat. Ran one very bad rapid where there was no foothold to make a portage. Walls of canon at camp 89-1800 feet, always in two, often in three or four terraces. First terrace 400 feet, canon not over . . . top. Camped on right bank behind some rocks, just below a huge rapid that made a most infernal roaring all night. Rain at intervals during the day and at night.

Monday, August 19th. Camp No. 90. Ran 4¼ miles, making one portage, letting down past 3, and running two rapids, all big. Camp on soft bank. Took five pictures. Canon 2000 feet. Four terraces below camp 90, first terrace 685 feet. River average width, 125 feet. Camp just below a big rapid and in sight of another.

Tuesday, August 20th. Camp No. 91. Ran 9⅞ miles, making one portage and running rapids. Generally four terraces. Canon 1¼ miles average width at top. River 125 feet. Ran most of the day, with marble for walls near water's edge. It is a grayish drab very hard veiny stone. A good deal of chert, often jaspery. Camped on right bank just below the mouth of a dry gulch and just above two springs pouring out of the face of the cliff 50 feet above the river. Ivy, Red bud, grasses, and a few other plants grow on the wall around the springs. There is the appearance of other springs having burst through the cliff in their vicinity. The Major thinks that the place is called "Vasey's Paradise"[59]

[59]Named by Powell in 1869. George W. Vasey (1822-1893) was botanist of the U. S. Department of Agriculture (1872-1893).
[58]Dellenbaugh records that the reorganized river party comprised Major Powell, Jones, Hillers, Dellenbaugh in the Emma Dean; Thompson, Hatten, and W. C. Powell in the Canonita. The Nellie Powell, the boat least fit for the trip, was left behind.

but if it is, it is a Hell of a Paradise.   Intend making Colorado Chequite [Little Colorado] in two days.

Wednesday, August 21st.   Camp No. 92.   Ran 10⅜ miles, passing some rapids—one very bad in the P. M. run.   Walls of canon getting higher, 2700 feet at camp 92.   Generally the walls have had four terraces—the lower or first increasing in height until it is 800 feet.   Walls have been for a long distance vertical from water's edge.   Stopped in an alcove of semi-circular form and took a swim.   Alcove about 600 feet deep and 500 feet high on river bank, running back to the sand.   Our camp is near the end of an eastern bend.   At the point of the bend the walls are broken back.   The tongue of rock in the bend is 600 feet at point, ¼ mile back, and 2500 back two miles.   Saw mesquite bushes just above camp for the first time on river.

Thursday, August 22d.   Camp No. 93.   Ran 17⅞ miles, letting down past one rapid and running 17.   The walls are broken more than heretofore.   That is more of a valley near the river, but little vertical wall from the water's edge.   Fewer terraces. In lower part of day's run occasionally two 1000 feet.   We are now through marble canon.   Have made it 60⅞ miles long.   Has at the present stage of water 69 rapids.   We ran 60, many very bad .   Made four portages and let our boats over five by ropes. Have had more walls vertical from the water's edge on both sides than in any other canon.   Current very swift.   Whirlpools and eddies very strong.   It is so far the typical canon.   Answers the ideal better than any other.

Friday, August 23rd.   Camp No. 93.   In camp taking observations for latitude.   Saturday, August 24th.   Camp No. 94. Ran 4⅞ miles, passing five rapids.   First day in Grand Canon. Camp at the mouth of Quagunt [Kwagunt] Creek, a little stream coming in from the west.   The cliffs offside camp are 3500 feet. Up the valley the end of the Kaibab is 7 miles distant, 8000 feet. A few miles south both walls of canon are 7000 feet above river, I think.   We are at the base of Carboniferous-devonian.   Shales rise unconformable to the Carboniferous.   River really is ¾ miles wide, 3 long.   Climbed 2500 feet this P. M.

Sunday, August 25th.   Camp No. 94.   In camp.   Fred and I climbed and made map of Quagunt Valley.   Monday, August 26th.   Camp No. 94.   Climbed with the Major, Fred and Jones up 2600 feet.   Could see the "Fold" on the Buckskin [East Kaibab Monocline].   The cliffs on East side of river are 3500 feet, but are near the river.   The Kaibab is 6 miles back, 5500 feet.   The valley "Quagunt" is much broken.   Up the river from the point to which we climbed is another valley that evidently runs back to the Kaibab.

Tuesday, August 27th.   Camp No. 98.   Ran 7½ miles passing

ten rapids, two bad. Camped on left bank. Valley averages two miles to foot of an elevation of 2000 feet. Canon at top of wall 6 to 8 miles. Have named it Red Shales.

Wednesday, August 28th. Camp No. 96. Ran 6 miles, 6 rapids, getting past one and making a footage over part of . . . . Are camped on south side in middle of last rapid. It is the largest and has the most fall of any so far on river, ½ mile long, fall 40 feet. We have made portage of half it and shall run the other half. The granite rises at the foot of rapid. The river seems to bear more to the west; from this point the walls are becoming more vertical, the river narrower and altogether the whole aspect of the canon is wilder, more savage and grander. The upper canon is 8 miles wide, rises on the north to the Kaibab, on the south thus far 1000 feet lower, but we can see that a few miles to the west is as high as the Kaibab. The heads of the high plateaus are covered with timber. We are camped at the mouth of a gulch bearing 190 degrees that usually runs a little stream. Call it Dyke Creek. It runs back with but little elevation for five miles.

Thursday, August 29th. Camp No. 97. Ran 7¼ miles. Ran the rest of the rapids and through a narrow canon for three miles, when we came to a rapid of 130 foot fall in ¾ of a mile, with no chance to make a portage. Landed at the head of north side. Looked it over. Took three pictures of the thing, then ate dinner, pulled up the river a little, turned the bow down and went into it. The waves tossed us like feathers, but our boats rode them finely, and we went through all right, shipping but little water—not as much as in some other places no half as bad. A mile below we came on a curious rapid. It was in fact a whirl, and turned our boat completely around. At 4:00 o'clock we came to the worst rapid by far that I have seen on the Colorado—but little chance to get along the north side, none on the south. Worked above the wall and managed to get a third of the way down before night. Climbed on the rock, each one rolling up in a blanket and curling up on the rocks as best we could. River has been very narrow, walls of granite varying from 500 to 1000 feet high, often standing in pinnacles. Granite seems a kind of gneiss with dykes of quartz and veins or dykes of other special kinds of granite intersecting; often red feldspathis.

Friday, August 30th. Camp No. 98. Made not quite ¼ of a mile by noon, when we got to a place where we could set out, but by this time had so jammed our boats that we were obliged to haul them out and repair. While doing this, the river commenced rising, and before we got through, rose 3 feet. As it was nearly dark, concluded to haul our boats out of water entirely and camp. By hard lifting we have got them some 3 feet above water and propose to curl up among the rocks again. Have had rain every day for the last five. The color of the water coming down indicates that the rise is caused by these rains, probably a "cloud burst" and if so, it will soon fall. It must rise fearfully fast in these narrow canons. We have found driftwood at least 100 feet above the present level of the water.

Saturday, August 31st. Camp No. 99. Ran 8⅜ miles. Passed eight rapids. The river this morning was about the same height as last night. Concluded to set out after breakfast. Set our boats down in the water and held them from the rocks all we could while putting the loads in. The Dean got so pounded that she commenced leaking badly. Hurried all we could and tumbled in her cargo, fastened down her hatches, and with her cabin half full of water pushed her bow out into the current and away she went. About 50 feet below our starting point is a projecting buttress of granite against which the current dashes with great force. It is necessary to pull on the left to avoid it. The Dean made the offing finely and away she went. Now our boat must be drawn up to the farthest point and pushed out by her own crew alone. At this junction one of Clem's oars could not be found so I cut down one of the spare ones, made all as tight as I could, pulled the boat up stream as far as we could, and while Andy and I held her, Clem bailed her out and got his place in the bow. I now went to the stern. As quick as I got in, the current proved too strong for Andy to hold against, and the boat dragged him off his feet. Clem pulled as hard as he could, but down she drifted, stern first, toward the rock. When half way down, I decided to let her stern strike the rock and then try to throw her bow out into the stream. Just then Andy got his oars. The eddy seemed to carry us up 25 feet. We swung her bow to right, the current caught her, two vigorous strokes of the oars, the point was cleared and away we went over the long waves like a deer. At the foot of the rapid, found the Dean landing and the crew engaged in unloading so as to repair the leak. Pulled in and helped them. Had dinner, got through repairs, loaded up and started out at 4:00 P. M. Rapid succeeded rapid in quick succession, and we could see they were clear of rocks, so away we went riding them like ducks. Stopped once to examine one, but went through it. Passed two portages of former trip without thinking them bad. At 5:00 P. M. came to Bright Angel Creek,[60] 7⅞ miles from noon camp. The walls of granite have been getting lower and here we ran them under. River has been 150 feet wide, walls vertical for ⅔ way and standing in pinnacles and buttresses. Camp 99 is on a sand bank at the mouth of a nice little creek bearing 16. Canon seems 8 miles wide at upper terrace. Creek occupies a deep gulch in the Kaibab, probably drains DeMotte's Park.

[60]The clear waters of Bright Angel Creek were contrasted by Powell in 1869 with the mud laden Dirty Devil (Fremont River).

Sunday, September 1, 1872. Camp No. 100. Ran 7⅛ miles, passing 10 rapids—running 9 and making a short portage at the other. For the first three miles from camp 99 the river was a continuous rapid. Could not land. Ran through waves that tossed us, filled us half full, and before we could get the water out, repeated the process. Three and a half miles passed in 15 minutes, when we came to a heavy rapid. Ran it, but the waves were fearfully bad; came from all sides at once. At the lower part it was a feast of whirls; around we spun in waves large enough to swamp us. A rod or two away was the Dean in like condition. Down toward more whirls we drifted, stern first, into the whirls, and as her bow swung, I gave the boys the word and out we came alright and away the current caught us, leaving the Dean still waltzing. As soon as possible I landed, climbed back on the walls toward the rapid, but met the Dean coming down. They lost two oars in the whirls and stopped to pick them up again. The poor Dean had a rough time of it this A. M. Jones lost his balance and fell, or rather his oar knocked him overboard in a rapid. He caught the boat but nearly capsized her in the waves, getting in. Had dinner and ran ran 1½ miles down, when we came to a portage. Made repairs on the Canonita, took pictures and camped. Granite getting lower, and sediment, tiny rocks coming down to meet us. River 150 feet, current averages 6 miles. The first or granite terrace stands in craft pinnacles and buttresses, the second in bold heads. At the "Gulches on Left" where we are camped, the lower terrace is much broken.

Monday, September 2d. Camp No. 101. Ran 15⅛ miles, making two portages and running about 20 rapids. Camp on left bank. River has been about 150 feet, current very strong. Many of the rapids bad. We ran one that set against the cliff so that we ran within an oar's length, but came out alright. We seem to have less height of ground than two or three days ago. Occassionally we see the high headlands of the "table on either side." Upper terrace seems about eight miles wide.

Tuesday, September 3rd. Camp No. 102. S.B. Ran 8⅛ miles, eight or ten rapids. It has been a day of adventure. While running a rapid ¾ of a mile below camp 101, the Dean filled and capsized. The crew stuck to the boat, righted her and pulled in to shore. They bailed her out, and found they had lost two kettles and an oar, but otherwise no damage done. In the same rapid we lost three oars and broke oar lock, but found two of the oars again. Stopped 1⅜ miles below camp 101 to examine rocks. Started again about 3:00 o'clock. Ran 6½ miles when we came to a rapid that looked bad. While trying to land in very rapid water Fred was thrown from the boat by a lurch. The Major and Jones jumped to help him and hold the boat, but could do neither and away into the rapids went the Dean with Jack aboard and Fred dragging by the bow—

line. Fred soon got to the boat, climbed in, and Jack and he landed
her about half way down the rapid. We had landed above and
now let down to them and went into camp. The river has been
very swift and full of white pools today, worse than ever before.
At times it is impossible to land. The water seems to be coming
up still. Must be eight to ten feet higher than when the '69 trip
was made, and our danger increased. We are camped near the
southern end [Ives Point] of the long ridge [Powell Plateau]
that was east of us when we first saw the river on the Kaibab
trip, think not more than 5 miles from the "notch". [Saddle to
Powell's Plateau.]

Wednesday, September 4th. Camp No. 103. Made 13¾
miles, passing some dozen rapids. River for first 5 miles very
swift, narrow and full of the worst whirl-pools we have seen.
Water rose 3 feet on the rapid last night. The Major and myself
walked three miles down the cliff before starting, to see what kind
of river we were coming to. Ran the Granite under 4⅝ miles
from camp 102. The upper terrace comes close to the other at the
foot of Station 2 of P. M. run, then as the river sweeps north,
keeps close. While on the tongue the canon is same depth and
not more than 4 miles at top. Walls on left slope this P. M. run
back from a mile to a mile and a half before reaching full height,
4000 feet.

Thursday, September 5th. Camp No. 104. Ran 9 miles in
a N.N.E. direction. Eight or ten rapids, one let down and one
portage. Eight miles of the river in Granite again. River in one
place 50 feet wide. Current very swift and full of bad whirlpools.
Wall of first terrace not over 600 feet. Generally the upper terrace
has been nearer on left than right. Whole height of walls about
2000 feet.

Friday, September 6th. Camp No. 105. Ran 4¼ miles,
making portage and running four rapids. Stopped at a creek
thought to be the outlet of "Surprise" valley and got six pictures.
Just above our camp on the right is a fine creek 20 feet wide, and 2
feet deep—clear and cold. Call it "Ta Pits Creek" [Tapeats,
name of a friendly Piute]. The immediate walls of canon today
have been for 200 feet a trap rock, then sandstones. Long walls
and broken, and slope quick at an angle of 75 degrees. River is
80 yards wide and with fewer bad whirlpools. The water has
fallen 3 feet in the last three days.

Saturday, September 7th. Camp No. 106. Ran 12¼ miles,
passing 12 rapids. Ran the granite up and down. Extent of
granite two miles. Character of rise changes as soon as granite
is struck, becomes narrow, short bends full of whirlpools and
eddies. Passed a clear, cold stream, pouring off a cliff 100 feet into
the river. Got to Kanab Wash at 5:00 P. M. Found George, Mr.
Adams, and Joe Hamblin with rations. The Major talked with me

tonight about stopping trip at Mount Trumbull. Think he is in favor of so doing. It is nonsense to think of trying the "lower land" with this water. We have run 164¼ miles since leaving the mouth of Paria, alright. Can map 89 miles further by running to Mount Trumbull and using the Major's notes, and perhaps more. This being the case, there is no necessity for going entirely through, and I am in favor of doing the work around Mount Trumbull and letting the rest slide.

Sunday, September 8th. In camp at foot of Kanab Wash. Talked about leaving the river with the Major in the morning. I told him that I thought we had better run one boat to Mount Trumbull, but finally, about night, we decided to quit where we are.[61] I have told the Major that I can map the river from this point to a point 30 miles *by river* below the bend to the south of the river, near Mount Clinton. From this point hope to be able to reach mouth of Diamond Creek. I would much rather explore the country on south side by land than by water. Found both barometers broken today. We have decided to leave Clem and Jack here to photograph while the rest of us go to Kanab and send back for them.[62]

Monday, September 9th. The Major told the boys of our decision this morning. All very pleased. The fact is each one is impressed with the impossibility of continuing down the river. After breakfast we packed up part of the "plunder", and leaving Clem and Jack, went to the "Fern Spring" [in Kanab Canyon]—seven miles to camp. Canon very narrow, average width six rods. Trail poor. Tuesday, September 10th. Broke camp at 8:00. Made "Cedar Tree" at 4:00, when we camped, 12 miles. Canon walls getting lower. Fred and I climbed out. Many caches. Found old human bones at tree.

Wednesday, September 11th. Fred and I left "Cedar Tree" at 8:00. Made old camp at 12:00 and at dark, camped for supper, nine miles below Kanab. After rest of one hour, saddled and came to Kanab at 10:30—40 miles. The Kanab Canon commenced about 14 miles below Kanab. A few buttes mark its commencement. It has numerous branches in upper part. Below Pipe Spring wash are two large washes. The first comes in four miles below the "Cedar Tree", and the second [Hack Canyon] between it and the mouth. Below the Shinimos Canon [Shinumo; Snake Gulch] are three, one 1 mile below, one 6 miles, and one 8. The country is cut in a vast system of net work by these canons.

----

[61]The unusually high water stages of the river which made boating more dangerous than on the 1869 trip and a reported plot of the Shivwits to ambush the party were factors in making the decision to discontinue the river traverse at the mouth of the Kanab. As no scientific observations of value could have been made, the risk seemed not worth taking. Dellenbaugh remarks, "We were in the field to accomplish certain work and not to perform a spectacular feat."

[62]In accordance with arrangements, George Adair, Nathan Adams, and Joe Hamblin with provisions had arrived at the mouth of the Kanab September 4. "They had grown very anxious for we were several days overdue."

Thursday, September 12th. The trains got in about noon. Telegraphed to Mr. Austin about longitude.[63] Friday, September 13th. The Major and Jones got in at noon. Got answer from Mr. Austin. He will assist any night about 10:00 P. M. Telegraphed to Bishop Musser in regard to moving Table and Key to Tent. [A. Milton Musser, Supt. Deseret Telegraph Co.] Saturday, September 14th. At Kanab. Got no word from Bishop Musser. Started Adams and Joseph Hamblin with ten horses back for rest of things and Jack and Clem. Sunday, September 15th. At Kanab. Got word from Supt. D. T. C. that I could move table, etc.

Monday, September 16th. Had stones, etc. hauled to the place where I wish to put up tent. Ran the line to town. Tuesday, September 17th. Andy started for Beaver. Sent by him to get things to trade. Gave him $150.00 to use for us. Paid him $20.00. Put up transit and tent. Wednesday, September 18th. Located meridian line for Bishop Stewart. Got first observation tonight, but on account of wind and sand blowing, not satisfactory. Major and Jones left.

Thursday, September 19th. Work on observations. The observation better, but still not cleared. Inst. in meridian.

Friday, September 20th. Observed tonight. Boys got in from field. Good results. Saturday, September 21st. Sent telegram to E. P. Austin, telling him I would be ready Monday, the 23rd. Got answer "all right". Got good observation tonight. Sunday, the 22nd. Got observation the latter part of night. Windy the first. Monday, September 23rd. On account of bad results last night, telegraphed Austin that I would not be ready before the 24th. Settled with Adams. Tuesday, September 24. Got good observation. Exchanged [time] signals with Salt Lake. Line worked badly. Wednesday, September 25. Exchanged signals with Salt Lake. Thursday, the 26th. Exchanged signals with Salt Lake. Adams finished here. Friday, September 27th. Exchanged signals. Got good observation and good exchange. Adams got wood. Saturday, September 28. Let Clem have Dick and Fred, buyer to trade. Finished exchange of signals. Adams got wood. Mr. Austin is to write letter.

Sunday, September 29th. Observed for latitude by zenith distances. Went up the canon to "Cave Lake". Andy got home. Turned over to me vouchers to the amount of $103.85. Cash $21.25. Expense of trip $8.65. He spent for himself $6.60. Monday, September 30th. Observed. Worked on saddle, etc. Boys on saddles.

Tuesday, October 1, 1872. Let Jacob have $20.00. Wed-

---

[63]To make it possible to communicate with each other and to summon assistance when needed, the isolated settlements in southern Utah were connected by telegraph. As the line extended to Salt Lake City where longitude had been previously determined, it was used by Thompson in establishing the longitude of Kanab.

nesday, October 2nd. Let Joseph Hamblin have $2.00, Major and Jones got in. Thursday, October 3. Worked on zenith distances. Friday, October 4th. Work. Got two mules of Jacob, $150.00. Saturday, October 5. Major went to St. George, Frank with him. Sent Jack to Pipe for broncho. Sunday, October 6. At Kanab. Monday, October 7th. At work getting ready to start out.[64] Mr. Bintry works for us. Could not find horses.

Tuesday, October 8th. Worked, getting ready. Could not find horses until night, when Joe found them near Johnson. George Adair commenced work. Paid Mac $14.00 and Bunting $9.00 yesterday for work. Let Mac have $20.00 to get changed but he has not brought back the change. Bought a pistol of Robinson for $10.00. Paid him on account expecting $10.00. Wednesday, October 9th. Party for Moquis started this A. M. Jones and Joe *also.*[65] Told Jack and Jacob that if they could buy horses of Lee for $30.00 or $40.00, they had better do it, and take two or three over. Paid Jones $10.00 by check.

Thursday, October 10th. Enjoyed a sick headache. Last night word came at about 8:00 P. M. that the Navajo's had stolen 70 head of horses and mules from Parowan. Fred and Charley Riggs started about 11:00 to inform Jacob. The people have seemed to act the fool. Don't know what to do, nor how to do it. I advised them to raise a few men and cut the Indians off, but they objected. Fred got back at 11:00 A. M. having found Jacob at Navajo Well. Jacob and Charley went to the crossing of the Fathers to try and cut them off if the stock came that way. I do not think the Navajos have had a hand in it at all. It may be the Utes, but more likely is a scare. The men of the town have coaxed George to go to the aid of Jacob, and he left at noon without telling me, and I only found it out at night. Have engaged Adams to go with me.

Friday, October 11th. Left Kanab at 4:00 P. M. Camped at Navajo Well at 9:00. [Hired] Ang-E-quet and To-qui-tow for Indians. [Assistants.] An Indian came in before we started and told us that ten Navajos and four Utes had crossed at the "Ford" and gone up the old trail on the Paria with blankets to trade. This confirms the idea that the Parowan raiders are not Navajos.

Saturday, October 12th. Left camp at 9:00. Made Point D. at 12:30. Did work and made House Rock at 8:00 P. M. Sunday, October 13th. Climbed up near SS 11 this A. M. Some of Lee's people came here at noon. With them came James Wilkins. I hired him to take this trip with me for $10.00 per week, he to ride

---

[64]After returning from the river trip, Thompson resumed his systematic mapping, first along the Kaibab section of Grand Canyon (October 12-October 27), then in the region about the Uinkaret Mountain and lower Virgin River Valley (November 2-November 29). The months of December, 1872, also January and February, 1873, were given to plotting observations and records on maps.
[65]This was the annual trip made on behalf of the Mormon Church by Jacob Hamblin to the Hopi Villages and the Navajo settlement.

his own horse. Climbed to SS 10 this P. M. Put up flag and took angles. Monday, October 14th. Sent Jim and Humpy to put up a flag on the Kaibab. They are to get Mrs. Lee to bake some bread for them. Adams and I went to Point "E", and got back before dark. Tuesday, October 15th. Climbed to SS 11. Put up flag and triangulated. Did not get back until too late to go to Jacob's Pool.

Wednesday, October 16th. Sent Adams and Angequet to Jacobs Pool with pack animals while I went to SS 12 and triangulated. Got to Jacob' Pools' at 4:00 P. M. Thursday, the 17th. Climbed with Adams and Wilkins to Point east of Pools. Built monument triangulated. Very smoky. Friday, October 18. Left Lee's at 11:00 A. M. with John Doyle Lee, two sons and a son-in-law. Went to SS 11, and from there to Pa-quin-quin-a-pa spring fifteen miles.

Saturday, October 19th. Left our camp at 10:00 and traveled some 14 miles in a south direction until we came to a little stream from a spring up the valley. It flows down at least ½ a mile. Have made a sort of sketch of valley. Sunday, October 20th. Wilkins and I climbed to High Point on Ridge. I made a sketch of Nan-ko-weap Valley. The Little Colorado comes in just north of "Left Sharp Peak." Saw what is no doubt an overflow of trap in valley. Monday, October 21st. Left camp at 8:30. Climbed the Kaibab by a steep trail, traveled in a southerly direction some two miles to a spring. Went east ½ mile after supper and came to brink of canon of Nan-ko-weap Valley.

Tuesday, October 22d. Went south to the canon and then west. The valley we are in drains into Bright Angel Creek. Went on west side of valley of the creek. Saw from our west point the butte on which Quagunt [Kwaugunt] told us the Piutes killed the deer. Saw also the point on which we rode at the time. Made sketch of valley. There is a big spring, as the Indians say, at the head of one branch. Small springs in others. The Indians call the creek "Pounc-a-gunt" or "Beaver Creek" and say a long time ago the beavers lived in it, but that now all are killed. Can see the granite along the creek, and the granite capped by limestone on river.

Wednesday, October 23rd. Went to see the canon S.E. of camp in morning. Came to lake in DeMotte Park for camp. I wish to go from here to the spring west, but Indians do not seem willing. If they do not go I shall be obliged to go to Kanab. Thursday, October 24th. Indians concluded to go with us. Went in a direction a little west of south, to a spring in canon by noon. Had dinner and went to look at canon of Colorado. Made sketch and took bearings from two points. Have had little rain for the last two days. Some shower yesterday.

Friday, October 25th. Broke camp at 8:00. Made Rock

Spring at 11:00 and Black Water Spring at 3:00 P. M.   About four miles from latter place, met band of Indians, mining.[?]   There were only two old men with them, all the rest women and children —about forty.   The men were out hunting.   It was a novel sight.

Saturday, October 26th.   Sent Adams, Jim, and Andy out to camp at Work Spring, while Humpy and I went to see the Canon. Took bearing from two points, made sketch to mouth of Kanab Wash, and another to southeast bend of river, near Mount Trumbull.   Traveled in a divide 11 degrees east of river along the foot of the lower bench of Kaibab to Stewart's Ranch, then to camp. Rode at least 35 miles.

Sunday, October 27th.   Broke camp at 8:30, made Kanab at 5:00 P. M.   Found that the Major had gone to Paria.[66]   Monday, October 28th.   Commenced work on map.   Jones and Joe got in. Hired Adams for a month or six weeks longer at $40.00 per month. Paid Jim Wilkins $21.00.   Tuesday, October 29th.   Worked on map.   Paid off quite a number of bills.   Wednesday, the 30th. Worked on map.   The Major got in.   Bought mule, $140.00. Thursday, October 31st.   At Kanab.

Friday, November 1, 1872.   At Kanab.   Saturday, November 2.   Left Kanab for the Mount Trumbull trip.   Camped at a spring eight miles from Kanab.   Sunday, November 3.   Went to Pipe Springs to camp.   Monday, November 4th.   Went to a spring about 18 miles to camp.   Saw a band of wild horses; two sick. Rain tonight.   Camped at spring in red cliffs north of Wild Band Pocket.   Tuesday, November 5th.   Came to Rock Pool or Witches Spring, as the Indians call it.   (Do-nu-pits).   Had a hard drive. Wednesday, November 6th.   Camped at Do-nu-pits Pocket.   Went with the Major east of the canon.   Took bearings of all the cones or Oo-na-ga-re-chits [Cinder Cones], on the north of Mount Trumbull.   Thursday, November 7th.   Climbed Mt. Trumbull. Took bearings.   Friday, November 8.   Climbed Mt. Trumbull again for more bearings.

Saturday, November 9th.   Moved camp to Oak Spring.   I went to the water pocket at the junction of the wash and................ Canon.   Climbed to the top of the Oo-na-ga-re-chits at the foot. Took bearings and made a sketch of river from the butte, run from the Kaibab to the turn southwest of the Oo-na-ga-re-chits. Saw and noted where the lava that dammed the canon flowed in. Climbed up a long, black ridge into Oak Spring Valley.   Saw a camp of Piutes.   Rode in and shook hands all around.   Saw them parching grass seed preparatory to grinding.   Found that the wagon had made the trip to the spring alright.   Very cold tonight.

Sunday, November 10th.   This morning the Major traded

---

[66]Before going to Paria, Powell had joined Jones in a study of Long Valley. Dellenbaugh writes that in October (1872) Major Powell, Jones, and Joseph W. Young traversed on foot the canyon of the Parunuweap between the present Mt. Carmel and the old ranch at Shunesburg. For some reason the date of the pioneer trip is given by Powell as September, 1870.

with the Piutes. Rode with him over the last basalt flow this P. M. Found that the last flow was over an older one that stood in the form of islands on the surface. The old rock is more compact than the latter. The flow of basalt at lower end (south) did not examine. Monday, November 11th. Went to the top of Mt. Logan. Triangulated. We can see a long distance to south.

Tuesday, November 12th. Divided rations this A. M. and went to top of Mount Ellen this P. M. Took angles and made sketches. Mt. Ellen is a few feet higher than any of the other peaks about. Looking south we can see to the western bend of the river, perhaps 35 miles in a direct line. The walls of the canon are not as high as above at the Kaibab—creek down where the fault crosses the river. The canons on the east side are short, but on the west they run back a long ways. The country to south and west is all plateau, with high hills and mountains on it. It is cut by canons and is quite rough.

Wednesday, November 13th. Left Oak Spring Camp at 8:00, and made camp at Salt Spring at 4:00 P. M., call it 22 miles. After leaving Hurricane Ledge (which we came down, south of Whitmore's trail) the valley is broad, slopes southeast at an angle of three degrees to the place where it slopes suddenly to the valley below Piute Spring. Barometer in valley read 24.7. The ridge west of valley rises at an angle of 5 with 3. The summit is higher. We then descend into another valley draining into a canon near 30-31 of November 11th. This canon is quite deep near 30-31 with vertical walls. We then cross the ridges running down from 32-33 round to south of it where spring is found halfway up mountain. The canon runs around as indicated on sketch of Nov. 11th. The mountain rises at an angle of about 25 degrees, is covered with a sheet of basalt 80 feet thick, which is vertical for 9/19 of the way around and shaped like this at V is vertical for 600 feet, 80 feet basalt, 200 feet white sandstone, 300 feet of sub—apparently limestone. Basalt appears covering ridges much lower down. There are some indications of a fault, ore gold, on east side of 32 and 33, but not enough for me to say certainly, without further examination. I do not see how the basalt can be on the top of these mountains and none in valleys unless there has been great erosion, or the basalt has been poured out on the top. No evidences of the latter. 30 and 31 seem basalt on the top, shape seems to have more basalt on it than 32 and 30. There is a butte between Diamond and angle of Hurricane Ledge. Is lower than Diamond. Diamond has basalt on the top, the inside butte not quite as much. Diamond is 3 miles from angle of ledge. Have talked with Indians tonight.

Thursday, November 14th. Left camp at 8:00 A. M. Arrived at camp 6500 feet. Passed over ridges of 32 and 2 into canon. Camp near head of a canon a little east of south from Dellenbaugh's mountain, distant perhaps five miles. Canon, the Indians say, runs into Colorado west of southern bend. The basalt is at least 500 feet in canon, and to all appearance covers the entire country, since climbing cliff at Pine Spring. It is exactly like the basalt that caps 30-31 and 2. The upper stratum of sedimentary rock is the light grey 200 feet above red. I think now that the whole country has been covered by basalt from Mount Trumbull here and a large part eroded.

Friday, November 15th. Moved our camp about 1½ miles this morning, then Pa-an-tung and I went some eight miles to south and climbed a high basalt ridge that I have taken from both Layer [Logan?] and Ellen. The basalt is 400 feet thick on the top and apparently the ridge was once an old crater. Is at least 1800 feet above lower terrace of canon. The point south is evidently another crater. Could see a few miles below Garden at point marked S, what I suppose is granite. At 20 is the point where boys left the Major. The upper terrace is much wider on west than east, no deep canons on east. The cliffs on both sides are much cut and worn. At bend of river the cliffs on south seem lower. The river swings around so that at point marked N. the neck is not more than 1 mile wide. Think the first jump is at least 2000 feet, then slopes to river, then is 2000 more. The cliffs continue to the S.W. about the same height on north, gets lower and lower all the time on south. The plateau seems quite smooth except when cut by canons running to river, and these in a short distance become very deep. The basalt is evidently at least 200 feet deep all over the plateau. I think I can see granite at S. Pa-an-tung says that some "no sense" (cat-i-sure) Cherriots killed three American men where we are camped. At Wimp-u-run-cent, pocket in south branch of canon, to Av-e-ku-net, pocket at point marked DR, Pa-an-tung says a creek comes in where Americans hunted gold. It must be Diamond River. At point S. is Sacramento mining district. It may be that at point B. is the bad rapid where Bradley went over.

Saturday, November 16th. Broke camp at 8:00 A. M. Adams and George took the trail, while Pa-an-tung and I went to Dellenbaugh Mountain, climbed it, and noted barometer. Took bearings, etc. Pa-an-tung did not want Adams to climb the mountain with us. We were within about eight miles of the river when on the mountain, the view same as yesterday except the basalt does not seem to continue as far west. As I thought, the mountain being on its western edge, Mount D. has evidently been the seat of an old outburst. Found the ruins of an old Moqui's building on the very summit. It had evidently been used as a lookout or temple of worship. It was circular in shape, and perhaps 20 feet in diameter, with walls now standing—5 feet high. We descended by the west and struck limestone within 3 miles of the base.   Traveled in a N.W. direction around the base of basalt. Came to a spring in a valley, and find Adams and George.   The spring had "played out"; not water enough for the horses.   After supper we saddled up and traveled until after midnight in a west of north direction for the first half of the way, and were on low ridges of loose rock, mostly basalt, and valleys of limestone.   We then entered a canon with a general course a little west of north; limestone walls.   Came at last to a spring flowing out of a sand-stone stratum.   Camped and got something to eat.

Sunday, November 17th.   The Indians went to the Cherroits [Shivwits] camp last night, and about 9:00 this morning, came back with Q-ne-tive and another captain.   Talked.   Left at 11:00. Traveled down the canon, followed it a ways, then crossed a low divide into another canon which we came down into Grand Wash near the old Whitmore Ranch.   Found an Indian there with flour, sugar, and bacon.   Monday, November 18th.   Left camp at 8:30 A. M.   There is no doubt about the "Fault" or fold, I think the latter.   Came the "trail".   The white peak called Tanner by us is called Syconth by the Indians.   Camp on [Virgin].

Tuesday, November 19th.   Broke camp at 8:30.   Came to St. George.   Stopped at P.   Got telegram from wife.   Paid off Indians, sent telegrams to Kanab.   Wednesday, November 20th. At St. George, getting horses shod, etc.   Got telegram from wife this evening.   Thursday, November 21st.   At St. George.   Went to the top of a black miyer west of town.   Made sketch and took bearings.   Friday, November 22nd.   Came to Ft. Pierce.   Paid Pymm and St. George Co-op Adams for shoeing, etc.   Saturday, the 23rd.   Went out to Black Rock Canon, and then to top of Hurricane Ledge.

Sunday, November 24th.   Came to Pipe Springs.   Found John Renshaw; were Wheeler's men under Trent Dinnwoodie also.   Talked with them and gave them information.   Learned that the Major was not at Kanab.   Monday, November 25th.   Came to Kanab.   Found all waiting for Major.   Tuesday, the 26th.   At Kanab, getting ready to move.   Wednesday, November 27th. At Kanab.   Major got in from Shevroits.   Thursday, the 28th. Team from Shevroits got in—blacksmith shoeing horses.

Friday, November 29th.   At work getting ready to move north.   Decided that I would winter here, keep Fred, and with him and John, make the best map I could.   Am to pay Fred $400.00 when he is through.   Saturday, November 30th.   Major, Jack, Jones, Clem and Andy started for the East.   Major is to send me $1000.00 by Jack.   Settled with Stewart's.

Sunday, December 1, 1872.   In camp.   Traded narrow truck wagon to Jack Hamblin for 4200 lbs. corn.   Monday, December

2nd. Decided to stay in Kanab,[67] so commenced work on tents, etc. Got lumber of Stewart, and Rider worked for me. Rider is to let us have lumber to make tables.

Tuesday, December 3rd. Moving. Wednesday, 4th. Moving completed tonight. Thursday, December 5. Adams, John at work moving corn fodder. Friday, the 6th. Could not find Buttons, so did not start for Toquerville. Riley commenced work this morning at $45.00 per month. Saturday, December 7th. Started for St. George, went to Pipe Springs. Sunday, December 8th. Went to Sheep Troughs. Monday, the 9th. Went to Toquerville. Stopped at Nebekers. Tuesday, December 10th. Went to Berry Springs; Indians not here. Wednesday, the 11th. Went to Washington and from there to St. George. Stopped at Pymms. Thursday, December 12th. Distributed goods and came to Middleton to camp. Wrote to Major. Friday, the 13th. Came to Workman's Ranch for camp. Saturday, 14th. Went to Toquerville, sent team for rest of goods. Sunday, December 15th. Sent John to Toquerville with dispatch for Major. Gave Adams $5.00. Came to Sheep Troughs to camp. Monday, December 16th. Came to Pipe Springs, got Windsor's bill. Tuesday, the 17th. Came to Kanab after climbing Point H. Wednesday, December 18. At Kanab. Adams is hauling wood.

Thursday, December 19th. At Kanab. Adams hauling wood. Windsor brought one-quarter of beef. Bought stack of hay, some barley, and corn of Frost. Friday, December 20th. Settled with Windsor. He gave me $41.00 in money. I gave him a check for $104.00. He owed us $94.00 of it. Is to get the money and send it from Toquerville. We omitted to count 25 lbs. cheese @ 25c.

Saturday, December 21st. Hauled hay. Adams quit work. Paid Jacob. Sunday, the 22nd. At Kanab, Monday, the 23rd. At Kanab, working up observations. Tuesday, the 24th. At Kanab. Wednesday, the 25th December. At Kanab. Christmas. Thursday, December 26th. At Kanab. Rainy. Friday, December 27th. At Kanab, rainy. Paid Mac for making tables, Adams for work, and Mrs. Adams $8.00 for milk and butter.

January 1, 1873. Jack got in with goods from Salt Lake. January 16th. Jack got back from Toquerville with Charley and Thunderbolt. They are poor and crippled. January 20th. Jacob

---

[67]Dellenbaugh writes:

"Prof. concluded to make winter headquarters in Kanab and a lot was rented for the purpose. On December 3d. we put up a large tent in one corner, with two small ones for rations and saddles. The next day we put up one in the other corner for Prof. and Mrs. Thompson, and at the back of the lot we arranged a corral for the horses or mules we might want to catch. The large tents were floored with pine boards and along the sides heavy cedar boughs were placed in crotches around which the guy ropes were passed before staking. The tents thus were dry inside and could not blow down. A conical iron stove on a boxing of earth heated the large tent like a furnace. In the middle of the general tent we placed a long drafting-table and were ready for work. Another tent, half boards, was erected near ours for kitchen and dining-room, and Riley, who had turned up again, hired as cook and master of this structure. Prof. arranged for a supply of potatoes, butter, meats, and everything within reason, so we lived very well, with an occasional dash of Dixie wine to add zest."

bought corn. I have had of him 50¾ bushels. He owes now 24¼ bushels. January 23rd. Loaned Jack 2 Pack Saddles for 30 days. January 24th. Jack started for Mt. Trumbull with an Indian.

February 1, 1873. Sent letter and check for $12.00 to Bishop Thorne at Gunnison. Bought 20 lbs. mutton, $2.00 of Frost. Ordered ½ a beef of Windsor. Worked on map. Sunday, Feb. 2. Plotted trail up Kanab wash. Tuesday, February 4th. Worked on map. Got $200.00 in a registered letter from Bishop.

Wednesday, February 5th. Worked on map. Windsor brought two hind quarters of beef yesterday. I think that at least five inches of snow is on the ground this morning. Weight of beef 258 lbs. Thursday, February 6th. Worked on map. Boys made a jumper and we had a ride. Monday, February 10th. Jack got back from Mount Trumbull to night. In-mar-an-te-ki came with him. Got about a dozen views, but the weather was so stormy that he could take no more. Snow is three feet deep in Pasture Valley.

Wednesday, February 12th. Decided to let Jack go with Fred until he strikes some conveyance that will take him to the city faster than he can travel on horseback. Do this because the "Ipizootic" has obliged the Stage routes to take off their horses. Sunday, February 17th. Got map finished. Fred and Jack started [with it] for Panguitch or farther. Paid Riley $16.00, Stewart for Fred. Paid Fred $345.00 money, and gave Jack $25.00. Monday, February 18th. Worked on the diagram of Primary Triangles.[68] Traded the lumber, tables, etc., including stove to E. Brown for two horses. Wednesday, February 20th. Finished diagram and commenced work on St. George country.

Tuesday, February 11th. At Kanab. Got three papers by mail, the first mail matter we have had for four weeks. Thursday, February 13th. Jack got in tonight. Got Panguitch mail. No letter from the Major. Jack went to Salt Lake with Fred. His expenses were $64.00. I gave him on starting, $25.00. Monday, February 17th. At Kanab. Bishop Windsor brought 358 lbs. beef. Settled with him. Owed $53.15. Paid Eleazer Asay $10.00 for a colt that our mules killed. Got hay of Bishop Stewart.

Tuesday, February 18th. Jacob brought 25 bushels of corn for me. Jack up canon taking pictures. Saturday, February 22nd. Sent Riley and John to Eight Mile Spring with 19 head of horses. Jacob got home with harness, and I went and got it. Tuesday, February 25th. Jack got in from Canon. Got about ten negatives —good ones. Decided to have him print from them.

---

[68]After the map covering the work done in 1871-1872 had been dispatched to Washington, Thompson began preparation for the extension of the topographic survey northward across the High Plateaus, eastward beyond the Paria, and westward to Pine Valley Mountain. This involved trips to Salt Lake, to St. George, and the maintenance of general headquarters at Kanab. Under the supervision of Thompson, mapping in 1873 was carried on continuously by Hillers and J. H. Renshaw (assigned to topographic work in November, 1872), assisted by Nathan Adams, Joseph Haycock, George Adair, and Jacob Hamblin.

Wednesday, April 2d. Got letter tonight from the Major, dated Washington, D. C., February 19th. Sent him telegram saying I shall leave the 4th. Thursday, April 3rd. Hired Joe Hamblin at $35.00 per month. Traded the thin tent for a mare. Friday, April 4th. Stormy. Decided not to move until tomorrow. Decided to let Jack go down the Virgin river for pictures.

Sunday, April 6th. Went from Eight Mile Spring to Kanab for observations at head of Base Line. Bought corn of Frost, 7 bushels, paid $11.50. Got telegram from the Major saying "Appropriation to publish will be with you soon answer." Answered saying, "Team will be in Salt Lake the 25th." Paid $3.50 for telegram and $1.50 for wagon grease. Monday, April 7th. Went from Eight Mile Spring to Paria Settlement, with Riley and wife, leaving Joe and John.

Thursday, April 10th. Moved camp to just below Johnson. Went with John to PO. B. Friday, the 11th. Came to spring in Sink Valley [east of Alton]. Came to upper Kanab. Sunday, April 13th. Came over the Divide to a point below Asay's. [On Asay Creek.]

Monday, April 14th. Came to a point about 7 miles below Panguitch. Broke wagon tongue in the mud. Sent Riley back to get it fixed. Paid $10.00 for grain, $7.85 for wagon, and Riley $7.50. Wednesday, April 16th. Came to below Circleville. Thursday, the 17th. Came to below Alma. Bought $1.50 worth of grain at Marysvale, $1.00 coffee, and $3.00 grain at Alma. Friday, the 18th. Came to Salina. Paid $2.00 for grain. Saturday, April 19th. Came to Gunnison by noon. Got 235 lbs. of barley from Bishop Horne. Got check for $125.00, cashed. Paid John $1.30. Borrowed $55.00 cash of John for use expedition.

Monday, April 21st. At Gunnison. Got 669 lbs. of oats of Bishop Horne. Left Saturday noon for Salt Lake. Left John and Joe. Gave John $5.60 on his account and $3.00 to buy beans, etc. Came about 15 miles. Lost the road and went some ten miles out of the way. Camped on Cedar ridge. Tuesday, April 22nd. Came to Summit about 45 miles today. Wednesday, the 23rd. Came to Greenes., about 40 miles. Thursday, April 24th. Came to Salt Lake. Stopped at the Townsend House. Went to Captain Bishop's and got box. Saturday, April 26th. At Townsend until night, then moved to Mrs. Denholders where wife has engaged rooms and board for $15.00 per week. Got letters out of office for the Major. Sunday, April 27th. At Captain Bishop's for dinner.

Saturday, May 3, 1873. At Salt Lake. Paid Thompson $20.00 for keeping horses and grain. Mrs. Thompson paid Mrs. Denholder $24.00 for board tonight. Bought a magnet for use of expedition for $1.75. Major got here from Washington.

Tuesday, May 20th. Left Salt Lake at 10:00 A. M. Made Provo by 6:00 P. M., 50 miles. Stopped at the Lion House. Paid $2.00. Had dinner at Lehi, 50c for horse feed. Wednesday, May 21st. Left Provo at 7:00 A. M. Made Nephi at 7:00 P. M., 45 miles. Paid 60c at Payson for horse feed. Found the boys at Nephi. Thursday, May 22nd. Came to Gunnison by 6:00 P. M., 40 miles. Met Joe, hunting horses some 15 miles from camp. It seems that Choncho, Rowitz, and Jerusalem are lost. Joe will not come in for two or three days, if he does not find them sooner. Jack is at camp. Got some 30 negatives down the Virgin. Found letters from Fred, Brown, Walter and George. George has the P. O. order the Major sent on my order, $75.00.

Friday, May 23rd. Jack is going to print some pictures. All at Gunnison except Joe. Saturday, May 31st. Worked on birds. We are doing as well at Gunnison as anywhere. Thursday night the Assistant Geologist of Lieut. Hoxie's party of Wheeler's Expedition, came here. Had quite a talk with him.

Sunday, June 1, 1873. At Gunnison. The boys get birds in the forenoon, and put them up this afternoon. Saturday, June 14th. Got letter tonight from Major and wife. Major is going to Washington, ostensibly on Indian affairs, really to draw money to run things. Wife is going with him to Illinois on some sort of a junket. Have decided to go myself to Gunnison for grain and flour tomorrow.

Sunday, June 15th. Started for Gunnison, taking Henry with me. Made the bridge at Glencove [Glenwood]. Monday, June 16th. Made Gunnison, camped near the Bishop's. Paid 70c at Salina. Got check of $125.00 cashed. Wednesday, June 18th. Came from Glencove to camp. Agreed with Durkee to store some goods for me. Paid at Alta $10.00 for grceries. (Canned jellies and tea.)

Thursday, June 19th. Discharged Jim Jemmison. Paid him for work, $75.50 and expenses to Salt Lake, $15.00, making $91.00 in all. Got fifty cents of Jim's. Henry commenced cooking at Jim's ways. Friday, June 20th. Broke camp at 8:00 A. M. Came to Ford below Circleville, 22 miles. Got butter of Mrs. Van Buren, $1.50. Borrowed $15.00 of Jack.

Saturday, June 21st . Came to head of Panguitch canon, 18 miles. Sunday, June 22nd. Climbed the wall up head of Panguitch Canon. John made sketch. Got to Panguitch about 6:00 P. M. Camp two miles above town. Saw Bishop Lew Seavey. He thinks he can get me a cook.

Monday, June 23rd. In camp. Hired Thos. Haycock to cook at $45.00 per month. He commences today. Wrote Mr. Adams, offering him $45.00 per month to work. Wrote wife.

Sent picture of Marysvale. Paid Jack $2.50 that I had borrowed. Paid for milk and cheese, $1.75.

Tuesday, June 24th. Went to Panguitch Lake. Henry quit cooking. Wednesday, June 25th. In morning Jack made picture of lake. Climbed a high point. Went back to camp this P. M. Altitude Panguitch Lake 9,350 feet on barometer of Panguitch town 2306 m = 7940 feet.

Thursday, June 26th. Left Panguitch camp at 8:00 A. M. Came to two miles about Fred Hamblin's ranch. Set John to running levels and Henry trail. Paid $1.00 for Henry for washing. On east of road are the Pink Cliffs covered by igneous rock, for about ⅔ of today's drive. Friday, June 27th. Came to Upper Kanab [Alton]. Borrowed $1.00 of Jack. Paid 75c for butter. Saturday, the 28th. Came to Skoom Pa.

Sunday, June 29th. Came to Kanab. Camped near the Fort. Towsley caught up with us about 5 miles above Johnson. He was sent from Fillmore to change Beck for some other mule. He says that the party will probably leave F. in a few days, that the Major is expected in a day or two. I cannot take a mule out of the team until I get to Kanab, so took him along. In fact we did not catch the team until we got to Johnson, and his mule had been ridden so hard that she was not fit for work. Sent telegram to Fillmore.

Monday, June 30th. At Kanab. Went to Mr. Adam's Ranch. Mr. Adams has agreed to work for us at $45.00 per month. Commenced this afternoon. Henry and John hunting birds.

Tuesday, July 1, 1873. At Kanab. Sent Jack and Towsly up to Cave Lake to get pictures. Took observation with John to help. Henry hunting birds.

Wednesday, July 2d. At Kanab. Traded horses with Joe. Jack lost his mule, so did not get in. Ascertained today that the wire in main line was down, so my dispatch was delayed. Sent dispatch to operator at Fillmore, asking if first was delivered. Got answer from S. W. Ingalls about dark tonight, saying "Major left Washington 25th inst." Several weeks before reaching Kanab hired George Adair to go to Gunnison to get load of flour; furnishes his own wagon and harness and works for $12.00 per week. Is to start the 4th. Have decided that Towsly shall go with him as far as Panguitch, then to Fillmore. Shall go to Pipe tomorrow.

Thursday, July 3rd. At Kanab. Was ready to start for Pipe when dispatch came to Operator from the Major, asking if I was in Kanab, and a few minutes after, one from Office at Salt Lake, requesting me to stay at Kanab until I heard from Powell. Paid John Renshaw $15.00 for money spent for us, Rider $8.50 for work on wagon, and Robinson $9.75 for shoeing horses and repairs on wagon. Paid $3.20 for telegraph dispatches for Expedition. Got dispatch from Fennemore.

Friday, July 4th. At Kanab, waiting for message from Salt Lake. None came. Jacob got home tonight. Saturday, July 5th. Left Kanab and came to Pipe. Telegraphed the Major "that Jacob was at home." Paid $1.00 for telegram and 75c for butter. Left orders for any messages to be sent to Pipe and St. George. Sunday, July 6th. Got message at Pipe from the Major. He is at Salt Lake. Says "Moran and another artist wishes to join us."[69] Asks me to send to Marysvale. I sent answer saying, "Will send to Beaver for rations. Have Moran meet us there." Answer at Toquerville. Paid $2.90.

Monday, July 7th. Came to Sheep Troughs from Cedar Ridge. Tuesday, July 8th. Went from Sheep Troughs to Berry's Spring. Went to Toquerville. No answer from the Major. Sent dispatch to him, asking about rations. Paid $1.50 for message and 50c for corn. Wednesday, July 9th. Went from Berry's Spring to St. George. Got telegram from Major, saying to send to Fillmore instead of Beaver for Rations. Also send two riding horses. I answered, saying "Will send team. Cannot send riding horses. Take those at Fillmore." Got check of $200.00 cashed at St. George. Paid $58.85 for rations, etc. as per bill and vouchers. Paid Pymm $1.00 for dinner. Paid for telegrams to Major, and George $4.50. Paid for messages, $4.50. Paid John $1.00. Paid Joe Hamblin $2.75 cash. Agreed to be at Pakoon Spring on the 17th.

Thursday, July 10th. Left Berry's Spring and came to Washington in morning. In afternoon came to Diamond Valley. Paid $2.50 at Washington for beans. Paid Henry $9.00 for cooking before Haycock commenced. Friday, July 11th. From camp to top of Pine Valley Mountain. Camped at a seep spring on the top. Saturday, the 12th. Went to highest peak of Pine Valley. Made sketches, i. e. John and I. Built monument putting in Jones' record. Sunday, July 13th. Came from P. V. Mountain to Washington. Stopped in Tom Clark's lot. Addoms from St. George came to see me. Paid $1.65.

Monday, July 14th. Came from Washington to St. George this A. M. and from St. George to Rock Springs this P. M. Got word from Dr. Geib that George Adair was at Fillmore. Sent word to George to wait for Major Powell and rations, etc. Paid $1.50 for message. Paid $4.50 for shirts, and $4.00 for drinks, and $20.25 for provisions at Co-op, and $2.00 at Pymm's for fish. Had Dolly shod at Addoms.

Tuesday, July 15th. Came from Black Rock Springs to Pa-Koon. Thursday, July 17th. Came from Pa-Koon Spring to

[69]Thomas Moran (1837-1926)—Ranks as one of the ablest painters of American landscapes. His "Chasm of the Colorado" was purchased by Congress for display on the walls of the Capitol at Washington. The atlas accompanying Dutton's "Tertiary History of the Grand Canyon Region" includes paintings and sketches made by Moran under the auspices of the Powell survey. Mount Moran in the Teton Range, Wyoming, and Moran Point on the Colorado Canyon recall his many years of work in the plateau country.

Colorado River. Got observations. Friday, the 18th. Came from Colorado river to Pa-Koon Spring. Went to Mo-que-acks wick-e-up. Had watermelons and a big talk. Saw Quetus and other Shewits. When got to Pa-Koon Spring, found that Bentley's horse had given out. Saturday, 19. Came from Pa-Koon Spring to Cane.

Sunday, July 20th. Came from Cane Spring to Black Rock. Left Bentley's horse with the Indians at Cane Spring. They are to bring him in in five days to Bentley. I am to give them a hat, a shirt, a pair of pants, a box of caps, two bars of lead, and some powder. They think the horse is mine. I think the heat, no shoes, and some trouble with his water is what ails the horse. Indian's name that is to bring him in is Tar-mu-ga-towt.

Monday, July 21st. Came from Black Rock Spring to St. George. Rain this P. M. Camped near our wagon in Addoms yard. Got telegrams from Jack and letters. Sent telegrams to Major from wife. Tuesday, July 22nd. At St. George. Sent wagon to Ft. Pierce for camp. John and I remained to do some work. Could not get through so have concluded to stay at Pymms all night. Got telegram from Major, saying Adair would be at Toquerville tonight. Sent telegram to Jack and George Adair, telling the latter to meet me at sheep troughs. Paid $3.50 for canteens to C. S. Riding.

Wednesday, July 23rd. Came to Ft. Pierce. Paid Pymm $2.75 for horse keeping, etc. The water at Ft. Pierce is very bad. Thursday, July 24th. With John, climbed a high point near Black Rock Canon 9 miles. Was so sick on account of water that we could do no work. Sent team with orders to go to top of Hurricane Ledge, then sent a man to see if the water in gulch was better than at Ft. P. If not, go to Canaan Ranch. They found the water worse, so went for ranch 14 miles. John and I had a long ride and every mouthful of water made me sick. John looked as though he would drop from the saddle every rod. We had a small flask of brandy along, of which we occasionally took a swallow. Half-way up the Hurricane Ledge we stopped for a rest. After reaching the top went about four miles, then stopped for a rest under a tree. Four miles further on came up with Adams and the wagon. He was almost exhausted. Joe had been gone a long time for water. Henry and Frank with him. I urged my horse as fast as possible for three miles more when I overtook Haycock driving the loose animals. John had by this time fallen far in the rear. Caught old Utah and in a very few minutes passed four miles and reached the ranch. Found Joe starting back with water. Henry with his horse unsaddled. I talked with them a little, took all the loose things off my saddle and told Joe to "set old Utah up" until he reached Adams, and away he went. I waited at the Ranch until supper, when Col. Andrews insisted I should eat. Adams,

Haycock, and John came in while we were eating. I had sent
Henry after the water. When he got back had him fill it, and we
camped near the Kanab road. It will be a day long remembered.
Had we had a few miles more to have gone, some of us would
have given out entirely. Joseph Hamblin quit work today. Paid
him in money. Boys on map.

Wednesday, July 30th. Moran, Colburn, and George got in.
Gave Bishop Stewart a check for $300.00. He gave me cash,
$164.32. Is to give me $55.00 more, and in a few days $57.50.
Got rations, $23.15. John and Henry on map. Letter from Fred.
Thursday, July 31st. At Kanab. John and Henry on map. Paid
George, Adair for work, $28.00, and expenses of trip, $15.00.
Newman Brown commenced work at $30.00 per month. Friday,
August 1, 1873. Went with Jack Colburn. Moran, Newman, and
Frank out on Rockville trail. Dry camp. Wrote to wife.

Saturday, August 2d. Went west of our dry camp to brink
of canon on Rockville trail—fine view; then back to Cottonwood
Wash Spring to camp. Sunday, August 3rd. Came from Cottonwood Wash Spring to Kanab. Got in about noon. An Indian boy
had been bitten by a rattle snake. Sent to Johnson for alcohol and
whiskey. Got $4.80 worth, *charged*. Gave the Indian boy about
½ pint of alcohol. Beef came. Rain at night.

Monday, August 4th. At Kanab. Paid Young $47.80 for
beef and hides. Bishop Stewart paid me $112.50, being the
amount still due. Telegraphed the Major, asking him to send to
Marysvale for trunk of Indian clothing. Got 31-½ lbs. of beans
of Jacob Hamblin. Tuesday, August 5th. At Kanab. Got four
letters from wife. Jack and Moran started for Mount Trumbull.
Wednesday, August 6th. Got letter from Fred. Gave two checks
for $9.00 to telegraph operator. Got $8.50 in currency. Telegraphed Major.

Saturday, August 9th. Got the operator to telegraph to
Beaver and see if my last message had been delivered. Found that
it had. Hired George Adair to take one team and go and get the
flour he left at Richfield, $12.00 per week . Left Kanab at 4:00 P.
M. with Haycock-Brown, and John for a two or three day trip to
Long Valley. Paid Henry $1.00. Came to Cottonwood Wash
Spring for Camp. Sunday, August 10th. Came from Cottonwood
Wash Spring to Virgin River for camp. The country is very sandy,
the most so of any plateau I have been on. It often lies in bank of
clean, light orange color.

Monday, August 11th. Came from camp near Virgin River
to Kanab. Came up the creek until we came to where the road
out of Long Valley comes up the bluff. There we took the road.
Got to Kanab about 6:00. Found the Major at Kanab. Says he
answered my last telegram, but it has never been received at this
office. George Adair left today. Pilling and Towsly are with him.

Tuesday, August 12th. At Kanab. Paid John Renshaw $1.00 and Haycock $1.30. Jack and Moran got in tonight. Wednesday, August 13th. At Kanab. Went up to the Three Lake Canon with Major and Moran. Talked business matters with Major. He says the money is in bank at Washington.

Thursday, August 14th. At Kanab. The Major started with Moran, Colburn, etc. for Kaibab this P. M. Mr. Howell of Wheeler's Party, visited our camp today.[70] They have had a rough trip, leaving Spanish Fork about the 1st of June. They tried to come down the base of Wasatch Mountains. Got on Dirty Devil River and from that to a ridge or fold running to Colorado river a little above the mouth of San Juan. Found they could not come along the river and so retraced their steps as far back as the Dirty Devil, then went across to Glencove. Here Trent Hoxie left the party and went to Beaver for supplies, the amount taken with them having been consumed, and the party having lived on boiled corn for several days. Thompson, Howell and three others came back to D. D. River, then along my old trail to Table Mountain, and down the Paria to the settlement. After waiting a few days for Hoxie, Johnson and Howell came here. Hoxie came from Glencove to Beaver. Had some disagreement with his men and discharged them without payment of wages. They, in revenge appear to have stolen his mules, a fact that he did not discover for five days after the event happened. Hoxie is now trying to recover his stock.

Saturday, August 16th. Got telegram this A. M. from Ingalls, asking me to send team to Pipe to help his along. Sent Newman with span of mules. Ingalls and Roberts got in tonight. Got telegrams from Bishop, requesting loan of quadrants or compass. Paid Mrs. Plunkett $6.50 for bits. Sunday, August 17th. At Kanab. Paid $2.00 for fruit and Sunday Schools. Wagon with rations not in. Newman reports them at Pipe before Sundown. Wednesday, August 20th. Left Kanab and came to Navajo Well. Got telegram from Lund. Ingalls received one from Pymm. I answered, telling him to feed if necessary, 200 lbs. of flour per day until he heard from Ingalls. Thursday, 21. Came from Navajo Well to Paria.

Friday, August 22d. Came from Paria to Un-Car-Ca-On for camp. Saturday, August 23rd. Climbed from camp to point of observation this A. M. Came to a camp one mile below Paria. From the Crossing-of-The-Fathers the cliffs seem to continue about 20 miles east, then break around to next forming a sort of Table upon which Navajo Mountain seems to rest. Are 800 feet, nearly vertical. Are the Jurassic White Sandstones. The ridge

---

[70]The United States Geographic Surveys under the direction of Captain G M. Wheeler, U S. Army, covered northern Arizona, Nevada, and southern Utah, thus overlapping the surveys conducted by Thompson. Wheeler's party included the two able geologists, Edwin E. Howell and Grove Karl Gilbert, who afterwards became members of the Powell Survey in association with. Thompson.

or fold upon which point of observation is situated is 1250 feet above camp. The N. E. edge is line of fold of Echo Cliffs. From El Vado de las Padres there are first the Jurassic Cliffs, next the Cretaceous with coal beds showing at base, then above these other cliffs a short line stopped by the eastern edge of Kaibab fold, then back of that the line from "End of Cliffs" to "Ki-par-o-wits".

Sunday, August 24th. Came to camp 4½ miles up Cottonwood Wash. Climbed up Hogback on right of camp—Height 600 feet, Slope 45 degrees. Could not see what I wished. Monday, August 25th. Climbed to a point northeast 1½ miles from camp. The canon bears directly toward Kiparowits until within about five miles, then swings to left, and I think the fold divides, one branch continuing in about the same general directions, passing just west of Ki-par-o-wit's into Potato Valley, the other bearing more west at the foot of Table Mountain. This will account for less altitude of Pink Cliffs, and also of Kiparowits as compared with Table Mountain. The White Cliffs continue from near Johnson to the Paria river, and begin to appear as broken hills to the base of Kiparowits. The line of Cliffs from Kiparowits to opposite Navajo Mountain seems broken by canons and lies as indicated on Sketch. The White Cliffs are 600 feet vertical. Mollie's Nipple is at least 4 miles from White Cliffs and 5 miles from point of vermilion. The line of cliffs from Kiparowits to opposite Navajo are slopes to east and of first Set back after that vertical. Barometer at Station reads 7000 feet. Station is about same altitude as Plateau north of settlement and foot of White Cliffs, but the general altitude increases towards Kiparowits. Top of Mollie's Nipple is height of White Cliffs. Barometer at camp 6400 feet. Came to upper Paria crossing for camp. Went 6 miles up Paria Canon.

Tuesday, August 26th. Came from Paria Settlement to Swallow Park. Came up what is known as Buckskin Wash. Think I saw western edge K. F. Wednesday, 27th. Went down Swallow Park Canon today. Thursday, August 28th. Climbed the Pink Cliffs to what I called when on Table Mountain, Point N. Looking toward Kiparowits the general slope is down to the Paria, then up where John has written "Rough" on sketch. The cliffs are from 50 to 300 feet high on face, decreasing as they go toward Mountain, slope of face often 45. Can see first Dirty Devil Mountain.

Friday, August 29th. Came from Swallow Park to the former site of Stewart's Mill. Stopped at Skoon Pa [Skumpah, Clarkston] for dinner. There I sent Adams to Kanab for wagon. Gave him $5.00 to get a pair of shoes for Renshaw, pay Bunting 75c, and get the balance in yeast powders. Made an agreement with Adams to take care of our stock this coming winter. Am to pay him 30c per head per month, he to have the privilege of using any of the stock himself, but is not to let anyone else use them, nor is he to loan or hire them to anyone else. I am to lend him two sets of harness and two saddles. He is also to report to me once a month the condition of each head. Neither saddles or harness are to be loaned. Told Adams to be at Sink Valley in four days. In coming from Swallow Park to Skoon Pa. the foothills of Pink Cliff run nearly out to trail; are ridges rather than hills. Should think they were 600 feet high. ¼ mile from foot of cliffs. The Pink limestone seems to stand in Cliffs 1200 to 1500 feet, vertical height. Is worn in castles, towers, and pinnacles on a scale equal to the Canons. From the top of foot ridges to the foot of cliffs is say, 300 feet talus, at times often more. The canons between foothills rise say, 400 feet before reaching the point where ridges are 600 feet.

Saturday, August 30th. Rain last night. Moved our camp about a mile below the old mill site. The gray mare, Fanny, was found this morning with a wound six inches long and two deep on her left hip. It seems almost as though a bear or panther had struck her with its claw. Two small wounds on the right limb look as though the other paw had struck there. The wound is shaped "Y" thus. Bear tracks, old, have been noticed near camp. Threw her and sewed the wound up. Rain all day, so we could not climb. Clearer this P. M.

Sunday, August 31st. Camped on creek below "Old Mill Site." Went to "Highest Point Pinkbluffs" today. Bar. at camp 8200 feet at highest point, climbed 10,350 feet, making 2150 feet above camp. Rain all day. When we left camp clouds enveloped the crest of Pink Cliffs. We kept on hoping they would break away, but instantly thickened, and by the time we reached the top were so thick we could not see more than 150 feet. The feeling of the clouds was that of warm, moist, air. Soon rain fell. We built a fire and waited until about half past two, when seeing no appearance of the rain abating, came down to camp.

Monday, September 1st, 1873. Came from Camp 31st to Sink Valley.—Tuesday, September 2nd. Climbed to a high point on Pink Cliffs. Built monument and triangulated.—Wednesday, 3rd. Moved camp to Upper Kanab.

Thursday, September 4th. Climbed to points, Numbered 1 and 2. Took bearings. Adams got in. Paid 60c at ranch for butter and milk. Paid Adams $1.50 and 75c for baking powders. Got letter from Major and telegram from Lund at St. George.

Friday, September 5th. Came from Upper Kanab to camp near Fred Hamblins. Climbed a point near "Alkaline Spot." The cliff hills west of dinner camp are 400 feet above road. East higher at least 2000 to S. E. but slope gentle. Told Henry today that I should not keep him much longer. Told Brown how long I wanted him, viz, a week or ten days. Talked with John Renshaw. He agrees to stay until January 1st. I agreed to pay him $35.00 per month from first of last April, and $60.00 per month after January 1st, 1874, while we were in camp and $90.00 when we did not board him and were in some city, provided he could do final work on map.

Saturday, September 6th. Came to camp 6 miles above Panguitch. On account of stock being lost, I did not get to camp until 9:00 P. M. Went to Panguitch. Bought boots, $7.00, hat, $4.00, for myself, hat $2.00 for Henry, boots $7.00, socks $1.00, hat $2.95 for Renshaw, and tea, $1.90 for company.

Sunday, September 7th. In camp trying to take observations for lat. Poor success on account of rain. Wrote to wife, Major, and Jack.

Monday, September 8th. Came from camp on river to camp on East Fork, before noon climbed to an observation point on "Fold' 'this P. M. Made sketch and took magnetic bearings.

Tuesday, September 9th. Came from camp in East Fork Valley to about 6 miles above Panguitch. Climbed a point 9 miles north of camp this A. M., was 500 feet above camp. Took paintings and sketches. Our camp tonight is 1000 feet lower than on East Fork.

Wednesday, September 10th. Came to camp at head of Panguitch Canon. Discharged Haycock today. Paid him a balance due of $55.50. John Renshaw witnessed judgment. Got letters from wife and Fred. The latter seems disappointed at my last letter and seems to have thought he had made a bargain with the Major. He has also taken as facts what I gave only as opinions. Of course I like such bargains. I told John Renshaw today that I was obliged to withdraw from my offer of $60.00 and $90.00 per month at least until I saw the Major.

Thursday, September 11th. In camp taking observations; got "Lunar" Time and Latitude. Sent John and Adams to climb west of camp until they could get a view of country around Panguitch Lake.

Friday, September 12th. Broke camp at 8:00 A. M. Came to Van Buerens for camp.

Saturday, September 13th. Came to Marysvale for camp. Paid Durkee $40.00 for keeping horses. Paid Newman Brown $50.00, John Renshaw being witness. Took all things away from Durkee.

Sunday, September 14th. Got letter from wife. Came from Marysvale to a point 3 miles from Glencove.

Monday, September 15th. Came to bridge at Glencove. [Glenwood]. Found one of our wagon wheels so badly broken that I did not dare to go further without repairing it. Sent Adams with wagon to Richfield.   Paid $1.50 for grain, on account of poor grass.

Tuesday, September 16th.   Came to camp at Rocky Ford on the river.   Adams paid $6.50 for fixing wagon.

Wednesday, September 17th.   Came to Gunnison.   Saturday, September 20th.   Making boxes, packing and trading wagon.   Paid Bishop Horne $4.50 for lumber, used 50c for nails. Paid 75c for baking powders.   Paid $1.25 for milk and butter, 50c for potatoes, and $1.50 for herding stick and sheep vats.

Sunday, September 21st.   Came from Gunnison to Taylor's Ranch.—Monday, 22nd.   Came to Nephi.   Camped above town on Creek.   Have decided to stay here until first of January at least.   Paid $2.00 for hay.—Friday, September 26th.   At Nephi. Paid $1.75 for rations.   Engaged lot to camp on of Mrs. Howard.

Saturday, September 27th.   Put up tents.   Paid $5.00 for drafting boards, $3.25 for lumber to put in tents, etc.   Paid John Renshaw $1.00 and $4.50 for provisions as per vouchers, and $10.00 for ton of hay.   Paid $1.70 for rope and nails.   Paid $1.50 for potatoes and 75c for meat.

Wednesday, October 1st, 1873.   Adams left this morning with 6 animals.   Will have 19 when he gets to Kanab.   Will work until October 7th.   Paid him $130.00 in full.   Sent $7.00 to James Dwyer for Tracing Cloth.   Registered the letter.   Sent 3 months subscription to Salt Lake Herald.—Monday, October 6th.   Worked on map.   Wrote to Lee and Shepherd concerning Hookers Botany for wife.—Saturday, October 11th.   Captain Bishop came, left the Major on the 25th ult.   The Major was to go to Las Vegas to meet me.

Monday, October 13th.   Henry started for Gunnison for grain.   Got telegram from Major.   He was at St. George on his way north—answered at Fillmore.

Monday, October 20th.   Major got in tonight.—Tuesday, 21st.   Had talk with the Major.   We have decided that I shall go to Washington and we shall commence final work on the map. Paid $1.40 for telegrams.

Wednesday, October 22d.   Talked with the Major about John.   He agreed that we should employ him, give him $90.00 per month after he could do final work.   The Major said that the money was really to pay my salary; was at Washington, but he would have to go back and get a requisition through the Treasury Department first.   He told me August 13th when at Kanab that the money was in bank at Washington.

Thursday, October 23rd.   Working on Major's book.— Friday, 24th.   Working on Major's book.—Saturday, October 25th.   Paid the Major $100.00.   Owe Hayne $50.00 on account. Deseret Bank said we have no funds to our credit.

Sunday, October 26th. Left Nephi for Salt Lake this M. Rode all night. Wrote to wife.—Monday, 27th. Got to Lehi at 5:00 A. M. and Salt Lake at noon. Went to Walker House. Wrote wife. Thursday, October 30th. At Salt Lake. Got telegram from Hayne and son, Nephi, saying our check for $200.00 was returned.

Tuesday, November 4th, 1873. At Salt Lake. Paid Captain Bishop $5.00 for Indian Com. Paid H. C. Kiesel $10.00 on account. Major left for Corinne.—Wednesday, November 5th. Left for Grantsville, taking Roberts.—Thursday, November 6th. Went to Lee's at Grantsville. Paid $1.50 for dinner. Indians are not at Grantsville. Left Tuesday morning. Have decided to leave goods with Lee.

Friday, November 7th. Left goods with Lee. Gave him memorandum and made arrangements with him to send word to Indians, and arrange a meeting at Grantsville. He is to send word to Indian Commissioner when the meeting will be, and they will either come out or send him word what to do with goods. Paid Lee $4.00; paid $1.50 for dinner at Kislers. Went to Walker House.

Saturday, November 8th. Hunted about town for a room. Major got back tonight.—November 10th to 14th. At Salt Lake. Work on book. Major gave me $100.00.—Saturday, November 15th. Major started east this morning.—Sunday, November 16th. Left Salt Lake for Nephi. Wrote wife and Major. Paid hotel bill, $8.00, left key of box "D" with Bishop. He is to send mail. Stopped with Green at American Fork.—Monday, November 17th. Paid Green $3.00. Came to Spanish Fork.—Tuesday, November 18th. Paid $3.00 for entertainment.—Wednesday 19th. Paid Mrs. Hayne $20.00 for work on map.

November 20th, 21st and 22d. At Nephi. Worked on map. Wednesday, November 26th. At Nephi. Finished map; moved camp, storing things in Hayne's cellar the best place I could find. Borrowed $24.00 of A. Hayne. Paid $5.25 on meat bill. Paid I. Howard $5.00.—Friday, November 28th. Paid $5.25 for hotel bill at Spanish Fork. Paid $1.50 for dinner and $1.00 for grain. Stopped at Dunyon's.—Saturday, 29th. Reached Salt Lake and went to Walker House.

Friday, December 5th, 1873. Got letter and draft for $2800.00 from Major. Cashed draft at Salt Lake National Bank.

Sunday, December 7th. Left Salt Lake at 6:00 A. M. Paid $5.00 fare to Ogden, $2.00 for breakfast, $77.50 fare to Omaha, $8.00 sleeping car fare, $2.00 for dinner at Evanston, $2.00 for supper at Green River, $560.00 for 70 pounds luggage.—Monday, December 8th. Paid $2.00 for breakfast at Laramie, $2.00 for dinner at Cheyenne, $2.00 for supper.—Tuesday, December 9th. Paid $2.00 for breakfast, $2.00 for dinner at Fremont, $39.50 for tickets at Omaha, $6.00 for sleeping car, $4.75 for supper on train.

Wednesday, December 10th. Paid $1.50 for breakfast at Galesburg. Paid $35.25, balance due John Renshaw. Got to Aurora at 3:00 P. M. Phoned Brown at train. Monday, December 15th. At Aurora. Went to Naperville this afternoon. Paid $.60 for tickets. Got wife's statement of money had from the Major and Bram on the Major's account as follows: Of Major, including expenses of trip from Salt Lake, $153.00; of Bram, $323.00, making $476.00 today. Tuesday, December 16th. Went to Chicago this morning and came to Aurora tonight. Paid $3.80 for railroad fares and $7.50 for hotel bills Gave wife $50.00. Paid $59.00 for lace for wife.

Friday, December 19th. At Aurora working on map. December 20th and 21st. Aurora. Paid $58.50 for clothes. December 26th, 27th, and 28th. At Aurora working on map. Monday, December 29th. Came to Bloomington, stopped at Ashley House. Wednesday, December 31st. At Bloomington until night, then came to Normal.

Thursday, January 1, 1874. Came from Normal home— (Aurora). Wednesday, January 7th. At Aurora working on map. Paid $8.60 freight on books, etc. from Salt Lake. Friday, 9th. Got telegram from Major. Answered it, paid $1.50. Sunday, January 11th. Worked on map. The operator came to house today saying they could not find the Major at Washington. Gave him 910 M Street. Monday, January 19th. Sent Reservations Map to Major. Paid $3.00 for Major. Tuesday, 20th. Commenced work on Map of Canon of Desolation. (Working on map continually).

Monday, February 15, 1874. Went to Chicago to get Tracing Cloth; paid for fare $2.70, for dinner 50c, dress for wife $35.75, lace $18.50, opera glass, $10.00, tracing cloth, $2.50. Monday, February 22nd. Went to Chicago. Paid $1.35 for fare, 70c for pattern. Saw the Major and Jack. Went to lecture, bought fringe for wife, $4.50. Paid $3.00 for hat. Tuesday, February 23rd. At Chicago. Stopped at Sherwoods'. Bought lace for wife $3.75. Wednesday, the 24th. Came to Aurora. Paid $2.70 for tickets. Thursday, the 25th. At Aurora. Worked a little on map.

Tuesday, March 2, 1874. At Aurora. Finished map. Sunday, March 7th. At Aurora. Major and Jack came. Monday, the 8th. At Aurora. Major went to Wheaton. Tuesday, the 9th. At Aurora. Major lectures. Tuesday, March 30th. Bram paid me $100.00. Got all ready to leave Aurora. Was at the depot when the Major got off the train we were going on, so we did not leave until 5:15 P. M. Loaned the Major $100.00. Came to Gault House. Paid $4.05 fare. Wednesday, March 31st. At the Gault House. Went to the Comic Opera tonight—paid $4.00.

April 1, 1874. Left Chicago at 8:30 P. M. Paid $34.00 fare

to Washington. Loaned the Major $50.00. Paid bill at Gault,
$11.50. April 3rd. Came to Washington. Stopped at Metropoli-
tan House. April 5th. Have engaged rooms at 915 NZ Ave. N.
W. at $35.00 per month, commencing 6th. Tuesday, 6th. Com-
menced board at Mrs. Pipers at $20.00 per month each. Wednes-
day, 7th. Major got home. Went with him to Hayden's etc.
Major paid borrowed money, $150.00, also $50.00 on account.
Thursday, April 8. Decided tonight to work at Major's House.
Saturday, April 10th. Went to see Wheeler's Party. Sunday,
the 11th. At home. Went to see the Equestrian statues of Jack-
son and Scott. The latter is the finer. Wednesday, April 21st.
Went to circus this evening. Paid $2.00 for tickets. Thursday,
22nd. Went to Opera today, $3.35. Paid $1.50 for umbrella.
Saturday, April 24th. Went to Opera—paid $1.50 for tickets, and
$6.50 for shoes. [April 25 to June 7, no entries].

Field Season, 1874[71]

June 7th, 1874. Paid 75c for drayage on trunk of instruments.
Paid $5.00 for berth in sleeping car—for extra weight of trunk of
instruments 165 lbs. at $1.50 per cwt., $2.25. June 8th. Breakfast
at Altoona, 75c, Dinner at Pittsburg, 75c, supper at Alliance, 75c.
June 9th. Breakfast at Valparaiso, 75c, extra baggage, 165 lbs.
at .40, 66c, sleeping car to Omaha, $6.00. June 11th. Extra bag-
gage to Omaha, $2.80, dinner, 75c, supper, 75c, telegram to
Wheeler, 75c. June 12th. Seven fares at $38.75, $271.25, sleeping car, $11.00, extra baggage, 190 lbs. $11.70, breakfast on train,
75c, park bags at Omaha, $1.00, supper at Grand Island, $1.00.
June 13th. Breakfast at Sidney, $1.00, supper at Laramie, $1.00.
June 14th. Breakfast, $1.00, dinner at Wahsatch, $2.00, supper
at Ogden, $2.00, fuzz, $6.00, fares from Ogden to Salt Lake (3)
$6.00. June 15th. At Walker House. Went to camp, presenting
credentials and got order for rations. Paid $6.00 for truck there.

June 16th. Wednesday. At Walker. Went to Court and
signed receipts. June 17th. Bought articles. Had to go to Camp
Douglas. Paid carriage hire, $4.00. June 18th. At Walker House.
Paid $56.00 Hotel Bill. Expecting to go in the morning. Saturday,
June 19th. Mr. McCurdy commenced work at $35.00 per month
and Mr. Davis at $30.00 per month. Paid $2.00 for tickets to
York. Got a letter from Adams saying that we had but 3 saddles
and 2 blankets, so I stayed behind to buy more. Sunday, June
20th. Came from Salt Lake to York. Left Mrs. T. at Boro. Paid
Hotel bill, $8.00. Fares, $8.00. Found Adams, Hawkins and Mr.
Judd, the cook, at York. Monday, June 21st. Started a load of

---

[71]The professional personnel of the Survey during the field of 1874 was J. W. Powell, geologist,
in charge; Edwin E. Howell, assistant geologist; A. H. Thompson, geographer; J. H. Renshawe,
W. H. Graves, and H. C. DeMotte, topographers; O. D. Wheeler, assistant topographer; J. K.
Hillers, photographer.

rations for Gunnison while I came back to Provo. Paid $2.00 for Railroad fare, and $2.00 hotel bill. Tuesday, June 22nd. Bought a bill of goods at Provo, $21.00. Paid fare, $2.00 and came to York. Paid $1.50 for......................... Came to Nephi. Paid bill at Haynes, etc. Wednesday, June 23rd. Came from Nephi to Gunnison. Paid hotel bill at Nephi, $12.00, and paid for feed at noon, 50c. June 24th. At Gunnison, fitting up. Sent Hawkins to get load from York. Friday, June 25th. At Gunnison, fitting up. Hired Jerry Pickett at $40.00. Saturday, June 26th. At Gunnison. Spent for provisions, $5.00. Sent men up canon to jerk beef.

Field Season, 1875[72]

Thursday, July 1st, 1875. Paid bills at Gunnison and came to camp up Sahara Creek. Friday, July 2nd. Climbed the canon wall and made a station this A. M. Came ten miles up canon. July 3rd. Came to Howell's Hole this A. M. and to camp near Gilson's Ranch this P. M. Sunday, the 4th. Went to a point on the edge of Castle Valley. Tuesday, July 6th. Climbed Mount Hilgard. Made Station 11. Hillers took pictures of Marvine. Wednesday, July 7th. Came to camp 6 near Fish Lake. Found that Ward and party arrived last night, but did not bring all the load. Started Adams back. Thursday, July 18th. Prospected for road into Rabbit Valley. Found a good one. Adams got in. Divided rations. Captain Dutton climbed Fish Lake Mountain.

Friday, July 9th. Captain Dutton left the main party this morning. I agreed with him to be at Gunnison about the 10th of September. Gave him five head of horses. Hawkins for packer, Judd for cook. Gave Dutton $200.00. Paid Judd $25.00. Saturday, July 10th. Came from camp 7 to 8. Decided to locate supply camp on southeast side of Rabbit Valley. Tuesday, July 13th. Started for Thousand Lake Mountain. Camped on the shoulder of the mountain 650 feet below the summit. Wednesday, July 14th. Climbed the mountain and came for camp down a little Creek. Thursday, July 15th. Graves made Station on Aquarius Plateau.

Friday, July 16th. Renshaw [J. H. Renshawe] and I went down [Fremont] river. Sunday, July 18th. Hillers and myself climbed a ridge north of Tantalus Valley. Monday, July 19th. Camp 14 is in Tantalus Valley about ½ mile from the main creek. Bill [Robert Bell?] did not run a trail this morning. He is so faint hearted that I cannot rely on him, so I have given the trails to Renshaw and put Bill on stations with Walter. Bill gives up whenever he feels a bit poorly or tired. He never helps pack, the only

72The professional personnel for the years 1875 and 1876 was: J. W. Powell, geologist, in charge; G. K. Gilbert, Capt. C. E. Dutton (U. S. Army), and C. A. White, assistant geologists; A. H. Thompson, geographer; Robert Bell, J. H. Renshawe, and W. H. Graves, topographers; O. D. Wheeler, assistant topographer, J. K. Hillers, photographer.

thing so far that he has done is to cook a little or rather to let Mac do it. [July 17-23, no entries.]

Saturday, July 24th. Went across Aquarius Plateau. Bill says he did not feel strong enough, but I noticed that he ate as much supper as usual. [July 25-31, no entries; probably mapping along east base of Aquarius Plateau]. Sunday, August 1, 1875. When we arrived at Vagabonds Haven, found no water. Did find a pocket up a side canon of East Branch Last Chance. [?]

Monday, August 2d. [G. K.] Gilbert, [W. H.] Graves, Jack [Hillers] and myself started for the end of Kaiparowitz Plateau. Came about 25 miles down the valley. Climbed the first bench and up about 350 feet of the second. When we came to a place we could not get over, worked on it and got the Net. mule up; came down to the lower bench and camped. Tied the mules up on account of no water. When I was making the detail to come down to the end of the plateau, Mr. Bell said he would like to go, but when he had ridden six or eight miles his knee gave out and he did not know if he could stand the rapid ride. Of course I could not put him on the detail, even if I had desired.

Tuesday, August 3rd. Finished our trail and got on the top of the plateau at 9:30. Rode until 2:30, making 15 miles before we reached the end of the plateau. Was on the end about two house. [Opposite Navajo Mountain]. Got geodetic bearings and a few topographical. Jack could not get a picture on account of the late hour. Reached water that Walter had found in the morning about half past seven, P. M. when our mules had a chance to drink; the first water since yesterday morning. Fine grass. We made a fire, ate some bread that Gilbert brought for a lunch, rolled up in our saddle blankets, and went to sleep.

Wednesday, August 4th. At daylight Gilbert went for the mules. Soon after sunrise we were off. It took two hours to get down 900 feet off the first cliff and our camp was some 6 miles from the "come down". We reached our camp of the night of the 3rd inst. about 9:30 A. M., ate our "beans" and bread, and were off. Reached camp at 5:00 P. M. Thursday, August 5th. Came from camp on Last Chance [Collet Wash] to a camp on Pine Creek about a mile above its junction with the Escalante. Saw four Mormons from Panguitch who are talking about making a settlement here. Advised them to call the place Escalante. Jack took three views of the "Goblins". Monday, August 9th. Have decided to divide the party; to send Renshaw to do the work on the west of the Beaver Range, to go myself to El Vado, and put the main party under charge of Gilbert and send Jack with him until he gets to the Henry Mountains, they to let Jack take Jerry and make pictures when he pleases. Adams has beef. Gave all hands a rest. Adams expense, $3.50.

Tuesday, August 10th. Gilbert went on west side Thousand

Lake Mountain. Renshaw made a station, Graves on this sketch, Billy did nothing. Gilbert wished him to make a sketch on tracing cloth of Graves work, but he has slept, so he has not got it done. Wednesday, August 11th. Gilbert, Renshaw, Graves, and Ward made a station on "the Button". Shod the horses, paid Allen $5.00 on B———account. Thursday, August 12th. Main party under charge of Gilbert started for the Henry Mountains. I left camp supply with Renshaw and came to Grass Valley. Friday, August 13th. Came from Grass Valley to Glencove. Telegraphed wife and Bishop Horne. Left Renshaw and came 10 miles towards Green River. Gave Renshaw $35.00 for expense on his trip. Paid $4.25 for telegraphing.

Saturday, August 14th. Came to Gunnison. Hired Eric Larsen at $40.00 per month, he to furnish saddle horse. Paid him $5.00. Stopped at Bishop Hornes. Paid $2.00 expense. Came ten miles toward Nephi.

Sunday, August 15th. Came to Nephi. Met wife. Monday, 16th. Came from Nephi to Taylor's Ranch. Tuesday, 17th. Came from Taylor's Ranch to Gunnison. Bill at Taylor's $1.50. Wednesday, 18th. Came from Gunnison to Glencove. Thursday, August 19th. Paid bill at Glencove, $1.75. Paid for work at Glencove. Paid bill for trip at Richfield. Came to Salina. Saw Captain Dutton. He has a theory that will not hold. Friday, 20th. Came from Monroe to Marysvale. Paid bill at Durkees, $2.50. Hired Durkee at $2.00 per day. Saturday, August 21st. Came from Marysvale to camp in foot of Panguitch Canyon. Paid for grain and hay, $2.50.

Sunday, August 22d. Came to Panguitch, and stopped at Clarks. Met Renshaw and Larsen. Concluded to take them with me, so had them come to Panguitch. Monday, August 23rd. Hired John Clark at $2.00 per day. Bought two blankets of Jacob Hamblin at $17.00 for Captain Dutton. Got horses shod and bought fish, $2.00.

Tuesday, August 24th. Left Panguitch about 1:00 o'clock. Came to East Fork of Sevier for camp, 20 miles. Paid bills at Panguitch, $3.00.

Wednesday, August 25th. Came to a camp about 12 miles above Paria settlement. 25 miles. Thursday, 26th. Came to a camp about 9 miles below the old settlement. Camped with Navajos, 18 miles. Friday, August 27th. Came to a camp in Sentinel Rock Wash [Wahweap Creek], about 20 miles. Saturday, 28th. Came to El Vado. Sunday, 29th. Came from El Vado to camp on Warm Creek. Monday, 30th. Came from Warm Creek to camp below Paria settlement. Tuesday, August 31st. Came to camp on Paria. Paid $1.25 for meals at Paria.

Wednesday, September 1st, 1875. Came to Panguitch. Made the Kanarra herd ground on the East Fork at noon, Panguitch at night. Thursday, September 2nd. Sent John and Erick on their trip and came to head of Panguitch Canyon. Friday, 3rd. Came to Van Buerens. Saturday, 4th. Came to Durkees. Sunday, September 5. Came to Glenwood. Monday, 6th. Came to Gunnison. Tuesday, September 7th. At Gunnison. Telegraphed Dutton. Started for Nephi but came back. Wednesday, 8th. Dutton came. Went to P. V. but so cloudy could not work. Sunday, September 12th. Came to Nephi. Came to Ranch for camp. Gilbert left this morning.—Monday, 14th. Came to Salt Lake. Tuesday, September 15th. At Salt Lake. Settled with boys. Saturday commutation, $227.00.

Wednesday, September 15th. Paid bill at Walker House. Paid breakfast in Ogden, $2.00, sleeping car, $16.00, dinner at Evanston, $1.00, supper at Greenriver, $1.00. Friday, September 17th. At Omaha. Paid for sleeping carfare to Chicago, $6.00, supper, $1.50. Saturday, September 18th. Arrived at Aurora. [Aurora, Ill., home of Professor Brain Powell, brother of Major J. W. Powell and brother-in-law of A. H. Thompson.]

MISCELLANEOUS JOURNAL ENTRIES

Articles to buy: [Washington, April 1874] 3 doz. 6 H Pencils; 6 doz. No. 5 pencils; 2 doz. No. 4 pencils; 2 gross rubber bands; 1 doz. pencil ink erasers; 4 doz. Large Thumb Tacks; 2 Pencils Eye Lanterns; oil for Lanterns; 2 Metallic tapers for Dutton; A Magnet. Articles to take: Theodolite and Tripod; Gradientors; Mountain Theodolite and Tripod; Alt Azimuth Inst.; Prysmatic Compasses; Aneroid Barometers; Steel tape; Metallic Tapers for Dutton; Sextant and Artificial Horizon; Plane Tables Complete; Scales, 2 Protractors, 3 Dividers; Striding Level; 2 or 3 Letter Clips; 2 Packages Paper; Ink Stand; Chronometers; Pencils E; Erasers; Thumb Tacks; Rubber Bands; Gilbert's things; Nautical Almanac and Ephemeris; Table Logarithms; Loomis Star Catalogue; Loomis Tables; Chanrimts Tables; Davis Survey— Mes. Line; Maps; Books for Record; Lanterns; Thermometers; Voucher Books; Things to repair barometers; Drawing Paper and tracing cloth; Paper and envelopes; Barometer Tubes; Field Glass; Chronometers, Haversack; Mercury, 3 bottles; Note Holder with Dist.; Orders for tickets and Rating; Small Magnets; Medicines, Quinine pills, Opium pills, Dover's Powder, S. Powders, Cathartic Pills, Carbolic Salve, Camphor, Jamaica Ginger, Paregoric, H. Drops, Chloroform; Rubber blankets; Alcohol for lamp; Gin; Medicines; tweezers; pen knife; cork screw, if possible cartridges and ammunition for gun.

[Navajo Words]. Ma Koon Tow ep—Pink Cliffs; Paints a gunt—The Plateaus; Ki par o wits—Marshalls Peak; Oo wa ba—

Name of a spring Right Br; Pa go wh go ret—Name of a spring
Left; Oo wa weep—Name of the land, also of Creek; O pi munts
—Name of Plateau; Un tar re—1st Henry Mountain; Muchu
Karet, 2nd—Henry Mountain; Un cop a chune it—3rd Henry
Mountain; Nu as chub—4th Henry Mountain; Quay a chur—5th
Henry Mountain; A wish a chog—Henry Mountains; Pow oon a
pa—Spring between 1st; Pa o wats—Spring between 4th and 5th;
Pa rock a mits—Spring east of 4th; Pa ron gwan a quint—Stream
east of; Un car pa guve—Red Lake; Un car weet sim piah; Pa ru
—Stream from Table Mountain.

Kong wa—North branch; Shu awn a quint—1st West; Un
con a quint—2nd; Pa roon pi av—Aneast rock; Ka non a quitch
it—Another stream; Shu vi up—North Fork where—Shu vi up—
The country across Colon; Shu vi woon it—A Big Butte Mesa;
Cong Karet—Point of Observation August 23rd; O pi ment—
Name of cliff; Tshong we net—A long rock marked on Johns
sketch; Pe kar ga ret—A crag of rock; Tu a vats—A spring near
Point E.; Tu gua no net—A Point; Pa goo qua get—A butte-like
rock; To wich an a quint—Paria River; Pa woon a pa—Spring
near Table Mountain; Pow poor a pa—Spring near ....;
Ca mo ata—16 mile spring; Ma co bate—Navajo Spring; Kire a
karet—Navajo Mountain.

Nin is Kar de, means what do you call it; Nat is ahn, means
Navajo Mt.; Na tahn means corn; Pe Maw wa, means knife;
pocket to, means Colorado River; Na Kar Dit sa, means Talk; a
go tin i za, means where are you going; Se Kis, means Friend;
Ka te, means Good; Ha la ne se kis, means How do you do;
Ha dah nahl, means Where have you been; Nja go ta za, means
Where are you going; Tji, means Day; To que, means How many;
Kot ne kin-e-za, means Good-bye; Sin, means Sing; Nut to, means
Tobacco; Cha, means Peaches; Te-Jah, means Sheep.

John Clark account, commenced work August 23rd, 1875, at
$2.00 per day; account with Eric Larsen, August 15th commenced
work at $40.00; account with W. H. Graves, commenced work
July 1st, $18.74; fare from Omaha to Ogden, $38.75. Paid $305.00.
Paid at York cash, $905.00. Paid 9 Mo. from July 1st, $412.50.
Account with J. H. Renshaw, commenced work July 1st. Fare
from Omaha to Ogden, $38.75. Paid $310.00 at York. Robert
Bell, commenced work July 1st, fare from Omaha to Ogden,
$38.75, fare from Ogden to Salt Lake, $2.00. G. K. Gilbert, commenced work July 1st, spurs paid for, $1.50; September 12th paid
$400.00. Joseph Hamblin commenced work May 21st. Spanish
bit, $1.50. O. D. Wheeler commenced work June 10th. Ticket
from Omaha to Ogden, $38.75. Cash at Salt Lake, $22.00, ticket
from Salt Lake to York, $4.00. Paid at York, $205.00. Wheeler

has been allowed nothing for transportation above $100.00 per month.

To Buy [Field Season, 1875]: 10 bridles; 10 riding saddles; 18 halters; 24 jars, hobbles, 1 dozen; 4 pack saddles; 250 feet lash rope; 30 yards canvas; 2 sets shaving tools; 50 yards canvas for Jack covers ;4 sets curry combs and brushes; 20 pairs blankets; 2 nest kettles; 1-2 gal, 1-6 qt, 1-4 qt., 1 coffee kettle; 1 nest kettle, 1 coffee kettle; 2 bake ovens, 2 dozen tin cups; 2 dozen tablespoons; 2 dozen large spoons; 3 set knives and forks; 3 coffee mills; half dozen butcher knives; 3 axes; paper for packing; 3 lines, leather; half dozen canteens; rubber blanket; castile, 5 lbs; oil for lamps; gloves, Kit small; boots; cartridges, shells; cups, shot, powder, belt; tin cans; screw tops; dried apples, peaches; matches; cotton cloth; yeast powders, 5 dozen; rivets, punches, etc.; shoe thread, awls, etc.; match, safe, buckles, rings; bread pans; tins; buckskin; shears; knives, buckles; tea; Jamaica Ginger; salve boots; tin plates; kit, small; screws, copper wire; 1 quart lime juice; pair boots, 9; blankets, rubber blanket; lime juice; pair Horns; ore sacks; shot belt; match safe; farmers knife; table cloth; side leather; half dozen bridle bits; twine; nose sacks; monkey wrench; salt castors; shovel; 3 pairs spurs; boots Adams, 11; boots Hawkins, 9; Pins, fine comb; saddle; Spanish bit; 3 bridle bits; twine; tacks.

June 13th, 1875. Breakfast at Sidney, $2.00, Robert Bell, W. E. Graves, J. H. Renshaw, E. P. Thompson, O. D. Wheeler, J. K. Hillers, A. H. Thompson. Railroad Fare, $137 x 8, $1096.00; Saddles, 10x16, $160.00; Blankets, 30x5, $150.00; Pack Saddles, 5x8, $40.00; Pack Train, $150.00; Grain, etc., $250.00; Shoeing, $200.00.

Names of Horses Used	Riders
Utah Billy	Selz
Mapor	Captain
Servel	Gilbert
Charley	Bill
Annpits	John
Roxey	Wheeler
Sorrel	Walter
Mangin	Ward
Short Tail	Davis
Sorrel Fare	Joe
Prince	Adams
Dolly	Jack
Judd	Judd
Roan	Mac
Panter	Jerry
Bay	Enstine
Bay	Hawkins

St. George, Oct. 16, 1870.

President Horace S. Eldredge.

Dear Brother:

I am appointed to superintend the building of a fort, which the Church is building at Pipe Spring, the place where Dr. Whitmore was killed. It is to be a big affair, on the plan of Cove Creek Fort. It will be 152 feet long and 66 feet wide, the wall next the bluff 30 feet high, with two story dwellings inside, and the wall on the lower side 20 feet high, with milk rooms, &c., inside. This work will keep me out most of the winter, but it is a very necessary work, and I am willing to do my part in it. This Pipe Spring and Kanab country is right between us and the Navajos, and it is the best country for stock-raising that I ever saw, if it can be made safe against the raids of these marauding Indians. I start out to-morrow with a small company to commence the work. * * *

JOS. W. YOUNG.

(*Deseret News*, Salt Lake City, Thursday, August 24, 1871)

Geological Surveying Expedition. Mr. M. J. Shelton, Indian interpreter, called this morning. For the last month he has been traveling as guide and interpreter with Major Powell's exploring party, during which time they have had pleasant journeys from the Uintah Reservation to a point about two hundred and twenty-five miles southwest of it. In their rambles they have passed through many valleys susceptible of cultivation, and the Indians all through the country, are peaceable and talk nothing else.

The Major's party is seventeen in number, ten of whom have now gone down the Colorado with boats. The remainder go across the Pah-goo country, and will intercept the river party with supplies at the head of the Pah-goo. The trip thus far has been very pleasant!

(*Deseret News*, Salt Lake City, August 30, 1871)

"Brother A. P. Winsor arrived yesterday from the Kanab country, (Pipe Spring). He passed through Kanab City and states that the people there were very busy building rock, frame and abode houses * * The telegraph poles are being erected for the extension of the Deseret line from Toquerville to Kanab. Brother Winsor will take with him machinery for a cheese factory."

St. George, Dec. 11th, 1871.

Elder George Reynolds.

Dear Brother:—On the 20th Nov. our party left this city on a visiting tour to the settlements on the Rio Virgin. We passed through Washington, Harrisburg, Leeds and Toquerville, and reached Virgin City where meetings were held; we also had an agreeable meeting at Rockville and then we returned to Virgin City, thence rising on to the high plateau toward Winsor Castle Spring, in Arizona, where we arrived on the evening of the 23rd Nov. The next morning we continued our journey up the Cotton-wood Wash, or Canon, and over the divide into Long Valley, a distance of 30 miles, half the way through heavy sand. At Mount Carmel and Glendale meetings were held instructing and comforting to the Saints; the settlers in this valley are mostly those who vacated the Muddy settlements to get away from the vexa-tious taxation of the State of Nevada, and who left behind them the labors and improvements of years.* * *

On the 27th Nov. we drove to Kanab City, a distance of 25 miles, and held a meeting there in the evening. This city is lo-cated in a cove of the mountains, at the mouth of Kanab Creek Canon, and overlooks the country as far as the Buckskin Moun-tains through which runs the Colorado River; here is a vast range and an excellent quality of grass for stock; Kanab is the Indian name for willows, which grow along the creek.

The Telegraph Line has been extended from Toquerville to Rockville, thence onward over these highlands to Kanab City. On the 28th Nov. we drove to Winsor Castle Ranche, and stayed overnight with A. P. Winsor, who is in charge there; the next evening we camped at Shadow Rock. On the 30th inst.* * we reached St. George about 5 p. m., having travelled a distance of 250 miles.* * * We are engaged visiting and comforting the Saints, exploring and developing the resources of this land, and seeking out and locating secure resting places for the Saints among the rugged recesses of these majestic mountains.* *

BRIGHAM YOUNG.

(*Deseret News*, Salt Lake City, December 16, 1871)

By Deseret Telegraph. Winsor Castle, Utah. (Now Pipe Springs, Ariz.) December 15, 12:31 p. m. Editor NEWS. We have opened a telegraph office here this morning, Miss Luella Stewart, operator. Winsor Castle is progressing rapidly towards completion; it will be a very creditable structure, and will afford security to its occupants, should friend "Lo" attempt to contest the right of possession to this dry country's flocks and herds. Bishop Winsor with his estimable lady, is now absent at St. George. . . . A. M. Musser.

(*Deseret News*, Salt Lake City, Monday, June 3, 1872)

"Kanab. * * The Colorado River gold excitement has almost entirely died out. The river is very high. A number of Piute In-dians are gathering here to receive presents of blankets, grubbing hoes and so forth from Major Powell's exploring company. We have not had a visit from the Navajos for some time."

(*Deseret News,* Salt Lake City, February 14, 1872)

"Major Powell. We had a pleasant call this morning from Major Powell, the Colorado explorer, who arrived in town on Monday night (12th). He is well and hearty. He left his party at the camping ground about six miles south of Kanab, to which he intends to return in a short time.

We learn from him the following particulars concerning his late operations. He has been engaged this winter establishing a meridian base from Kanab south, and erecting monuments, on conspicuous points, one hundred miles from that place, in every direction, making a topographical map and examining the geology of that region   *   *   *

Placer gold has been found in many places on the Colorado. The gold is very fine, but it is not yet known whether it would pay for working. * * * Major Powell was on the Colorado, at the mouth of Kanab Creek, during Christmas week, where at that time, the grass was green and flowers were in bloom."

(*Deseret News,* Salt Lake City, July 17, 1872)

Major Powell, who has attained distinction as the great scientific explorer of the Colorado, is in town. He is trying to arrange to obtain the exact longitude of Kanab. He will soon be in the field again.

(*Deseret News,* Salt Lake City, August 30, 1872)

"Returned. We had a pleasant call yesterday from Brother James Fennemore, who arrived on Wednesday evening, (28th), accompanied by Professor H. C. De Motte and Captain F. M. Bishop, from the Colorado, the three gentlemen being members of Major Powell's expedition. They left the river August 15. We learn from Brother Fennemore that the expedition will take a trip through Grand Canyon to Grand Wash,—which will take them about three weeks.

The reason why Brother Fennemore will not accompany the expedition as photographer, is because his health will not permit of his taking the trip. Only think of the thermometer at one hundred fifteen degrees in the shade in the daytime, with dry hot sands at night, and cool piercing breezes in the morning.

Major Powell being Indian Commissioner for the Southern tribes, will hold a grand council with the leading chiefs at Kanab about the first of October, after which he will proceed to Washington, where he will remain for the winter, while Professor Thompson and assistants run a base line from the Upper Sevier. After this latter work is done, the results of the labors of the expedition will be compiled and published, not the least interesting portion of which will be the two hundred fine illustrations, the work of Photographer Fennemore, who is a well known talented artist. Major Powell was highly pleased with his labors in his department. The work, when published, including maps and so forth, will be one of the most interesting of the kind.

We have also, since writing the above, had a pleasant visit from Professor De Motte and Captain Bishop.

(*Deseret News,* Salt Lake City, Wednesday, October 2, 1872)

"A Narrow Escape." We are informed by Brother John Rider, who lately arrived from Kanab, that Major Powell, the Colorado explorer, came very near losing his life a little over two weeks ago. The Major, Professor Thompson and several members of the expedition were "shooting" the rapids of the river, a very dangerous feat, and the Major was standing up in the stem of the boat, giving directions, when by a sudden lurch of the little craft, he was thrown headlong into a seething whirlpool. The boat was upset and all who were in it were also thrown into the water; all but the Major however, were cast into a place from which they scrambled without much difficulty, and were enabled to rescue the Major from his perilous situation. After he was safely landed, he remarked that he thought for certain that the time had come for him to "hand over his checks".

(*Deseret News,* Salt Lake City, October 14, 1872)

The Colorado Country. Mr. E. O. Beaman, recently photographer to the Powell Exploring Expedition, called on us this morning with a number of interesting stereoscopic views of various scenes on the Colorado, and of the Moquis villages and residences, which accompanied by Mr. James Carlton, Mr. Beaman visited for two or three weeks. These views can be obtained at Savage's fine art gallery, and other places in town".

(*Deseret News,* Salt Lake City, October 29, 1872)

The Wheeler Expedition. Kanab, October 28. A detachment of Lieutenant Wheeler's expedition of twenty men and three government teams, Lieutenant Mott in command, arrived here last Friday, (25th), and are expected to remain one month. Three other detachments have gone on, via St. Thomas, across the Colorado, one up the Virgin River Canyon, and one branched off at Winsor to the Grand Gulch. They have contracted for grain at Long Valley.—J. L. Bunting.

(*Deseret News,* Salt Lake City, December 6, 1872)

St. George. The Southern Division of Lieutenant Wheeler's expedition arrived at Washington, (Washington County), a few days ago. It met with brilliant success. One man, F. Kettleman, was wounded in the Narrows of Pareah Kanyon. Lieutenant Wheeler's officers and assistants will return to Washington, D. C., about December 20th.

(*Deseret News*, Salt Lake City, February 28, 1873)

The Powell Colorado Expedition. F. S. Dellenbaugh, Esquire, assistant topographer of the Powell Exploring Party, called this morning. He reports that a party of four men, under Professor Thompson, have been encamped at Kanab for the last eight or ten weeks, unable, on account of the unfavorable weather, to continue their explorations. They are now awaiting the return from the East of Major Powell, before any attempt will be made to resume spring work. Mr. Dellenbaugh left the party on the 16th.

(*Deseret News*, Salt Lake City, April 30, 1873)

Pahreah. R. A. Smith writes April 13: "This settlement is thirty miles north of the ferry, which has lately been started on the Colorado. It has been supposed by a great many that we were in Arizona, but Professor Thompson, who has lately been here, has taken observations and decided that our place is twelve miles north of the southern line of Utah, which leaves us in Kane County * * There are about ten men and eight families here."

(*Deseret News*, Salt Lake City, May 12, 1873)

Shoshones. Several principal men of the Shoshone tribe of Indians were in town today, and were being piloted around by Major Powell. There was an unusually respectable air about them, for Indians. One of them in addition to an ordinary suit of civilian's clothing, wore a regular stovepipe hat. We understood they desired and had an interview with President Young.

It will be remembered that Major Powell holds the appointment of U. S. Commissioner to locate reservations for the Indians in this region of the country, a position which we would judge him to be well qualified to fill. After locating reservations for the Shoshones and some other tribes, and getting the Indians upon them, it is the intention of the Major to resume his explorations in the South.

(*Deseret News*, Salt Lake City, May 17, 1873)

Movements of Major Powell and Party. Major Powell, Dr. Gibe, Mr. Roberts and a number of men left today for Skull Valley, where they will probably remain about two weeks. The object of their visit to that valley is that they might come to a conclusion as its adaptability for an Indian Reservation.

On their return here the members of the above party will await the return of United States Indian Commissioner Ingalls, now in this city, and who proposes shortly to visit Fort Hall and vicinity, in the interest of the Indians in that region. On his arrival here he, in company with Major Powell and the others mentioned, will proceed to the winter camp of the Powell Expedition, near Gunnison, and there join Professor Thompson and party.

The last named gentleman, accompanied by Mr. H. C. Kiesel, as draftsman, and a number of camp hands, also left the city today, it being their intention to proceed direct to Gunnison, where they will soon be joined by a photographer, another draftsman and a number of camp hands.

When all the fragments that will constitute the entire party, are concentrated at Gunnison, they will either proceed up the Sevier over to the Colorado, or go directly south, about four hundred miles. The place of operations has not, we understand, been definitely decided upon. The surveys will be geological and topographical, besides which, Indian matters will receive considerable attention. The Major has some idea of establishing one or two Indian Reservations on the Muddy.

MAJOR POWELL'S PRELIMINARY REPORT

Prof. Joseph Henry,   Washington, D. C. April 30, 1874.
    Secretary Smithsonian Institution,   Washington, D. C.

I have the honor to submit the following statement of the progress made in the survey of the Colorado River of the West and its tributaries. It is a summary of all the work which has been performed from date of beginning to the present time. * * *

That portion of the Colorado between the mouth of the Rio Virgin and the junction of the Grand and Green had never been mapped, before the one made by the parties under my charge was constructed. The river had been crossed at two points by Lieutenant Ives, and at another by Father Escalante, and such points approximately determined. Nor had that portion of the Green between its junction with the Grand and the crossing of the Union Pacific Railroad ever been mapped; but its position at three different points had been determined by Government explorers, viz. at the mouth of Henry's Fork, at the mouth of the Uintah, and at Gunnison's Crossing, on the old Spanish trail.

During the years 1867, 1868, and the first part of 1869, I was engaged with a small party of naturalists, volunteers like myself, in the exploration of the mountains of central and western Colorado about the sources of the Grand, White and Yampa Rivers. After exploring a number of canons through which these streams run, I determined to attempt the exploration of the great canons of the Colorado. Boats were built in Chicago and transported by the Union Pacific Railroad, which was then running construction-trains, to the point where that road crosses Green River, and from thence in our boats we descended Green River to the Colorado, and the Colorado through the series of great canons to the mouth of the Rio Virgin.

On starting we expected to devote ten months to the work; but meeting with some disasters, by which our store of rations was greatly reduced, we were compelled to hasten the work, so that but three months were given to it.

On this trip astronomic stations about fifty miles apart were made, and observations taken for latitude with the sextant, and also for longitude by the method of lunar distances. The meandering course of the river was determined by compass-observations from point to point, with the intervening distances estimated, thus connecting the astronomic stations. For hypsometric data a series of tri-daily barometric observations were recorded, taken at the water's edge, and using this as an ever-falling base-line, altitudes on the walls, and such adjacent mountain-peaks as were visited were determined by synchronous observations. The results of this hypsometry were used in the construction of the geological sections. The course of the river and the topographic features of the canons only were mapped. It should be remarked here that a portion of the records of this trip were lost at the time when the men, who had them in charge, were killed by Indians.

Having demonstrated the practicability of descending the river in boats, it was determined to make a more thorough survey of the series of canons along the Green and Colorado Rivers, and of the more important side canons, and also to include as broad a belt of country as it was possible from the river, and application was made to Congress for the necessary funds to carry on the work. The assistance asked was granted, and the work has been in continuous progress from July, 1870, until the present time.

It had been determined that it would not be practicable to perform the elaborate work projected, depending on such supplies as it was possible to take with us on the boats from Green River Station, but that it would be necessary to establish depots for supplies at a number of points along the course.

Between Gunnison's Crossing, on Green River, and the foot of the Grand Canon of the Colorado, a distance of five hundred and eighty-seven and one-half miles, it was not known that the river could be reached at more than two points. One of these, at the crossing known at El Vado de los Padres, where Father Escalante had crossed the river in 1776, by following an old Indian trail; the other but a short distance below, at the mouth of the Paria River. This route had been discovered by Jacob Hamblin, a Mormon missionary. These were so near together that only one of them could be used as a depot for supplies.

The last part of the year 1870 was given to the exploration of routes from the settlements in Utah to the Green and Colorado on the east and Colorado on the south. These lines of travel were mapped by fixing astronomic stations with the sextant and connecting them by the methods usually adopted in a meandering reconnaissance.

Early in the spring of 1871 boats were provided at Green River Station. The latitude of this point was determined by observations with the zenith telescope, and the longitude by telegraphic signals, with an astronomic station at Salt Lake City, previously established by officers of the United States Coast Survey. The altitude of this point above the sea had also been determined by the railroad surveys, so that the altitude, latitude and longitude of the initial point of the survey were fixed with a good degree of approximation.

In descending Green River, astronomic stations were established at distances averaging forty-five miles by river, or about twenty-five miles by direct lines, the instrument used being the sextant. At each of these stations the variation of the needle was determined. The river was again meandered by two observers, working independently, and their work compared.

The lines between stations on the river were used as a series of base-lines, the lengths, of course, only approximately determined and an intricate net-work of triangles was projected to salient points on either side of the river. From a vast number of points thus fixed, the surface contour of the country was sketched so as to include a belt from twenty to fifty miles wide, the parties making frequent trips from the river into the interior of the country. At each of these astronomic stations barometric readings were recorded in hourly series, and as we proceeded down the river tridaily barometric readings were made, all referred to the water's edge. With the river as a base-line for hypsometric work, altitudes were determined by triangulation and by barometric methods, using both mercurial and aneroid instruments. Thus all of our altitudes in this region are related to the river.

Our time during the spring, summer and fall of 1871 was thus occupied until we arrived at the mouth of the Paria, a stream entering the Colorado from the northwest, a little below the Arizona line.

Such was the character of the astronomic, topographic and hypsometric work done up to this time, methods not absolutely correct, but giving valuable approximate results.

But the wonderful features of the Grand Canon district had yet to be mapped, and it was determined to do the work in this region by more thorough methods. A general reconnaissance was made for the purpose of selecting a site for a base-line, and the valley of the Kanab was chosen. Then a point midway between the extremities of the proposed line was selected, and an astronomic transit mounted for the purpose of determining the meridian direction and fixing the extremities of the line. This accomplished, the alignments were made with a theodolite. The latitude of the northern extremity of the line was determined by an extended series of observations with the zenith telescope, and the longitude by telegraphic signals with the previously-mentioned astronomic station at Salt Lake City. The base-line was measured with wooden rods, leveled on trestles, and aligned by sighting on small steel pins in either extremity. The rods were trussed to prevent sagging and warping, thoroughly seasoned, oiled and varnished, and the extremities were shod with small metallic cones, for the purpose of securing accurate contact. The rods were measured with a standard steel tape, at a temperature of 52 degrees. Three rods were used, two always remaining in position as a protection against accidental movement. The leveling instrument was a plumet, or an inverted T, the base of which was the same length as the rods. Every hundred feet of distance was marked off by a stake, in the top of which was inserted an iron wire sharpened to a point, and this point connected with the point at the end of the rod by a plummet, and each hundred feet of the distance was re-measured with the steel tape.

The ground selected for the site of the base-line was very good, being nearly level and quite smooth, and we found that the work could be done more rapidly than had been anticipated, the only delay being due to windy weather. When the wind was blowing briskly it gave a trembling motion to the rods, which rendered it impossible to make that correct alignment and accurate contact between the points which was desirable, and for that reason the work was carried on only during still weather. The line was found to be 48,099.4 feet in length. Then a system of triangles was expanded from the extremities of this line, so as to embrace all of the country from the Mar-ka-gunt and Pauns-a-gunt Plateaus on the north to salient points a few miles south of the Grand Canon, and from the Beaver Dam and Pine Valley Mountains on the west of the Navajo Mountain beyond the Colorado on the east, and still farther to the northeast, so as to embrace the country from the Sevier River on the west to salient points immediately beyond the Colorado on the east, and as far north as the southern tributaries of the Dirty Devil River. The angles of these triangles were measured with a seven-inch theodolite. At the geodetic points mounds were built and flag-staffs erected, and in that clear atmosphere it was found that it was practicable to make the sides of the triangles from twenty-five to thirty miles long, and occasionally, when the artificial points were on very salient natural points, the sides of the triangle could be made much longer.

Six of the more distant and important geodetic points were used as astronomic stations, where observations were made with the zenith telescope for latitude, for the purpose of checking any serious error that might occur in the triangulation.

From the points thus established a number of observations were made with the theodolite or gradientor, and from these observations a vast net-work of secondary triangles was constructed.

Thus the position of all the salient topographic features were deter-minded, courses of streams and lines of cliffs were meandered, and the position of the observer constantly checked on the determined points, and *pari passu* with this the topographical features were sketched. The great features were Marble Canon and the Grand Canon of the Colorado, and many salient points on either side of the great chasm were fixed by triangulation.

The following summer we descended through these canons in boats, and fixed the course of the river and the topographic features of the canon wall by compass and gradientor observations on the points thus previously determined. The same system of barometric observations carried on in the canons above was continued through these canons, and occasionally hourly observations of eight-day series were made.

The parties engaged in geodetic and topographic work carried with them barometers, and made a vast number of observations over the country traversed. All of these and all of those in the canons were synchronous, with a continuous series made at the northern extremity of the base-line in the valley of the Kanab, so that the altitudes along the river and on the walls of the canons, and over all the country embraced in the triangulation, are refer-able to this hypsometric base. We have compared this base of altitude with other points whose altitudes have been approximately determined by other observers, as at the mouth of the Rio Virgin, Saint George, Beaver, Salt Lake City, and so forth; but it is hoped that before this work goes on permanent record the altitude of Kanab above the level of the sea will also be determined by the levels of the railroad survey, which is now in progress.

We have one unbroken series of observations at this point (Kanab) of three months' continuance, and another of ten months, and several shorter series. These were tri-daily, except that occa-sionally they were expanded into hourly series.

By the methods last described, an area of country has been surveyed embracing twenty-five thousand square miles, and by the less accurate methods first given, an area of country embracing twenty thousand square miles, making in all forty-five thousand square miles.

Preliminary maps have been constructed on a scale of two miles to the inch, but the final result of all this work will be shown in a series of maps on a scale of four miles to the inch, giving the topographic and geological features of the region surveyed.

(From [Preliminary] "Report of Explorations in 1873 of The Colorado of the West and Its Tributaries," by Professor J. W. Powell, under the direction of the Smithsonian Institution, Washington, D. C., 1874.)

COLORADO RIVER GOLD

*By Cass Hite**

Rincon, thirty-five miles above the mouth of the San Juan River in southeastern Utah, is as far as a road can ever be taken down the river (from Green River, Utah), and is about ninety or a hundred miles to where it empties into the Colorado River. From that point the San Juan enters and plunges through three canyons that are dark and appalling as the mighty canyons of the great Colorado.

I see by the papers that they are claiming coarse gold in those places. I look upon that as an impossibility. The Elk Mesa on the north, and the Mesa Calabasa on the south are entirely sedimentary formations, and all gold that has ever yet been found in the sedimentary rocks is fine gold. Coarse gold does not travel far from the leads.

The whole country has lost several thousand feet of its surface. The great process of erosion has worn the gravels, bedrock and all, down, down to the sea! Gold being soft and heavy has naturally been ground very fine in its travels.

The only show, according to my belief, for coarse gold in that region would be in the short gulches on the north or west of Navajo Mountain, which is at the junction of the San Juan and Colorado. They head in the trachytic formation of that island-mountain, and unless they have found coarse gold in shale, marl and sandstone, then there is no show for nuggets outside of those few little short gulches heading up into the Navajo Mountain. You ask me my opinion, and, although I may be wrong, I do not think there is any coarse gold in the country.

But for fine gold, and large areas evenly distributed as fine gold most generally is, that (industry) has a great future. That entire country is sedimentary rocks. Erosion has caused that great box canyon country, and left between them high mesa formations, which show in the most distinct manner the great markings of Time. The stupendous belts of the sedimentary often cut 2,000 to 3,000 feet in depth. A stratum of quartz pebbles many feet in thickness constitutes one of those great blankets that cover that entire country, and with that stratum I contended for two years.

I never found anything that a poor man could work, although I am convinced I know of much good gold property in that section that could be worked at a good profit with capital enough to put it in good working order. The gravel in that quartz stratum, the water levels of the strata for miles, would suggest that it is formed by glaciers.

The great canyons of the lower San Juan and the Colorado have performed the functions of mighty sluice boxes. The fine

*(In Beaver Utonian, January 13, 1893, for Associated Press.)

gold and the richest of the black sands, owing to their gravity, have dragged along behind all other matter and deposited wherever they had a chance in large and small bodies, and in some instances very rich. From the mouth of Moonlight Canyon it is about thirty-five miles to the confluence of the San Juan and Colorado Rivers. That is a very rough canyon, and with but few gravel deposits. Coming into the San Juan from the south are Moonlight Canyon, Copper Canyon, Foote's Canyon and East Canyon, the latter being the last, and it drains everything to the east of Navajo Mountain.

That is a good gold country, and the fact that I did not strike it rich in there is no reason in the world why others may not. I drifted over on the Colorado and struck Dandy Crossing (Hite on present day maps), Tickaboo and Good Hope, where I could and did live for years with a 'rocker'. I believe that the beds of those streams are yellow, but it is the easiest bars or deposits we are always after. The gold deposits on those streams will last for a century of active mining. It is a barren, desert country, and the great mass of poor adventurers who go there will likely suffer great disappointments, as well as for 'chuck'. The waters of the San Juan and Colorado Rivers are hard to take out for mining and irrigation purposes, owing to the walls and banks and seasonal rise and fall of the waters in the rivers.

Green River, January 13, 1893.—The excitement over the valuable placer finds on the Green River still continues. Prospectors are staking every promising bar both up and down the river. A party has just come in for supplies, bringing considerable gold, which goes to Salt Lake for assay. An outfit left the bars at Wheeler's Ranch (San Rafael), eighteen miles south Tuesday. These bars have been worked in a desultory way for some time. Small boats are in great demand, and every possible conveyance is pressed into use. Green River parties are deluged with inquiries by mail and wire as to the accessibility and value of the placers. Supplies of every description can be obtained here. Every man in the vicinity has claim stakes driven. Reports from placers on the Colorado Rver in Utah show that the original statements have not been exaggerated. A large amount of machinery goes to Hall's Ferry.—*Herald.*

January 13, 1893.—The road from Green River all the way to San Juan via Dandy Crossing is in good condition. The distance from Green River to Dandy is 105 miles, and from Dandy Crossing to the placers on the San Juan is 50 miles. The trip can be made by wagon from Green River, in six or seven days' time. Tom Farrer of Green River is prepared to take care of all parties desiring to reach the gold fields. He will furnish horses and teamsters and all supplies. The rate overland from Green River to the San Juan River, for parties of four, will be about $15 (each), and for parties of seven about $10 (each).—*Beaver Utonian.*

INDEX
Vol. VII Nos. 1, 2 & 3   1939

Smith, R. A., 133
Snake Gulch, Ariz., 70, 99
Spanish Crossing (Green River), 41, 42
Steps cut in sandstone, Colo. River, 57
Steward, J. F., 11n1, 22n4
Surveys of Southern Utah, 136, 137

T

Tannery, 182
Tapeats, (Name), 98
Terminology, (Geographic names in So.
   Utah), 9, 110
Thompson, Almon Harris, (Diary of), 3,
   biog., 5, portrait 10
Thousand Lake Mountain, 125
Time Signals, Telegraphic, 137 Toroweap,
(Meaning), 9
Townsend House, (hotel), Salt Lake City,
   109
Traverse, Southern Utah, 8

U

Uinkaret, (meaning), 9
Uinta Basin, 29
Undine Springs, 43
Ute Ford, (Colo. River), 57, 135

V

"Vasey's Paradise," 93
Vocabulary, Indian, 126, 127

W

Waweap, 125
Walker House (hotel), Salt Lake City, 122
Wheeler's Expedition, 110, 115, 132
Wheeler, O. D., 122n71, 123n72, 127,
128 Wheeler's Ranch, 140
Whirlpool Canyon and Rapids, 23, 24
White, C. A., 123n72
White, James—(First through Colo.
   Canyons), 75
Wilkins, Jim, 103
Winsor, Bishop A. P., 108, 129, 130
Winsor Castle (see Pipe Springs), 129,
   130
Wonsits, (meaning), 9

Y

Yampah River, 22, 26n10
Young, Brigham S., 70
Young, Joseph W., 129
Young, John W., 103